LEADERSHIP IN THE KINGDOM

To Frank and Ginger:
With great appreciation for
your hard work and
friendship.

[signature]

8, 31, 2008.

LEADERSHIP IN THE KINGDOM
Sensitive Strategies for the Church in a Changing World

REVISED EDITION

IAN A. FAIR

Abilene Christian University Press

Abilene, Texas

LEADERSHIP IN THE KINGDOM

ACU
PRESS

Cover design by Mark Decker
Interior text design by Sandy Armstrong

For information contact:
Abilene Christian University Press
1648 Campus Court
Abilene, Texas 79601

1-877-816-4455 toll free
www.abilenechristianuniversitypress.com

"Leadership" is a word on everyone's lips....

Everybody agrees that there is less of it than there used to be....

Often the enormousness of present-day challenges and the pace of change seem unaccompanied by great notions and the great people to implement them....

...leadership is the pivotal force behind successful organizations...to create viable organizations, leadership is necessary to help organizations develop a new vision of what they can be, then mobilize the organization change toward the new vision....

The new leader...is one who commits people to action, who converts followers into leaders, and who may convert leaders into agents of change. We refer to this as "transformational leadership."

WARREN BENNIS & BURT NANUS
Leaders: The Strategies for Taking Charge (1985)

CONTENTS

PART FOUR: DEVELOPING LEADERS IN THE CHURCH

PREFACE TO THE REVISED EDITION

When this book was published in 1996 I opened the preface with Basil Mitchell's observation about his book *Morality: Religious and Secular*: "I don't think of writing a book as if it were the last word on the subject. I seek only to further the discussion." This revised edition is written in the same spirit. I want it to further the discussion of leadership among church leaders, with the additional purpose that it will ultimately bring glory to God and Christ through the church.

Although the first edition was published primarily with the Churches of Christ in mind, the book has found a wider readership among churches of different origin. I am gratified for this, and hope that this revised edition will also be of help to other churches interested in biblical leadership in the kingdom.

Those familiar with the first edition will note that I have added a new chapter, "Developing Leaders in the Congregation," chapter 20 in this revised edition. I trust that this addition will enhance our understanding of *Leadership in the Kingdom*.

Since the original publication ,we have entered a new century, not only in time, but also in church growth, generational makeup in our churches, and worldview. We no longer live in what scholars have identified as the age of modernity but are part of a postmodern culture. Many, especially in a post-Boomer generation, are not given to serious reading. They have been raised with visual aids, and now are tied to video games and video simulation learning. The video "gene" is so widespread that even those of a "post Boomer" and possibly a postmodern age are more interested in hands-on participation in learning.

We can respond to the changes that surround us at every turn in several different ways. We can be confused and frustrated by the fact that the "good old days" are gone forever, leaving us without tried and tested comfort zones in which to live. Or we can look at the changes as though they are external to our world, and merely go on as before. These two alternatives will ultimately leave us frustrated and pessimistic about opportunities for church growth.

Most, however, realize that many of the dramatic changes taking place in our world present exciting challenges and opportunities for the spread of the gospel. Although we fully recognize that growth in many regions of the church has slowed—and in some cases reversed—we still believe that the Gospel of the Kingdom is powerful and can reach across generational and cultural boundaries. A decade or more ago J. J. Turner expressed this optimistic mindset:

> We are living in exciting days for the Lord's church. Throughout our great brotherhood, progress is being made in all areas of the work assigned to the church by

the master. Across the land, congregations are moving forward by faith as more and more people are becoming involved in the growth of the local church.

Why is this happening? In a word—Leadership! This is the key. Men of outstanding ability are involved in leadership on all levels in local congregations. This has produced a renewed interest in leadership training as the man in the pew has become excited about the work of the church and his role in it. He is no longer content to sit still and "let George do it."

Workshops, seminars, classes, training sessions, and a host of other efforts are being used to prepare members of the Lord's church to be more productive leaders. As one elder put it, "We are taking leadership training more seriously now than we have ever taken it."[1]

Thoughtful Christians are enthusiastic about church growth and evangelistic opportunities and pray daily with a deep passion for growth of the kingdom on earth, that the Lord's will might be done on earth as in heaven, that the church might be multiplied as in the days of the early church in Jerusalem and Judea.

Exciting indigenous church leadership in Africa, notably in Accra,[2] Ghana, and many areas of Nigeria and East Africa, has convinced us that the church of our Lord still has a powerful and effective message. Fresh leadership and leadership models can rejuvenate the church. The Kingdom of our Lord still has powerful influence in lives willing to surrender to his will.

In spite of the fact that many congregations of the Lord's church are moving forward and taking advantage of the challenges presented by dramatic changes in our world, many churches continue to struggle. Everywhere, and seemingly on every front, the world appears to prosper while many churches struggle to make a significant impact on the lost in their community. For reasons not easy to define, the church is not multiplying at a pace concomitant with its inherent potential, with the challenging opportunities being presented by the rapid sociological changes taking place in the world, or with the transcendent power of its message.

A leading conservative religious journal once declared that the 1980s would be the decade of the evangelicals in which evangelical churches would enjoy numerical growth unprecedented in recent experience. Only the extreme optimist would agree that this prediction has been even moderately realized among Churches of Christ. In a front page article of *The Christian Chronicle* (vol. 64, No. 2, 2007), Bobby Ross, Jr. writes:

> The U.S. population is growing. And fast. The nation's nearly 13,000 Churches of Christ—as a group—are not. In a nutshell, that's the challenge facing a fellowship whose membership has increased only about 1.6 percent since the beginning of the Reagan era.

In the same quarter-century, America as a whole nation grew at a rate of twenty times that.

"In my experience the church is growing in relatively few places," said Mike Rhodes, minister of the Pine Street church in Vivian, La. "With few exceptions, congregations are doing well just to keep attendance stable. Even more are losing membership rapidly."

The original edition of this book grew out of concern for the slow church growth being experienced by most Churches of Christ at the close of the last decade of the twentieth century. At the time I was working with the College of Biblical Studies at Abilene Christian University. We had conducted a summer seminar for church leaders with the purpose of identifying and studying critical leadership issues the church would have to address in the 1990s if it was to experience once more the exciting growth of its past. The seminar was comprised of experienced elders and ministers, each with at least five years of ministry and leadership experience. Although the seminar recognized that a number of sociological factors impact church growth, three concerns surfaced. Without attempting to prioritize these three concerns, those attending the seminar identified poor or unimaginative leadership, lack of church identity and direction, and creeping secularism as significant concerns needing serious attention in the coming decade. The original edition of the book addressed one of these concerns, namely, the need for innovative, creative, and informed leadership.

A primary concern addressed in the first edition of *Leadership in the Kingdom* was leadership style. An autocratic leadership style was stifling new ideas coming from a more professional Boomer membership. I am gratified that *Leadership in the Kingdom* challenged many leaders and congregations to be more open in their leadership style and to move from an "eldership-management" style to a shepherding, leading, and caring style. A decade has passed and we are pleased to learn of new dimensions of dynamic leadership that are apparent in many congregations.

Surrounded on every side by change, younger generations are calling for changes in church function, or at least flexibility and less structure in church life and worship. Unfortunately, many are uncertain as to what changes are most desirable, while others of an older generation are suspicious or concerned over the pleas for change. Calls for change in worship, notably in preaching style and congregational singing, are perhaps the most pervasive and disturbing concerns faced by church leaders today, especially those of a traditional or conservative nature.

In his characteristic thought-provoking style, Peter Drucker in 1989 drew attention to the fact that, almost surreptitiously, contemporary society has moved away from traditional ways of understanding itself. Drucker refers to societies moving historically through "passes" in much the same manner as roads or railroads move through mountain passes from one geographic terrain to another or from one nation to another. He feels that con-temporary society has recently moved through such a pass or sociological shift. The "topog-raphy" of contemporary society has indeed changed radically over the past decade. It is no longer axiomatic that we can depend on people to accept "tried and tested" ways that in past generations have provided for many a stable system of security. Our postmodern soci-ety has adopted new pluralistic worldviews which reject centralized sources of institutional authority and government. Worldwide geopolitical and socioeconomic shifts have intro-duced major challenges and new paradigms for corporate and other institutional leaders. Young people have grown accustomed to multiple choices. "Cafeteria style" has become a new concept in our vocabulary taking us far beyond our food menus.

Centers of authority are an additional factor in which paradigm shifts are being experi-enced. In place of a single national or centralized source of authority, contemporary society in every sphere ranging from business, education, health, family, and religion now depends almost exclusively on localized or personal forms of leadership and authority. Heretofore major institutional centers are no longer the "magnetic north" to modern society's com-pass. Drucker explains that organizations and institutions in the new "apolitical" society have developed new, localized, functional forms of authority and leadership in place of centralized political, hierarchical, bureaucratic centers. He argues that not only will busi-ness and political leaders have to adjust to these "new realities," but so too will educational and religious institutions.[3] The impact of this shift in "magnetic north," or in the traditional safe havens of authority, for church leaders and non-profit organizations is profound.

One weighty new reality presently challenging all institutional leaders, especially in economic and geopolitical sectors but also in religious circles, is the rapidly chang-ing face of American society. Poverty is becoming a serious political and sociological issue. The *graying* and the *coloring* of American society pose unique problems for all leaders. The firming of ethnic and generational segmentation are realities demanding serious understanding and adjustments. Once a melting pot for all wishing to become "Americans," society has taken on a strident diversity. Someone has observed that America is no longer a melting pot of immigrating European peoples, but a mosaic of ethnic groups held together by a dream of freedom and democracy.

Traditional views of the family have been shaken to the very root. The number of unmarried couples living together in 1990 had quadrupled since 1960. Of all children born in 1990, sixty percent will live in single parent households at some time before they turn eighteen.[4] Each of these disturbing "new realities" impacting traditional family mores not only poses challenges for churches with long-standing traditions comprising family units, but also challenging and disturbing opportunities for minis-try. In almost every edition of the major news releases today we learn of states redefin-ing marriage and civil unions. New realities are confronting leadership on every front!

How do churches, structured along traditional family unit models, minister to those whose family units are dramatically different?

One of these new realities that presents serious challenges to Churches of Christ is the change in the socioeconomic makeup of the church. Whereas in the past the church had in many ways a predominantly rural character, the move to urbanization following World War II and the upwards socioeconomic movement of urban church members has changed the character of the church and presented church leaders with several weighty challenges. Most churches hold services whose schedules were determined fifty or more years ago along rural needs. Lifestyles in large metropolitan communities are considerably different today from those in rural America in past generations, yet churches still keep to patterns determined by a bygone age.

Noteworthy among these sociological changes, and perhaps more significant than most are willing to admit, are the generational and gender segmentation of society. The maturing of the Baby-Boomers[5] was evidenced in 1993 in the presidency of Bill Clinton, who for the first time in the American presidency represented a Boomer interest in the White House. With the inherent distrust of traditional authoritarian structures, coupled with the graying of American society, the shift in power structures introduced significant concerns for older generations, especially those drawing social security benefits, and introduced challenging new scenarios. A cover article in *Fortune 500* stressed that "There's a new generation gap, and it can hurt a company's effectiveness. To overcome the tension, begin by understanding each side's point of view."[6] Church leaders ignore the generation gaps within their congregations only at considerable cost. Since the first edition of the book, we now have to deal with a growing new generation gap: two newer generations are pressing for attention, Generation X (Busters) and Generation Y (The Millennials). We ignore them to our own demise! This revised edition of *Leadership in the Kingdom* continues that concern but broadens its scope of awareness.

Concern over increasing demands from women for an active leadership role in society, with considerable impact on church leadership roles, causes traditionalists considerable discomfort and trauma. Young Christians, both men and women, are better educated than their peers of twenty to thirty years ago. In secular life women are moving up the corporate ladder. Many now hold executive, corporate, and leadership positions in society and desire to contribute in meaningful ways to the life of the church. Yet in church life these dedicated capable young Christians are often ignored. They yearn for a greater role in planning, organizing, and directing church life. In many instances they are spiritually, experientially, and administratively capable of supplying insightful and creative leadership ideas. Yet church leaders are often threatened by these young "Turks," and at times are even distrustful of them.

Some "traditional" church leaders, threatened by the pleas for greater involvement coming from the Boomers, Busters, and Millennials, become even more entrenched in the comfortable authoritarian leadership style inherited from their forebears in the belief that such "traditional" models are biblical. The results often lead to unfortunate church splits or in most cases a mass exodus of the new generations to community and Bible fellowship churches where they are permitted a significant voice and where their needs, especially in regard to worship, are addressed. This has caused some churches and church leaders to retreat further into their traditional shells and cry out in frustration and anger at these shifts. In contrast to this, some church leaders are expressing understanding for the concern of their young leaders and are seeking to adjust their congregational leadership roles to meet the new and exciting challenges presented by the bright young minds available to them. Such openness to new leadership style causes older traditional church leaders to mistrust the new style, leading to conflict among congregational leaders, and often congregational trauma.

The distressing dilemma in much of the congregational conflict caused by generational and gender concerns is that both leadership groups are seriously striving to be biblical. The one group is bound by traditional, comfortable leadership models, while the other seeks, within the biblical model, creative ways in which to keep pace with the rapidly changing socioeconomical and cultural needs of their community. The tragedy is that too often even within the same congregation the opposing group concerns become polarized, and the church slowly grinds down to a malaise of mistrust.

The difficulty in adjusting church leadership style to meet the rapidly changing sociological developments need not necessarily be related to doctrinal convictions. We often forget that the eternal gospel is dynamic enough to transcend even the widest cultural and sociological gulfs. Most often the discomfort and problems encountered by churches facing calls for change in leadership style or church structure, are due to insensitivity to the sociological and cultural structures of our church life. Although driven by a passion to structure church life along New Testament "patterns," we are often unaware that much of our church life and structure are derived by adapting biblical principles to cultural needs.

We should be aware that in speaking of *leadership style* we are not addressing *leadership "models"* which relate to one's understanding of biblical teaching on church polity, biblical examples, or biblical authority. *Leadership style* has reference to *how* leaders function, not to whether the church should have elders, or what their "qualifications" should be. To some, steeped in traditional models of rigid authoritarian leadership, the distinction between *pattern* (which addresses biblical authority) and *style* (which addresses function) is, however, unfortunately not readily grasped. Furthermore, for some traditionalists, neither is innovation in style readily accepted. It is either openly resisted or, more often, immediately branded as "liberal" or "unbiblical."

To those concerned leaders who are open to new concepts of leadership style within the biblical pattern of leadership, exciting, stimulating, and creative leadership opportunities are abundant. The problem is that little help is readily available to those willing to explore new directions in leadership style.

The new section on developing leaders we have added in this revised edition, we hope, will address the issue of developing a dynamic style of leadership that will not be a panacea to all church growth issues but will challenge churches to raise up a new generation of leaders with an optimistic vision for the future and a new confidence in the church.

I am personally grateful to our heavenly Father for the way in which he has led my life and ministry to this point in time. Since my conversion to Christ some thirty-seven years ago in Southern Africa, I have been blessed by his grace to work among churches of all sizes: both mission churches and local domestic American churches, rural and urban. The experience of working as a minister and missionary across several cultural gaps has enabled me to see that much of what we do is culturally shaped as well as biblically determined. As a missionary, minister, deacon, Bible professor, college administrator, and elder in the church, God has created opportunities in which I have been able to observe church leadership from many perspectives. He has also surrounded me with loving Christians, church leaders, and professional colleagues who have nurtured me through the years. He has placed me among colleagues in the College of Biblical and Family Studies who have stimulated me to careful disciplined study, and most of all, to constructive concern for the church.

This revised edition of *Leadership in the Kingdom* is dedicated to several wonderful people who continue to make my ministry both possible and rewarding. It is dedicated first of all to my devoted and loving wife, June, who has supported me through years of searching and discovery; to my three sons, Deon, Nigel, and Douglas; and to my three wonderful daughters-in-law, Susan, Sherri, and Joy, all seven of whom have shared with me both the good and the not-so-good times of my ministry. I owe much to them for their patient understanding when I was gone from home for periods far too long for their and my good. But in keeping with what I am calling for in this revised edition I am also dedicating this revised edition to my "five" grandchildren, Rachel Cooke and her husband, Casey; Kevin Fair, Shelby Fair, and Ian Michael Fair; and three "other" family grandchildren, Amber, Chris, and Cassie Lehmann, with the prayer that they will mature into the dynamic new leaders we believe are needed for dynamic church growth.

Theological reflection during many hours of running and backpacking with Anthony Lee Ash has challenged me to look deeply into the overarching message of the text, and to see the text in the larger context of the Bible itself. Tony was a constant encouragement when administrative demands and bureaucratic minutia in my role as dean of the College of Biblical and Family Studies intruded into matters of much greater significance, such as the relation of God's word to church life and the Christian struggle to be more like Jesus. In our "retirement," which term he refuses to admit, he continues to be a ready support and encouragement to me in my new ministry.

Many of the thoughts reflected in this book have been stimulated through my association with Wilson C. (Dub) Orr, my friend, brother in Christ, mentor, and confidant. As fellow elders we shared concerns for the flock we shepherded and for other shepherds who struggle like us to be effective leaders and bishops. We have shared our concerns and instruction in countless leadership seminars, and have tested our ideas on each other in our travels. In many ways I have been a student of his wisdom. He has patiently listened to me as I have tested my thoughts on him and as I have struggled to articulate them in our leadership seminars. From Dub I have been introduced to the depths and the true meaning of leadership through serving. He has been, and continues to be, my model of an "elder-shepherd."

The rationale behind the writing of this book and its revision is the conviction that there is within the inspired biblical example of leadership through elders, ministers, and deacons space for challenging and stimulating leadership opportunities. The problem is not with the biblical *pattern* of leadership, but with the *style* many leaders have adopted in the name of being biblical. Members of Churches of Christ have not always been able to see clearly the distinction between what is biblical and what is traditional. This book seeks to clarify this distinction and focus on leadership style as a fundamental ingredient of church organization and polity. This book is written, therefore, from within the context of a theologically conservative stand, a deep love for the church of our Lord, a belief that there is a biblical model for the church, and a dedication to the restoration of the New Testament church in the conviction that we still have much to learn about being disciples of Jesus.

Since this book is written for a popular audience and not for scholarly circles, I have suppressed the scholarly temptation to use extensive footnotes. However, when I have felt the pressing need to document some discussion, I have included some limited references. In the place of copious notes, I have indicated in a bibliography those works which I have found helpful and out of which I have done much of my research.

This book is revised and offered with the prayer that those reading it will be stimulated to search deeply into the biblical models of leadership for inspiration, and to examine carefully those successful models of leadership style unfolding before us in our contemporary society. May the combination of our study and prayer lead to much growth in the kingdom of our Lord and Savior!

Ian A. Fair
Durango, Colorado
December, 2007

PART ONE

THE CHURCH AND LEADERSHIP IN THE KINGDOM OF GOD

Remember your leaders, those who spoke to you the word of God, consider the outcome of their life, and imitate their faith.

HEBREWS 13:7

CHAPTER 1

THE CHURCH AND LEADERSHIP IN THE KINGDOM OF GOD

———

Whoever would be great among you must become your servant.

MATTHEW 20:26

This book explores leadership in the context of the church. We begin with a brief study of the nature of the church in order to understand more fully the character of the leadership defined in Scripture for that "organization" of believers commonly called "the church."

THE CHURCH

The term "church" occurs in the Revised Standard Version of the Bible 74 times in 73 verses. The term occurs three times in the Gospels, and only in Matthew, 17 times in Acts, and 43 times in the Pauline corpus. In Revelation it occurs as "church" seven times in seven verses and as "churches" 13 times in 12 verses.

The Greek word from which the English word "church"[7] is translated is *ekklesia* (an *assembly, congregation,* or *gathering*). A broad definition of this term often adopted by members of Churches of Christ has unfortunately been "a called out body of people." However, the word is better understood as "a body of people organized into a somewhat autonomous community of believers in Jesus." The essence of the term as it is most often used in the New Testament should, therefore, be "an organized community of believers in Jesus," or a congregation.

This community of believers is organized into a congregation of believers often referred to as the *body of Christ* (Col 1:18, Eph 1:22 - 23) with Jesus Christ as the head of the body. The body—or better referred to as the congregation or community of believers—is led through Scripture into a life of obedient faith and service. Members are initiated into the body through faith in Jesus and by being baptized into the body (1 Cor 12:13).

As head and Lord of the church, God has given Jesus "all authority both in heaven and on earth" (Matt 28:18) and put all things under him. He has made Jesus "head over all things for the church" (Eph 1:22). Jesus has passed on his will for the church through the inspiration of apostles who in turn have recorded that will in Holy Scripture received by the church as the New Testament. Living under the headship of Jesus through Scripture, believers form separate congregations or churches under the overall headship of Christ and the immediate care of local leaders identified in the New Testament as elders, shepherds, or bishops. Along with these elder/shepherds, the congregation is served by evangelists and deacons.

Briefly speaking, the purpose of these local congregations or churches is to bring glory to God through Jesus Christ (Eph 1:11, 12; 3:20, 21). They do so by following a lifestyle reflecting their faith in Jesus, by worshiping God through Jesus, and by carrying out his purpose of reconciling the world to God through Christ (2 Cor 5:18-20)—in other words, through evangelism or sharing the message of Christ with the world.

In summary then, the term "church" or "congregation" is used to describe followers of Christ as they are "organized" into *a corporate body of believers with a specific purpose*. The term emphasizes the corporate unity of the believers. It defines their "organizational relationship" to one another in a community of believers under the headship of Christ.

Vital to the organizational relationship of the members, and their relationship to the headship of Christ, is the role played by the leaders of the community. The purpose of this study is to explore the scriptural nature of that leadership. Broadly speaking, the biblical picture of the church is *a local congregation serving under the headship of Christ*. In the early formative years, the church was served by apostles, prophets, evangelists, elders, and deacons. In time, as the New Testament Scriptures became "canonized," and the apostles and early prophets passed on to their Lord, the local congregations were served by elders (bishops, shepherds), *deacons*, and *evangelists* (1 Tim 3:1ff., Titus 1:5ff., Acts 20:17-30, Phil 1:1, Eph 4:11ff.). It is this model of leadership, with local churches under the headship of Christ being led by elders, deacons, and evangelists, that will form the pattern of church polity for this study.

THE CHURCH AS THE KINGDOM OF GOD

The term "church" is but one of several used in the New Testament to define the community of Christian believers. As we have already noticed, the believers are also identified as the "body of Christ." This concept explains the relationship of the believers to Christ. Each believer, drawing on the analogy of the human body, serves the other members of the body, and the overall purpose of the body, under the headship of Christ.

Christians often draw on the concept of the "family of God" as a means of defining their relationship to God, their Heavenly Father, and to one another as "brothers" and "sisters" in Christ. Christians are "children of God" (Jn 1:12; Rom 8:16; 1 Jn 3:1), having been born anew (Jn 3:16) into the family of God through faith, repentance, and baptism.

The biblical term "kingdom of God" best defines the nature of believers in Christ and their relationship to God. This concept in three related forms, "the kingdom of God," "the kingdom of heaven," and "the kingdom," occurs over two hundred times in the New Testament in reference to God's people.

The New Testament, and especially the Gospels, presents the kingdom of God breaking uniquely into history in the person of Jesus. Jesus came preaching the "gospel of God" proclaiming "the time is fulfilled, and the kingdom of God is at hand" (Mk 1:14, 15). He added, "But if it is by the Spirit of God that I cast out demons, then the kingdom of God has come upon you" (Matt 12:28). This kingdom became a reality in human experience, with power, on the day of Pentecost when the Holy Spirit came upon the apostles (Acts 2:1-21).

Upon surrendering their will to God through faith in Jesus, repentance, and baptism, believers are born into the family of God, become members of his church, and come under the reign of Christ. By being united with Christ in baptism, believers are united with him in his death and resurrection, their "old self" is crucified with Christ, their sinful life is destroyed, and they are no longer enslaved to sin (Rom 6:1-14). Paul adds in regard to his own life, "I have been crucified with Christ: it is no longer I who live, but Christ who lives in me" (Gal 2:20). In this sense, through dying to self and being born again in Christ through faith, repentance, and baptism, members of the church are also members of the kingdom or reign of God in Christ. The unique emphasis of the kingdom is the "reign" of Christ in the life of the believer. The believer no longer reigns in his own life, but through dying to self, Christ reigns in the believer. This is what it means to be a member of the kingdom of God.

This kingdom notion relates to leadership in a profound manner. Due to the influence of several factors, there is at times a tendency to associate leadership with position or power. In some circles leaders draw on the unfortunate term "office" in 1 Timothy 3:1 in support of status or position. When leadership is set in the context of kingdom, a balance is introduced into the relationship of leaders to their followers. Jesus' disciples, and those close to them, on several occasions confused their relationship with Jesus as an advantageous one in regard to position. In Matthew 18:1-4, 20:20-28, and Luke 22:24-27, Jesus gently corrected them by stressing that the greatest in the kingdom would be the ones who served others. Leadership in the kingdom is not one of position, power, and office, but one of humble service.

In one of the most profound passages in Scripture, Paul in Philippians 2:5-10 stressed that it was on account of Jesus' humble service that God highly exalted him above every other person. Jesus did not "count equality with God a thing to be grasped (desperately clung to), but emptied himself (of self and all claims to position), taking the form of a servant...he humbled himself and became obedient unto death, even death on a cross."

In the fullest yet ironic sense, Jesus became the *king* over God's kingdom through becoming the *servant* of all men. In one simple yet meaningful statement Matthew drives this point home: "He came not to be served but to serve" (Matt 20:28). Likewise, Luke stresses that before everything else he is a servant (Lk 22:27).

If church leadership can be understood in the light of Jesus, the King who was a servant of others and in the context of the kingdom, the church will be enriched beyond measure and led in a manner worthy of the kingdom.

THE CHURCH AND THE BODY OF CHRIST

A super-spiritual group in Corinth created several major problems for Paul and the church in that city. One problem that relates to leadership was their tendency to consider themselves more important to the cause of Christ than other "ordinary uninitiated" Christians. Paul discusses this in 1 Corinthians 12:1—14:39. Paul's conclusion is that it is those characterized by "faith, hope, and love" who are the mature Christians and true leaders, not merely those whose gifts included some of the supposedly more spectacular or glamorous gifts such as tongues, special knowledge, and healing.

Of particular interest to our study of biblical leadership is Paul's analogy of the church to the human body. His argument in 1 Corinthians 12:12-30 is that like the human body the church has many individual members. No one member is more important to the body than any other. Each member has an important role that is vital to the proper function of the body. All members are special servants of one another in the body.

The lesson we learn from this in regard to leadership in the church is that all members of the body are servants of other members. In the church it is more meaningful to describe leadership and service in terms of ministry. The emphasis falls on mutual service or ministry, not position or power. Authority to function is involved in the ministry, but this authority is inherent in the particular ministry or service, not in a position or superior "office." The primary consideration is, therefore, on ministry, not position or authority.

We are constantly reminded of Jesus whose kingship was secured by humble service rather than by birth or position. As we continue this study on leadership from a biblical perspective and through the contributions of leadership theory, our primary consideration will be exploring the implications of humble servant leadership rather than leadership from positions of power and control.

PART TWO

CONTEMPORARY LEADERSHIP STRATEGY

I think the ideal leader for the 21st Century will be one who creates an environment that encourages everyone in the organization to stretch their capabilities and achieve a shared vision, who gives people confidence to run farther and faster than ever before, and who establishes the conditions for people to be more productive, more innovative, more creative and feel more in charge of their own lives than they ever dreamed possible.

> ROBERT CRANDALL,
> CHAIRMAN AND PRESIDENT OF AMERICAN
> AIRLINES

People will be asked more and more not just to manage; they will be asked to provide leadership.

> JOHN B. KOTTER,
> PROFESSOR AT HARVARD BUSINESS SCHOOL

The first aspect of leadership for the future is openness to, and maybe even eagerness for, change.

> BLENDA J. WILSON,
> PRESIDENT OF CALIFORNIA STATE UNIVERSITY

What it takes to be a leader in the 1990s and beyond is really handling change.

> ROBERTO GOIZUETA,
> CHAIRMAN AND CEO OF THE COCA-COLA
> COMPANY

Chapter 2

Leadership, Vision, and the Future

Leadership is like beauty: it's hard to define, but you know it when you see it.

Warren Bennis, *On Becoming a Leader*, 1989

What Will It Take?

Along with all who are concerned for the future of the church in a world that is changing almost too rapidly to keep abreast with the challenges being presented, we are disturbed that many churches seem unable to break out of a pattern of "no growth." For whatever reasons, many traditional mainline Protestant churches are not experiencing the exciting growth found in some of the newer evangelical Bible or community churches. In many instances, whatever growth has taken place in mainline churches is from "transfers" or from within the church family itself.

Reluctant as we might be, we simply have to admit that many Churches of Christ are likewise not reaching the world of our unchurched neighbors through conversion. In many cases we are merely preaching and ministering to ourselves. We do this very well! However, when it comes to real evangelism we are not very gifted. The traditional model of ministerial training among "Church of Christ" colleges, universities, and schools of preaching is one of church "chaplaincy," not missionary evangelism. This is not to deny that shepherding the flock is a major function of the church, but shepherding or "pastoring" the church is the role of elders, bishops, or shepherds (pastors), not the evangelist. For whatever reason, elders have abdicated their role as shepherds to the minister who visits the sick and the hospitals, does most of the counseling, and administers the office staff of the church. Focusing most of his attention, by demand, on the church itself, the minister assumes the role of the church chaplain or shepherd (dare we say "pastor"), leaving no one to be the evangelist of the church.

29

In many instances the ministry of the church has simply turned inward upon itself. At this point, we merely wish to emphasize the fact that the church of our Lord Jesus Christ is intended, by divine commission, to be a missionary evangelistic church—one that goes out into all the world and preaches to, and makes disciples of, all nations. A new and timely term has arisen in recent years among Churches of Christ: "missional churches"! The intent is to become, plant, and develop churches that are church-planting churches, not church rest homes. The "all nations" in the great commission is intended to include our own neighborhoods and cities, as well as those in distant places. In stressing the nature of the church as an evangelistic, missionary body, we do not overlook the fact that the church must minister to its own. Our purpose at this point is merely to refocus the church's mission on the "missional" ministry of reconciliation to which it has been called by God (2 Cor 5:18-20).

It is not that the Lord has not provided for the needs of the church members. He has set "pastors and teachers," namely, *elders* or *bishops*, into the church to *shepherd* the church. The predominant model for elders for many years in Churches of Christ has been one of church administration in which elders take care of the financial or fiscal needs of the church. This involves being caught up in endless elders meetings in which they make the decisions for the church. Time demands upon elders, who in secular life are often high-pressure business leaders, in many instances, leave little quality time for serious attention to the spiritual needs of the members. We are gratified to learn that, since the publication of the original edition of this book, this situation has changed and elders are acting more like shepherds and less as managers, and involving capable members of the church as ministry group leaders who share the load of leadership and take care of management issues.

Biblical elders are intended to be shepherds who teach, not board members who simply attend meetings to make decisions. Biblical shepherds should be freed from administration in order to spend more time in members' homes and lives. Elders meetings need to be liberated from administrative concerns in order for the shepherds to devote time to prayer and the spiritual needs of the members. Preachers, as evangelists, need to be unfettered from shepherding roles in order to lead out in the ministry of evangelism to which God has called them.

Our research has led us to believe that leadership, properly understood, plays a significant role, although not an exclusive one, in leading the church of the future into a life of missionary outreach and fruitful evangelism. Dynamic leadership, properly focused by its biblically defined ministry, is essential to leading the church with vision in the twenty-first century. Biblical leadership is indispensable to ensuring that the church of the next generation is recognized in its community as a caring, evangelistic community church driven by its concern for its neighbors, rather than one generally perceived today as a dormant church, given mainly to preserving its past and holding on to its present members.

A basic premise of this study is that a careful re-examination of the biblical ministry roles of leadership and of recent leadership theory is essential to dynamic growth and outreach in the church of the twenty-first century. *This book, therefore, is devoted to exploring dynamic biblical leadership in the church.* By leadership we include all those in the church who provide some form of ministry or service. We will be addressing elders, deacons, ministers, ministry group leaders, Bible class teachers, parents, and all those concerned Christians who love their Lord to the point of desiring to serve him actively and effectively in his kingdom.

LEADERSHIP THOUGHT

Drawing on recent leadership research, Warren Bennis and Burt Nanus have observed: "Leadership is the pivotal force behind successful organizations and ...to create vital and viable organizations, leadership is necessary to help organizations develop a new vision of what they can be, then mobilize the organization to change toward the new vision."[8] They add that although "'Leadership' is on everyone's lips...everybody agrees that there is less of it than there used to be."[9] Since their pivotal research, nothing much has changed. We still struggle to understand leadership and the difference between leadership, management, and "pasturing."

For whatever reason, it seems that outstanding leadership in history has arisen in extreme occasions of crisis or urgency. We observe this especially in the case of national leadership. Mahatma Gandhi, Winston Churchill, and Martin Luther King, Jr., exemplify the emergence of transformational leadership in noteworthy manner. Abigail Adams' comment in a letter to Thomas Jefferson seems as relevant today as it was in 1790: "These are the hard times in which a genius would wish to live. Great necessities call forth great leaders."[10]

Concerns for dynamic, transformational leadership in times of economic stress and uncertainty have been heard from corporate business publications. One of the most prestigious publications in this field, *Fortune 500*, has repeatedly addressed the need for paradigm shifts in business management style and philosophy. In a December 1993 issue of *Fortune 500* the cover title was "Managing in the Era of Change," with the cover story, "Welcome to the Revolution," addressing four business revolutions that corporate leaders must take seriously if they are to survive. In a February 1994 issue, the cover article, "The New Post-Heroic Leadership," argued that serious attention should be given to servant leadership: "...Don't dismiss it. It's real, it's radical, and it's challenging the very definition of corporate leadership for the 21st century." Drawing attention to the crises many corporations are experiencing, the cover article of April 5, 1994, "Managing in the Midst of Chaos," argued that "The entire corporate world seems to be going crazy as companies cut costs but demand more.

The ability to deal with the resulting upheaval and turmoil has become a crucial new skill for executives."

Our world community has undergone a series of rapid crises and changes in recent years. Significant world changes took place in rapid succession after the tearing down of the Berlin Wall. Following the collapse of the Soviet Union, the face of Europe has been transformed into a new world power, and the European Common Market is now a world reality and challenge to United States "hegemony." Following "9/11" and the catastrophic terrorist attacks on New York and Washington, D.C., the growing political crises faced by the United States in Iraq has given rise to strident cries for radical political changes in the United States. Crises in education and college athletics have shaken even those bastions of traditional stability, namely, our institutions of higher learning. Even our traditional mainline churches are searching for means of addressing both the speed of the changes and the insecurity and uncertainty presented by the changes themselves. For many the future is uncertain, and if not threatening then certainly it is intimidating.

It is in the context of urgent need and the uncertainty of the future that dynamic and fresh leadership stakes its claim. Kouzes and Posner in 1987 correctly maintained:

> The domain of leaders is the future. The leader's unique legacy is the creation of valued institutions that survive over time....The most significant contributions leaders make is not to today's bottomline but to the long-term development of people and institutions who prosper and grow.[11]

In a 1983 editorial, former vice president Dan Quayle encouraged the presidency of Bill Clinton and the Democrats to provide the vision and leadership necessary to take America into the leadership of a world desperately seeking direction in the post–Cold War era.

> QUAYLE'S ADVICE FOR BILL CLINTON: Provide a vision in which the United States would lead the world....Vision is especially critical at a time when virtually every major leader has approached the (economic) summit in an economically and politically emaciated state....America can once again offer a vision that will lead the world....[12]

In the closing years of the George W. Bush presidency two popular voices in the Democratic presidential primaries called for radical changes in American political leadership. A major challenge to the almost two-decade Republican dominance of the highest office in the United States is came from a woman, Hillary Clinton, who if elected would be the first woman in United States history to gain that office. A serious challenger was Barak Obama, a young, articulate African American. These candidates introduced a new "face" and voice in the prevailing political scene in America. Furthermore, Congresswoman

Nancy Pelosi, the first woman in American political history to serve as Speaker of the United States House of Representatives, is exercising considerable political power as she calls for changes in how the House of Congress runs its business, notably in the area of House Ethics. The point is that new voices from previously unheard ethnic and gender circles are demanding attention.

A Paradigm for a Vibrant Future

In the following pages we will attempt to present a vibrant paradigm for growth based on essential biblical principles and focused by values-directed dynamic leadership principles. *We will stress that clearly articulated values, creative and innovative leadership style within biblical principles, teamwork, flexibility, vision, a sense of mission and purpose, well defined goals, faith and courage, and finally, sensitivity and concern for people rather than tasks are concerns common to dynamic leadership development.* Each of these components will be explored in this study and integrated into a biblical model of church leadership.

CHAPTER 3

CHALLENGES FACING LEADERSHIP STRATEGY

—◦◦◦—

Leadership...was an American game. The competition may have been fierce, but it was knowable. If you played your cards right, you could win.

But that game has changed—dramatically....The deck has been shuffled and jokers added. Never before has American business faced so many challenges. Uncertainties and complexities abound. There are too many ironies, polarities, confusions, contradictions, and ambivalence for any organization to understand fully. The only predictable thing right now is unpredictability. The new chic is chaos chic. Yogi Berra had it right: "The future ain't what it used to be."

In his new book, Adhocracy: The Power to Change, *Bob Waterman tells us that most of us are like the characters in Ibsen's play* Ghosts. *"We're controlled by ideas and norms that have outlived their usefulness..."*

WARREN BENNIS, *Leaders on Leadership*, 1992

...the next century is already here...Some time between 1965 and 1973 we passed over...a divide and entered the next century....

PETER F. DRUCKER, *The New Realities*, 1989

NEW DIRECTIONS AND NEW REALITIES

In 1982, John Naisbitt's *Megatrends: Ten New Directions Transforming Our Lives*[13] suggested with remarkable foresight that a number of sociological developments already taking place would have profound impact on American lifestyle in the next decade. These, Naisbitt warned, would bring about significant changes that business and other organizations would have to negotiate if they were to be successful in the decade of the 1990s. Although two decades have passed since Naisbitt's research, many of the same challenges he identified still remain and in some measure have been magnified by generational and sociological shifts. Naisbitt's implications were that a number of profound shifts would have to be made by successful organizations as society faced the new realities of the twenty-first century. In fact, in the two decades since Naisbitt's succinct observations, the leadership world has been stretched to the limit to maintain contact with the sociological developments that seem to morph every year.

Many of the changes predicted by Naisbitt's *Megatrends* in 1982 within ten years became an integral part of the established global business and sociological structure. This has, in some measure, created numerous problems for the American business leader as America has moved from an industrial manufacturing economy toward an information and service economy. Cheaper labor costs and the reality of modern technology in many developing third world countries have forced American manufacturers to move manufacturing plants out of the United States. Challenges from the European Common Market appear as an even more threatening challenge to the American economy. The rise of a new world economic power in China looms sharper every year. New threats from the Muslim-controlled Middle East oil-producing nations and the radical socialist Hugo Chavez, president of Venezuela, have given rise to calls for new diplomacy in dealing with these emerging radical threats. American gunboat diplomacy of the past is a moribund leadership style in a rapidly changing new world.

As Naisbitt predicted, American technology has developed toward a new information and service sector in a global economy. The changes from manufacturing to information service have caused major upheavals in some areas which in previous years had depended on heavy industry for their financial base. This was especially true in Texas where the energy crisis beginning in 1974 radically transformed the state's financial base from one which relied almost exclusively on oil and gas into a diversified global information economy. Reinforcing this opinion, Thomas A. Stewart, in an edition of *Fortune 500* entitled "Managing in the Era of Change," notes four "revolutions" which must be embraced by leadership in the coming decade if organizations are to prosper. They are 1) Globalization, 2) Computers, 3) Management, and 4) An information economy.[14]

The industrial challenge from Europe, the Far East, and the developing nations has already made significant impact on and redefined American business. The rise of American information technology to take the place of its ailing industrial might has already become an established reality in American business. High tech, however, is no longer an exclusive American domain. It is now also rapidly becoming a global reality.

Although in some measure we still await the final maturing of the unified European economy and its challenge to the world business market, we are already living fully in a world economy in which America no longer provides exclusive leadership.

The breakup of the Soviet Republic into smaller independent states in which nationalist interests predominate merely reinforces the political pluralism that pervades modern society on an international scale. Ethnic segmentation, ethnic cleansing on an almost global scale, political pluralism, and the shifts in the world economic base are present realities; they are no longer merely "megatrend" predictions. These realities are the very fiber which gives the modern global society its texture.

Almost without exception, Naisbitt's predictions have already become the shape of a new American mindset. The South has successfully challenged northern domination. All three presidential candidates for the 1992 campaign were from the South (if both George H. W. Bush, Sr., and George W. Bush, Jr., are permitted to be identified with their Texas roots). With some recognition of former Northern traditional political power enclaves the South can no longer be treated as a political novice. With Southerners from Arkansas and Texas at the head of the most powerful nation in the world, the South has staked its claim as one of the new realities to be dealt with in the changing scene of American politics.

Traditional hierarchies have given way to networking systems in almost every sphere of organizational theory. Most business strategists have lamented the short-term thinking of American corporations and have identified Japanese long-term strategy as a major factor in the rise of Japanese business supremacy. Rampant individualism and a society almost totally absorbed in self has seen the demise of an either/or authoritarian mindset. The anti-institutionalism of the pluralistic Boomer[15] has shaken confidence in all hierarchical forms of institutional control. The mindsets of Generation X and the more recent Generation Y (the Millennials) continue to challenge outdated leadership paradigms.[16]

What has been emerging with alarming rapidity over the past two decades is a totally new way of thinking about and reacting to the changing world. In a time characterized by a transitional socioeconomic framework, the age of modernity (the age of absolutes and rational progression) has given way to the age of postmodernity (the age of subjectivism that reacted to rational progression in society).[17] In some measures almost imperceptibly, yet again with remarkable rapidity, a new worldview has been emerging. This new worldview is presenting the traditional model of doing business with strident challenges that refuse to be ignored. The new realities demand new answers. Old traditional solutions no longer are able to adequately address the new and rapidly emerging realities. On every front today leaders are confronted by change. In many instances, how we respond to the challenges presented by the paradigm shifts of contemporary society will determine how successful our organizations or businesses will be in the coming decades.

Peter Drucker, specialist in the "science of management," and an astute analyst of global sociological and political superstructures, spoke with remarkable foresight of these new realities as he described the restructuring of modern society. He observes that the many significant "new realities" that presented themselves in the closing years of the twentieth century needed to be confronted courageously and integrated into American business and institutional leaders' worldview if America is to provide successful world leadership in the Twenty-first century (which century Drucker believes actually began as early as 1973!).

Drucker observes that societies, like history, pass through "divides" from one era to the next. Referring by analogy to the Brenner Pass in Europe, which "is the lowest and gentlest of the passes across the Alps" and which from "earliest times...has marked the border between Mediterranean and Nordic cultures," Drucker maintains that "some time between 1965 and 1973 we passed over such a divide and entered the 'next century.'" Although Drucker speaks more directly to the phenomenon of political restructuring, it is obvious in the total context of his book that the same could be said of religious and sociological restructuring. With particular application to the religious sphere, Drucker adds, "We passed out of creeds, commitments, and alignments that had shaped politics for a century or two. We are in a political *terra incognita* with few familiar landmarks to guide us."[18]

Charles Kaiser and Os Guiness, cited by Doug Murren,[19] conclude that the social upheavals of the closing years of the 1960s, and especially the riots and student unrest of 1968, ushered in one of the most turbulent periods in American history, perhaps the most sociologically disturbing era in American history. It is generally conceded that the traumatic years following 1968 and the closing years of the Vietnam War had as great an impact on the American culture and psyche as did the Civil War one hundred years earlier. In September 1988, *Newsweek* ran a front page article raising the question, "Will We Ever Get Over the '60s?" The article dealt with the stormy impact of the student generation of the late 1960s, which generation has been referred to as either the "yuppie" generation, or more recently, the Boomer generation. Murren observes that the "Boomer power" of the 1990s is nothing less than the "coming of age of the spirit of 1968." And now we have moved on to two new generations that demand to be addressed, Generation X (the Busters) and Generation Y (The Millennial Age).

Many established traditional organizations and conservative leaders, noteworthy among them churches and private institutions of higher learning, have failed to recognize these "signs of the times," that is, the sociological "divide" through which American culture passed in the period following 1968 (the student and civil rights unrest) and 1973 (the oil embargo and energy crunch), and the pivotal impact this has had on society. The decline in student population following the "baby boom," the demands of the Boomer generation to be heard and pandered to, the energy crisis of the '70s and economic turmoil it generated, and the competitive challenge of foreign business, are merely some of the significant new realities which impact the contemporary scene. If American businesses, churches, and private universities and colleges are to be successful in the twentieth century, they must *know the rules* by which society, both American and global, will be playing in the coming decades. *These new rules are the "New Realities."*

THE SHAPE OF THE NEW REALITIES FOR CHURCH LEADERS

Successful leaders in the "new American society" that has been developing over the last two or three decades must stay constantly informed regarding the demographic shifts that have been working, sometimes unobtrusively, to move the texture of American thinking beyond the familiar traditional mores with which we have been comfortable in past generations. These "new realities" form the arena in which leaders must develop strategy for the future.

It will serve church leaders well to remember that the church, although established on biblical principles, is an integral part of contemporary society and is shaped significantly by its sociological environment. Although the church in some measures is a safe enclave away from the stresses of secular society, in reality the church is an integral part of that society. Churches which in the past have attempted to withdraw from secular responsibility have come to recognize that the call of Jesus to be a light to the world and the salt of the earth must operate within society in order to have an impact on society. Churches of Christ, which have for many years eschewed any involvement in social issues for fear of adopting a "social gospel," now recognize that their witness is severely restricted by their withdrawal from the social structure of their communities. Christians now understand that although they are guided and shaped by a transcendent message they are part of the secular world in which they live and serve. The church must not only live in its contemporary world, it must impact contemporary society, but as it does so it is in turn shaped and colored by contemporary developments.

Christians are correct in observing that what they do in Christianity is primarily *supra-secular* or *supra-cultural*, and that their ministry and lifestyle have eternal roots that transcend this world. Unfortunately, this conviction often leads church leaders to conclude that they should shun contemporary secular culture, or at least demand that it meet them exclusively on Christian ground.

Christians are fully convinced, and rightly so, that what they do must resist, make an impact on, and transform contemporary society and its secular lifestyle. It has been correctly observed that the church must be a *counter-cultural* movement. But what church leaders often fail to realize is that the church *lives in* this mundane environment, that its ministry is to be *conducted in* this world, and that the church is in many respects *shaped by* the culture in which it lives. To be effective in *Christian* ministry this ministry must take place *within* this world, while resisting this world's secular demands. Christian ministry must competently address the prevailing worldview, *from within* that worldview, while resisting its secular character.

Furthermore, if the church has any intention of leading this lost world to Christ, it must realize that it is working with secular people with secular persuasions. Although disturbed by the secularity of its society, the church simply must seek to understand its worldly neighbors: how they think, what motivates them, and what *turns them on and off*. Christians must make every effort to meet their secular neighbors where *they* are. Many churches expect their worldly neighbors to come to them, to be like them, but if there is one lesson to be learned from the incarnation of Christ, it is that Christian witness will not take place until Christians are willing to go to their neighbors and seek them where they live, and in the language and sociological framework in which they live.

Although many Christians are uncomfortable with what some call the postmodern or post-Christian mindset, church leaders should realize that this non-traditional, postmodern worldview is here to stay! The church simply will have to deal with it, not ignore it, or wish it would go away. To deal with it the church must make every effort to understand it. The church cannot go back over the "Brenner" pass of sociological history and live in a previous generation or sociological structure. Church leaders simply cannot canonize the past and be effective in a future that is already present.

Many challenges facing church leaders today are related to generational differences. Most church leaders are either of a generation born before World War II (the G.I. Generation), or they were at least born during the war era (the Silent Generation). Most difficulties encountered by church leaders with the "younger generation" have their roots in generational differences. Much research has been conducted in the field of generational segmentation, and considerable emphasis will be given to this matter later in the study.[20] At this point we merely wish to stress that generational differences are a reality that must be considered in church leadership.

In addition, although they might not realize it or define their faith in this manner, most conservative church leaders are either neo-Thomistic in theology or, in the language of the American Restoration tradition, are Baconian-Lockean and Campbellite in their theology. We are not commenting here positively or negatively on these theological presuppositions, merely making an observation. The problem we are emphasizing at this point is that many contemporary mindsets are neither neo-Thomistic nor

Baconian-Lockean, but predominantly existential, individualistic, and postmodern in structure. That conservative church leaders do not think in the same manner as do some of our contemporary world neighbors does not necessarily imply that church leaders must change their conservative worldview or abandon their theological heritage and presuppositions. It does mean, however, that church leaders must understand how others think and in what manner their different mindset will impact their leadership. Leading a church in a particular community of believers involves understanding generational, cultural, and philosophical differences, and how these impact leadership style. Church leadership today is profoundly a cross-cultural (or at least cross-generational) phenomenon.

THE IMPACT OF POLITICAL UPHEAVALS AND GLOBAL REDEFINITION

We have already mentioned the intriguing challenge mounted by H. Ross Perot in the 1992 presidential campaign. Experienced political observers have expressed surprise that Perot should build so strong a challenge in such short time. That he has no formal political experience has merely added to the astonishment of many. But this should be no surprise. Both Naisbitt and Drucker have drawn attention to the Boomer dissatisfaction with traditional institutions, and the political infrastructure of our political system. Although the Boomers voiced their concern and dissatisfaction with traditional institutions, the Busters and Millennials have simply ignored them and "walked away from them." We must recognize that our traditional "political" systems, in both the secular and religious environments, are primarily centralized and hierarchical, both concepts being rejected as archaic by the postmodern Boomer, Buster, and Millennial mindsets.

If in other spheres of social experience many are finding alternate solutions to their needs, so why not in the political arena? Traditional hierarchies and centralized forms of authority have in many instances experienced the anger, frustration, contempt, and rejection of today's multi-layered Boomer, Buster, and millennial dominated society. Convinced that the establishment has both betrayed and failed them, many have lost confidence in the established two-party system, believing that it is a self-serving entity. During the crisis of the post–Iraq conflict and the fall of Saddam Hussein, frustration with the continuing struggle to impose a democratic culture on a radical authoritarian Muslim culture has led to strident demands for changes in the American political philosophy, and a rejection of presidential "hegemony."

The political climate of the United States is by no means unique. Political "individualism" in the form of rampant nationalism, or ethnic myopia, is rapidly becoming a global phenomena. One form in which this phenomena surfaces is the international struggle for freedom. Although recently unsuccessful in Nationalist China, individualism and nationalist ethnic freedom has expressed itself with astonishing force in the Soviet Union as the monolithic block of Marxist communism collapsed in ruin all over Eastern and Central Europe. The geo-political boundaries of Europe, Asia, Africa, and the Middle East are in constant flux.

What has this to do with the church and the challenges faced by church leaders? The answers to this are staggering. Astonishing opportunities for world evangelism are being presented as new nations are openly expressing their quest for spiritual values. Many previously monolithic societies and institutions are now being replaced by new, vital forms of political, social, religious, and educational opportunity. Some of these challenges are positive. Others are not. The unstable political climate in many nations, especially third-world nations, presents Christian mission theory and strategy with serious challenges and uncertainties. Political and cultural naiveté will not carry the day in the twenty-first century.

An alarming factor surfacing in the contemporary political turmoil and pluralism is the *role* of the church in society. For centuries the Christian church has been seen by many as one of the stable institutions in society. Now, along with challenges to the traditional political infrastructures of society, the very nature, role, and necessity of the church itself is challenged. As an integral part of the social infrastructure, the church has itself come under scrutiny, being perceived by a rampant secular society as one of the moribund traditional institutions to be rejected—or at least desperately needing revitalization and restructure. Rather than accepting the church as a stabilizing factor to the community, the "take it or leave it" mindset of modern secularity, influenced and shaped by the political pluralism and anti-institutionalism of the contemporary mood, is ready to jettison a church system it perceives to be out of touch with the needs of modern society.

It is not the mere *fact* of political transition and repositioning that is intriguing and challenging today. It is the *rate* and *extent* to which the political boundaries and philosophies of our world are being redefined that defines the new realities of contemporary society. The complexity of the rapidly shifting political and national boundaries has in many cases resulted in doors being opened, even if only marginally so, to potentially rich and rewarding economic and religious mission fields. The question faced not only by our political and business leaders, but also by our church leaders is, "Are we emotionally and strategically prepared for the challenges being presented by the sociological, economic, philosophical, and political restructuring of the world?"

GLOBALIZATION OR ISOLATION?

The comfortable isolation and "island" mentality of economic and political leaders has been dealt a serious blow by the rapid political, economic, and social globalization of contemporary society. On many fronts today we read of concern over "foreign" investors that are taking over our businesses and "buying up" our land. Calls to "buy American" strike a harmonious note for many. Calling on Americans to buy American cars is, however, short sighted. Although sounding patriotic, the call is misguided to say the least. It overlooks the fact that many components of "American automobiles" are manufactured overseas. In addition, a high percentage of the so-called "foreign cars" are now being built in America by Americans. As never before, we are learning that a leaf falling in the quiet of the forest effects the very universe itself! Contemporary business institutions are competing daily in an international market. American investments overseas and foreign investments in America have produced an international market in place of an isolationist "domestic" market.

In startling, dramatic fashion, the world experienced first the Persian Gulf War and the war in Iraq as wars had never before been experienced. The experience was dramatic in that for the first time the scenes before us were in the present tense; live in the comfort of our own homes, the war scenes were enacted before our very eyes. We no longer read news as history, but become part of the news in our own private world! The world has shrunk in less than a lifetime from "a world far away" to a "world within my living room." We can no longer afford to think in terms of our own community or our own nation. We are forced daily to think and plan in global terms. Strategic thinking on a global scale is not unique to the world of political and economic strategists. It must become the lens of church leaders as they face a rapidly changing and intrusive world that presses into the "living room" of our churches.

Church leaders must "seize the moment" to plan their ministry on a global scale before the moment is lost. This will call for creative, innovative, and bold congregational leadership style that is willing to explore new methods of engaging in strategic mission planning and operation that will stretch the boundaries of our present mission philosophy, convictions, and style.

THE EFFECT OF URBANIZATION ON CHURCH LIFE

In the early 1960s Harvey Cox, a student of the sociology of religion at Harvard Divinity School, published his *Secular City* in which he lauded the radical urbanization of American society. Cox naively lauded this phenomenon as one aspect of secularizing God. He was, however, accurate in identifying urbanization as one of the striking developments of the 1950s and 60s. He was also correct in proposing that this urbanization would demand new models of church life if the church was to minister effectively in this new environment.

The impact of this rapid urbanization on American culture is not overstated when we conclude that prior to World War II America was predominantly a rural society, or at

least rural in its fundamental psyche. Since the 1950s, the urbanization of American society has brought about a profound shift in American thinking and lifestyle. Unfortunately,
many of our churches are still living in a rural, cocooned mentality. We tend to live in a
world remote from the changes that are taking place around us.

Well-established paternalistic patterns of authority have eroded with the breakdown of the traditional extended family. Many of the ethical constraints of living in a
small community where the individual is identified through family connections have
evaporated. Individuals in the secular urban setting no longer live shaped or controlled
by parental or extended family mores. Children no longer graduate into the family business, but move away to the city to build their own lifestyle. Family ties are weakened.
Family commitments are redefined. It is no wonder that the traditional American family
is under siege. Those involved in family studies have not yet effectively addressed the
challenges experienced by most families as they move to a new urban setting. The rapid
urbanization of American society and its impact on the traditional American family
presents serious consequences as well as challenging opportunities to church leaders.

Leith Anderson, citing Vance Packard, observes that the mobility inherent in
urbanization "that gives freedom, socioeconomic rise, and social excitement can
severely damage social structures and traditional values."[21] Radical individualism,
personal freedoms, individual anonymity in the secular city, and the loss of the stigma
of divorce, have led to a radical new reality in the American lifestyle: the single family
parent, or "live in" unmarried couple households. Anderson observes: "When parents,
grandparents, and grandchildren are thousands of miles apart, extended families no
longer share child-rearing responsibilities. Traditional values that were reinforced in
small towns and established neighborhoods often dissipate in a community of new-
comers and strangers."[22]

Many familiar "rural" models or structures have undergone radical reinterpreta-
tion as a result of contemporary urbanization. Notable among these is church worship
structure and church meeting patterns. We do not have reference here to the *doctrinal*
character of the church, but simply to the *pragmatic* character of how church is "done."
In a striking manner Leith Anderson demonstrates how the shift from a rural to an
urban church has not normally been a smooth or "economic" transition. He begins
a chapter of his book, *Dying for Change*, by stating, "I have never milked a cow. Only
twice have I seen anyone milk a cow....Yet many churches still hold their Sunday morning services at eleven o'clock, an hour originally chosen to accommodate the milking
schedule of farmers."[23] Church meeting times have fundamentally remained the same
from one generation to another, from a rural pattern to an urbanized society.

Recently, while visiting a son in a large metropolitan city, we attended morning worship with him in a fairly large and highly esteemed congregation. The attendance board

in the front of the auditorium indicated that the attendance for the past week was 1,245 for the AM assembly, 585 for the PM assembly, and 356 for the Wednesday night Bible class. The dramatic fall-off in attendance was disturbing. It appeared to one unfamiliar with the congregation that there was a lack of commitment in this church. My son's response was equally disturbing. "Dad," he answered, "I am not one of those who attend on Wednesday night!" How could this be? The son of a missionary, minister, elder, and Bible professor not attending Wednesday night Bible class? The explanation should have been apparent. Young professionals working in the inner sanctums of corporate America cannot leave their office at an early enough hour to get to church in time for midweek Bible study. "After leaving work at 6:00 PM, wrestling the interstate traffic for 60 to 90 minutes, then driving from home to church, it is practically impossible to get to Bible study before the closing hour at 8:00 PM." Many urban churches have been unable to shake the rural model of "doing" church, and continue to impose a rural model on an urban community without understanding the difference. Obviously a new paradigm for "doing church" in an urban community is called for if we are to minister meaningfully to an urban society. Fortunately, many urban churches are already making such changes, but alarmingly, not without serious opposition from some of the older generation.

Urbanization, with all of its hidden agendas and demands, is one of those challenging *new realities* that necessitates a new paradigm or model of "doing church" in a modern secular society. The church doctrinally must obviously remain the same, but the manner in which it operates must adjust to changing times. Insightful church leaders will be flexible enough to meet the challenges and opportunities presented by the new realities among which the church must function in order to effectively reach the postmodern world in which it lives with the saving gospel of Jesus.

Drawing a fence around our own preferences and comfort zones, or canonizing a familiar past, and refusing to make those adjustments necessary for effective communication and dialogue with a generation that has shifted considerably from our traditional mindset, will surely result in an ineffective and stagnant church manifesting no real growth and effective mission outreach. A "circled wagon" mentality will merely preserve a past heritage for a while, but will in the end result in a church incapable of ministering to its own shifting community of believers, and incapable of communicating with a lost world in which our Lord has left us as his witnesses and ministers of reconciliation.

Changing leadership style in order to meet the new realities of a "new world order" does not necessarily mean surrendering one's cherished doctrinal commitments. It merely means seeking new and flexible paradigms of ministry that are meaningful and challenging to a new generation that has grown up in a world of new realities. Are church leaders capable of making those changes necessary for effective ministry in the new realities?

CONCLUSION

In this chapter we have examined a number of new directions and realities challenging leaders on a macro-leadership scale. We have considered economic, political, and general sociological changes that have forced successful leaders to adopt new leadership style and strategy. We have stressed the fact that the rapid sociological changes on both the global and domestic horizons must be studied carefully by concerned church leaders. Unless church leaders are willing to be more flexible in their leadership style and creative in their strategic planning, many of these wonderful and challenging new opportunities opening daily before us will have passed before we determine to "seize the moment."

In the next chapter we will consider further new realities of specific interest and concern for church leaders. We will explore the profound implications of ethnic, generation, and gender segmentation on church life.

CHAPTER 4

MORE NEW REALITIES

———

The pace of change is swift. Institutions that have lost their capacity to adapt pay a heavy price. Yet the impulse of most leaders is much the same as it was a thousand years ago: accept the system as it is and lead it.

JOHN W. GARDNER, *On Leadership*, 1990

To meet the demands of the fast-changing competitive scene, we must simply learn to love change as much as we have hated it in the past... Today, loving change, tumult, even chaos is a prerequisite for survival, let alone success.

TOM PETERS, *Thriving on Chaos*, 1987

ETHNIC SEGMENTATION

For almost two hundred years America has been the great melting pot of Western civilization. People immigrating from Europe, Asia, and Africa, either voluntarily or by force, were identified simply as Americans or United States citizens. Perhaps naively, it was commonly thought that being "one nation under God, indivisible," would through time and along rational lines melt all those seeking a new life in the United States into one "American" people. The idea of one people, not divided along ethnic lines, was a lofty and grand concept conceived among the rationalist minds of the Founding Fathers and worthy of serious pursuit and defense.

During the period of reconstruction in the South following the Civil War, it soon became apparent that the human element often betrayed lofty ideals. Although free, the emancipated slaves of the South soon realized that freedom did not mean equality. Emancipation changed very little in the life of the slave, and freedom "did not buy bread." Almost a century later the Civil Rights Movement of the 60s demonstrated

47

that the dream was not yet a reality. It cost the life of Martin Luther King, Jr., and then another decade before the cry "Free at last!" became more than a slogan.

Whereas for almost two centuries America had been perceived by most as primarily a "white" society of European descent, the last thirty years, seen either as the closing years of the twentieth century or as the first years of the twenty-first, has driven one point home with striking clarity. Ethnic prejudice and racial bias are realities that cannot be ignored and that will not be resolved simply by referring to a constitutional system of government. It has taken several Supreme Court rulings to drive home to a white majority that minorities of color are also Americans in the fullest sense, and are therefore entitled to all of the benefits of this great society.

Rather than being one *people* under God, or a predominantly "white" majority, the United States is rapidly becoming a diverse, "colored," multi-national nation, with ethnic and national pride a factor to be seriously dealt with. It is not uncommon these days to hear the terms Native American, Latin American, African American, and Asian American defended with pride. Our great democratic society has a long distance to travel down the road of ethnic and national tolerance, and international understanding. There are, however, encouraging signs of awakening. Many African Americans, Native Americans, and Hispanics are taking their rightful role in American political and civil life.

In spite of the fact that considerable progress has been made to recognize the varied heritages of the American people, the waves of ethnic segmentation that have become an integral component of American society are a reality to be contended with. Challenging and disturbing developments in ethnic pride and ethnic segmentation present themselves to corporate and church leaders. Perhaps it is to be the destiny of the United States to demonstrate to the world how a diverse people can live together in a community of people as "one nation under God." The essence of this issue is that in a manner not previously realized, American society is becoming, not only socially and ethnically diverse, but is also becoming socially and ethnically segmented. This segmentation must become a fundamental concern of all persons concerned with responsible and far-sighted strategy development.

One aspect of ethnic segmentation that demands attention in a society that has traditionally interpreted itself as a white community is that most mainline Protestant and Evangelical churches must be sensitive to the so-called "coloring" of society. This coloring of America can be traced to two causes. First, the population growth rate of the white majority was predicted to reach zero by the year 2000,[24] while the population growth among "ethnic" America continues to grow. Second, immigration over the coming decades will continue to change the complexion of American society. In the closing years of the twentieth-century America accepted more immigrants than all other nations of the world combined. America now has more Irish than Ireland, more

Jews than Israel, more blacks than any other nation except Nigeria, and ranks third in Hispanic peoples only to Mexico and Spain. Furthermore, it was predicted that whites would be a minority in California by the year 2000. Overall, the proportion of minorities will increase from 23 percent of the population in twentieth century to 26 percent in the twenty-first century. No creative purpose will be served by "white" Protestant America "wringing its hands in despair." The coloring of America is a fact of twenty-first century life and must be addressed by all responsible leaders.

These demographics pose serious challenges to American political and community leaders. Of major concern is the fact that increasing numbers of minority peoples will be living below the poverty level each year as we move deeper into the twenty-first century. Social problems in an increasing number will need to be faced seriously and with considerable urgency by every element of American community life in order to avert a major corrosion of society. Community, corporate, and church leaders will bear an equal responsibility in developing equitable solutions to this problem.

The ethnic segmentation and coloring of American society is one of the major new realities that all aspects of American society must deal with in the coming years. This will be especially true for those "border" states where the present minorities are rapidly moving toward a majority. Many present churches, now white enclaves, must make serious efforts to reach out to this burgeoning ethnic diversity, and seriously consider how to minister to this rich and diverse mission field that is right on their doorstep. This will demand sensitive, creative, innovative, and godly Christian leadership.

GENERATION SEGMENTATION

Jeff Magee insightfully observes that the next leadership paradigm shift is one in which we move beyond gender and race to one in which we have to recognize five generational segmentations.[25] We have at all times been aware of generational differences, for young people have always thought the older generation has not understood them. This is most likely true. However, it is only in recent years that generational differences have developed into a distinct segmentation that plays a powerful role in society and demands serious attention.

One major reason for the disproportionate role that generational segmentation has played over the past four decades of the twentieth century has been the powerful influence of the television media in entertainment and advertising. Fully aware of the fluid nature of the younger generation's move up the socioeconomic ladder, especially following the affluent decades of the 50s and 60s, corporate leaders have skillfully projected their marketing strategy at the individual tastes of the various segments of society, and increasingly at the younger generations. In response to this we have seen the growing power of the over 50s generation through AARP (*The American Association of Retired Persons*).

Another possible factor that has driven home the reality of generational segmentation has been the striking growth and increasing voice of that segment of the
population popularly known as the Millennials or Generation Y. Within the last three
decades the advertising media has moved in rapid succession past the Boomer and
Buster Generation (Generation X) to the Millennial Generation (Generation Y). While
the Boomer Generation is posing serious concerns for the Federal Social Security
Administration, the Millennial Generation is demanding respect and attention in
most areas of the economic and sociological sectors. Our society now has to take five
generations seriously.

In their seminal work on the history of generations in America, William Strauss
and Neil Howe[26] identified four distinct generation groups in contemporary society. The
nomenclature given by Strauss and Howe are descriptive of the makeup of these groups:

G. I. elders, born 1901-1924, age 66 to 89 in 1991;
"Silent" modifiers, born 1925-1942, age 48 to 65;
"Boomer" rising adults, born 1943-1960, age 30 to 47;
"13ER" youths, born 1961-1981, age 9 to 29.

Strauss and Howe demonstrated that these four generation groups manifest distinct preferences, prejudices, and characteristics. Their generational peculiarities are
illustrated in detail on the following pages.

Of particular interest to this study is the phenomenal loss of confidence in traditional institutions in contemporary American society. This decline in confidence
which began with the Boomer generation has continued unabated in the subsequent
three generations.

Although generational differences are not a new phenomenon in sociological
studies, they have become a factor of greater significance than in past generations in
shaping the fiber of contemporary society. It should be emphasized at this point that
we are not here merely highlighting generational differences. We are stressing that the
stratification of generational differences and generational segmentation must become
a major concern of church leaders.

For the sake of clarity, and to maintain some uniformity with the literature discussing the generational makeup of American society, we will be adopting the following nomenclature for the four major generation groups in contemporary American
society. The following vocabulary is an adaptation of Strauss and Howe's terminology.
For the sake of brevity and clarity we have presented the generational characteristics
in list form:

The G. I. Generation
• Born 1901-1929, 64-92 years old in 1993.

- The *Civic* generation, institutionally inclined.
- Typical representatives: Billy Graham, Tip O'Neill, Lee Iacocca, Ann Landers, Lyndon B. Johnson, John F. Kennedy, George Bush, Martin Luther King Jr., H. Ross Perot.
- They were raised during the Great Depression.
- They are the "get it done" generation.
- All U.S. presidents from 1961 through 1992 were from this cohort.
- They work together, are civic minded, and are team players.
- They are keenly impressed with progress in the "great society."
- They regard "government" as a benefactor.
- They are confident, left brained, pragmatic, rational problem solvers, technocrats, conformists, male dominated, trust in government and institutional authority.
- They fought and won wars.
- They represent the most "upbeat" generation.
- They see themselves as the powerful stewards and guarantors of the American way of life.
- They are uneasy with the Silent generation, and distrust the Boomers.

The Silent Generation
- Born 1930-1945, 48-63 years old in 1993.
- The *Adaptive* generation, somewhat institutionally inclined.
- They were born and raised during the Great Depression.
- Typical representatives: James A. Baker III, Andrew Young, Sandra Day O'Conner, James Dean, Ted Koppel, Pat Schroeder, Geraldine Ferraro, Walter Mondale, Michael Dukakis, Jesse Jackson.
- They have not, and probably will not, produce a U.S. president.
- They are interested in the system rather than the individual.
- They are sandwiched between two dominant groups, the G.I. generation and the Boomers.
- They are somewhat "confused," uncertain, subject to plasticity, look to G.I. as their role models, are willing to comply with G.I.'s, yet defer to Boomers, manifest no definite sense of direction.
- They prefer to defuse conflict, are flexible, and specialize in relationships rather than in grand or lofty ideals.
- They are the most considerate of generations, and admire fairness, openness, and due process.
- They are influenced by opinion polls, but reluctant to make decisions based on opinion.

• They often lack confidence and cohesion in relationships. They emphasize participation over authority, process over results.
• They matured during an affluent period of U.S. history.
• They gave birth to and raised the Boomer generation.
• They willingly accept the G.I. mindset, but are uncertain about Boomers.
• They lost wars and presidential elections.

The Baby Boom Generation (Boomers)
• Born 1946-1964, 29-47 years old in 1993.
• The *Idealist* generation, normally referred to as Boomers, having been born during the so-called "baby boom."
• They have lost confidence in institutions.
• The "Woodstock" generation.
• They were born and raised in affluent times, yet often reject materialism.
• They triggered a violent, reactionary period in American history, rejecting the Vietnam War as immoral.
• They are a confident, "smug" generation, and see little inadequacy or shortcoming in their generation.
• They were taught by the G.I. generation to think critically, to be critical of everything, especially the G.I. generation and its values.
• They are concerned with "principles," and launched the modern "Consciousness Revolution."
• They believe their parents' world needed a "spiritual overhaul," possibly even a "creative destruction."
• They reacted to the technological, materialistic worldview of their parents and grandparents.
• "The Boomer ethos remained a deliberate antithesis to everything G.I.: spiritualism over science, gratification over patience, negativism over positivism, factiousness over conformity, rage over friendliness, *self over community*."
• They manifest a mixture of high self-esteem and selective self-indulgence.
• They form a "narcissistic culture" with affixation on self.
• They are a generation with a strong religious feeling and idealistic sense of "perfection" that rejects formal, corporate, religious experience in favor of personal, subjective, religious experience.
• They are "spontaneous, imaginative, right brained"; they move from one form of internalized religious experience to the next: from the drug age, to "flower power," to the "Jesus movement," to evangelicalism, to the "new age."
• They represent the most active era of church formation of the twentieth century.

• They react to the male dominated G.I. generation, which reaction leads to an almost "oedipal" attachment to mothers.

• The Boomers reject the male-dominated society of the G.I. in favor of equal opportunity for women in every walk of life.

• They are characterized by an absorption with self and self-gratification which led to the "sex revolution" of the 1970s.

• Vietnam, the Kent State shootings, Watergate, the Iran-Contra episode, the failure of the savings and loan system, all led to an increasing distrust of institutional authority.

• Boomers are a strange mixture of "institutional criticism" and "individual toleration."

• They are an "explosive generation" and are intensely reactive.

• "If G.I.'s measure their worth objectively, by the works they leave to history, Boomers measure themselves subjectively, by the spiritual strength they see within."

• Boomers are a generation impressed with "self" and their own internal values. They consider their own inner "consciousness" to be higher than that of their "materialistic" predecessors.

• They disowned the only major war of their generation.

• Consequently, they lost confidence in the previous generation, and are concerned over the next generation.

The 13er or "Baby Buster" Generation
• Born 1965-1993, 1-28 years old in 1993.

• "Busters" are a *Reactive* generation. Their preferred nomenclature is "The Generation X."

• Typical representatives: Michael J. Fox, Eddie Murphy, Tom Cruise, Michael Jordan, Deion Sanders, Brooke Shields, Gary Coleman, Jennifer Capriati.

• They are a brash generation, with an "in your face" mindset; they rebel against being stereotyped by their elders as an inferior generation, especially the Boomers.

• They were raised during an age of national pessimism on the part of the older generation in the 1974-79 era.

• They sense that the older generation has lost control of life.

• They are defined by the older generation as frenetic, slippery, uncommitted, and without direction.

• They seem to be driven by appetites, not ideals.

• Jay Leno once observed, "We're not 'talkin' brain cells here. We're 'talkin' taste buds."

• They manifest little concern for *knowing* what is good or *doing* good; their major interest is in *feeling* good.

• They are generally considered by their elders to be a generation of "mediocrity" and a generation inferior to its predecessors.

• They have consistently scored lower grades than preceding generations.

• They are less college educated than previous generations.

• Busters have serious doubts over their economic future.

• They are being raised during a period of information overload.

• They have been raised to believe that there are no absolute truths that can be learned, therefore, they are not motivated to learn.

• Busters are faced with a multitude of options leading to a robust pluralism.

• They lack "ego" strength and tend, therefore, to react rather than to pioneer their own future.

• Busters are typical "Bart Simpson" underachievers: "Everyone expects me to fail." Busters are, therefore, not highly motivated.

• They are being raised in a period of great domestic dissatisfaction, divorced parents, and single-parent homes.

• Urban poverty and violence are characteristic of this generation—one in every five of them will live in poverty.

• Busters are experiencing major changes in a global society characterized by little stability.

• They are convinced that wars solve little.

• Busters are extremely cynical over the future.

• "We trust ourselves, and money—period."

• "The choices are ugly and few."

Since Strauss and Howe developed their generation categories, new generations and categories have developed. We now need to add the Millennial Generation, and list a few of their peculiarities.

Generation Y or the Millennial Generation

• They were born in the 1980/1990s and are maturing and entering the marketplace in the new millennium.

• They live in an age of personal electronic gadgets, electronic games, cell phones, iPods, and downloadable music.

• They understand the movie, "The Matrix."

• They are the skateboard generation.

• They dress casually in the marketplace and schools, and wear flip flops to work and school.

- They are highly intelligent, well educated, and informed.
- They are impressed by constant movement in music, advertising, and videos.
- They are extremely independent of family.
- They feel empowered as individuals.
- They live in an age of blogs and shared information.

In a more recent study (2006) Jeff Magee of *Jeff Magee International* (http://www. jeffreymagee.com/articles_show.aspx?categoryID=32&id=268) has drawn attention to the fact alluded to above that we now are dealing with five generations that demand attention. He lists the five generations as:

1. Centurions – those making up the elder statesmen end of the workforce, being about 55 years in age and older. Census information suggests that there are some fifty-five million of these individuals in the workplace, with many comprising the most senior leadership positions.

2. Baby Boomers (and the Eco Boomers) – those making up the bulk of the middle ground ranging from 38 to 55 years of age. Census information suggests that there are some seventy-three million of these individuals in the workplace, most with upwardly mobile career objectives!

3. Generation X'ers – those making up the more extreme-oriented and possession-oriented individuals of the workplace, ranging in age from late twenties to about thirty-eight years of age. Some fifty million individuals represent this demographic.

4. Generation Y'ers – those individual that are post-college in age and entering the mainstream workforce through about age 28. Some forty million occupants here.

5. Generation MTV'ers (or Mosaic) – are those individuals just entering the workforce as temporary and part-time workers and interns. Typically about age 16-21, this group comprises a staggering fifty-five million individuals or more.

SOME IMPLICATIONS OF GENDER SEGMENTATION

However we segment or denominate these five generations, we have to face the fact squarely that they do not think alike and that they are with us for the future. We must take all five into consideration in strategic planning if we intend to be effective in church planting and growth.

One of the major developments of the past thirty years has been the restructuring of the traditional family lifestyle. Whereas in the past, American society was structured around the traditional family unit, extended or nuclear, contemporary culture is rapidly becoming characterized by alternate lifestyles such as single-parent households and unmarried couple households. Single parent households are developing into a major sociological concern. Six out of every ten children living in the first decade of the 2000s will live for some period in a single-parent family. Unmarried couples living together and raising children are becoming vogue among the Baby Buster generation. The radical redefinition of traditional family lifestyles has dramatically shaken traditional family paradigms. The restructuring of the traditional family has consequently contributed to a challenging redefinition of gender roles in these non-traditional families.

A major driving force in the contemporary redefinition of gender roles is the Boomer rejection of a G. I. male-dominated culture in favor of one in which women have equal opportunities. This has created a mindset in which traditional gender roles are viewed as archaic and in need of serious redefinition. The distinctive male-female role differentiation of past generations has over the past thirty years become so vulnerable that what was once clearly perceived to be either male or female is now blurred. This is evidenced in the preference for unisex clothes, male earrings, unisex hair styles, and the breakdown of some male-dominated sports activities. It is possible that contemporary American society's comfortable acceptance of a gay lifestyle can be partially attributed to the breakdown of distinct gender differentiation and roles.

The church, as a historically conservative enclave and preserver of traditional values in society, is faced with profound challenges as it seeks to come to grips with the demands of both a secular and five-generational-dominated society. The role of women in the church will probably be one of the most difficult and traumatic problems faced by conservative churches for whom Scripture, not the strident demands of a secular society, must always be foundational to faith and practice. If church leaders are to successfully lead (however successfully is defined) the modern church out of the past into the future, they must understand clearly the nature of the changes being demanded by their constituents who live in a rapidly secularizing postmodern society.

Gender segmentation is a "given" with profound implications, both positively and negatively, for the church living in our postmodern contemporary society. Whether we like it or not, gender segmentation with its demands for increasing roles for women, will not simply pass away. Gender segmentation is a significant and challenging *new reality* with which the church must deal if it is to be successful in bringing this generation to Christ and his saving gospel. It is also a new reality that has enormous destructive and divisive potential if it is not handled in a sensitive manner. The church must find avenues through which to address these gender concerns in a manner that will be faithful to Scripture and sensitive to the concerns of women of a "younger" or new generation if it is to recapture its rightful place as a *moral* force in society.

CONCLUSION

Most leaders among Churches of Christ have their faith deeply rooted in a view of inspired Scripture. They are thus naturally "prejudiced" in favor of conservatism and toward preserving the traditional rather than hastily adopting new fads that appear from time to time. This is an admirable quality. However, in view of a commitment to being biblical, it is essential that church leaders regularly examine their *traditions* to determine whether their *firm commitments* are truly biblical, or whether, perhaps, some traditional elements have become biblical in the course of time. It is an easy step for the distinction between *traditional* and *biblical* to become *hazy* and for Christians to confuse their conservative *traditions* with *being biblical*.

In view of the challenges faced by a rapidly secularizing society, willingness to examine one's faith under a biblical lens is a necessary preliminary to being truly biblical. As the church moves steadily into a postmodern culture and is faced with distinct new realities that demand a hearing, church leaders need to "reinforce" their biblical foundations through careful, critical examination, while at the same time seeking to understand the nature of the society in which they must lead their followers effectively in an outreach ministry. It is absolutely necessary that church leaders seriously attempt to understand the secular nature of the world in which they minister while at the same time resisting all pressures to compromise their faith.

The church, along with its contemporary society, has passed—like it or not—through the modern "Brenner" pass into a new century where it is faced with new generational mindsets. The church simply cannot remain on the "other side" of the postmodern "Brenner" pass and still be in a position to minister to a culture on "this side" of the "Brenner" pass. The new realities of the twenty-first century cannot be ignored. The church, however, need not fear such "Brenner" passes, for the Christian gospel is not locked into any one generation, culture, or society. The true gospel and "power of the cross" have successfully survived many generational or sociological "Brenner" passes over the past twenty centuries. The church believes and proclaims an eternal gospel which transcends every secular development. It is the challenging responsibility of the church to seek to understand these sociological, ethnic, generational, and gender "new realities," and to explore avenues through which to address them while holding firmly to the eternal and enduring gospel message of the cross.

Chapter 5

Leadership in the Context of New Realities

—⁓—

Business in America has lost its way, adrift in a sea of managerial mediocrity, desperately needing leadership....Business executives erroneously believe that management and leadership are synonymous....The truth is that managing and leading are vastly different activities.

Abraham Zaleznik, *The Managerial Mystique*, 1989

The Leadership-Management Tension

In the closing decades of the twentieth century considerable attention was given to the differing management styles evident among American corporate leaders and their Japanese and European counterparts. Several highly qualified scholars in the field of corporate business and management style[27] addressed a perceived malaise in American corporate business performance. A common conclusion was that most American corporate woes could be traced to a conglomerate management style that was unable to adjust rapidly enough to successfully meet the challenges presented by a rampant global business challenge.

There was considerable opinion that much of the problem lay in a polarized leadership-management tension. Whether the fault lay in the traditional business school MBA mentality, as was charged by several leading scholars, lies beyond the scope of comment in this study. The thrust of this chapter will, however, focus on the leadership-management tension and attempt to identify those principles that are relevant to the study of church leadership. It is interesting to observe that much of what was being said in many leadership seminars, for instance by the Covey Leadership Center, regarding integrity, ethics, values, and people-centered leadership had remarkable affinity with what the Bible says regarding leadership. Perhaps it is both appropriate and ironic that those in biblical leadership roles be called back to their biblical roots by the business sector after a sojourn in a corporate management culture.

Before beginning this exploration into the leadership-management continuum, it is appropriate that we clarify one or two fundamental principles. *We must stress at the outset that this study is not arguing against sound management principles.* Every successful business or organization must be built on competent managerial principles. Failure to give serious attention to fundamental fiscal and fiduciary matters will eventually lead to disaster.

The point most often stressed in the leadership-management dialogue by those concerned with the apparent corporate malaise in American business had reference primarily to the *style* of management employed in many American corporations and organizations. Concern was expressed over the *emphasis* given to the management dynamic in the leadership-management continuum. It is of profound significance to the thesis of this study that we speak of a leadership-management *continuum* rather than a leadership-management *bifurcation* or *polarization* which could simplistically be read into the discussion. The leadership-management continuum and tension is clearly illustrated in the diagram below.

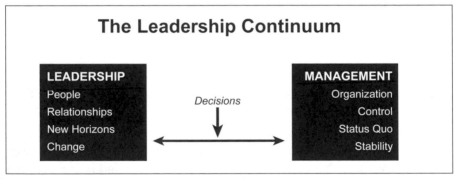

FIGURE 1

Such is the complexity of the business and leadership-management environment that all successful leadership-management decisions and the style of leadership demanded by that environment must be flexible enough to move back and forth along the leadership-management continuum as demanded by the situation. Certain situations, decisions, or opportunities will demand different leadership styles or degrees of management from others. Competent leaders will know when and how to determine which degree or style is most appropriate for the situation under consideration.

Kenneth Blanchard defines the ability to move along the leadership-management continuum as *Situational Leadership*.[28] In his unique manner, Blanchard identifies four leadership styles that demonstrate this movement. Blanchard's four styles of leadership are *Delegating, Supporting, Coaching,* and *Directing. Delegating* represents the leadership end of the continuum, and *directing* the management end.[29] As indicated in

Blanchard's model, the leader's style involves *followers* or workers. He observes, "A situational leader...changes his style depending on the person he is working with *and on the situation* (italics added)."[30] Two factors, therefore, impact the leadership-management dynamic: the character or maturity of the followers or workers, and the nature of the situation in which they function.

Appreciation of the nature and appropriate function of the leadership-management continuum is essential to understanding much of the discussion encountered in the leadership-management dialogue. Without a sensitive appreciation of this tension one could conclude that leadership and management are antithetical concepts in an either/or dichotomy. But this is not the case. Much of the concern being addressed by most leading business or management researchers is an imbalance or fixation in this continuum where management and management theory have become the dominant or sole element in corporate life.

Divorcing leadership from the leadership-management continuum, and allowing management to become polarized, degenerates into a Weberian[31] bureaucracy which slows an organization down, gradually and imperceptibly, to where it is unable to respond swiftly to the demands for change. Organizations encrusted with a bureaucratic culture are doomed to fail in today's rapidly changing global economy. Sadly, and all too often, this is what was happening to that sector of American corporate culture that was struggling to meet the challenges of foreign competition. Warren Bennis makes this thought provoking observation:

> Constant change disturbs managers. It always has, and it always will. Machiavelli's observation that "change has no constituency" still rings true. In his recent book *Adhocracy: The Power to Change*, Bob Waterman tells us that most of us are like the characters in Ibsen's play *Ghosts*. "We're controlled by ideas and norms that have outlived their usefulness, that are only ghosts but have as much influence on our behavior as they would if they were alive. The ideas of men like Henry Ford, Frederick Taylor, and Max Weber—these are the ghosts that haunt our halls of management."

> Most of us grew up in organizations that were dominated by these men, the fathers of the classic bureaucratic system. Bureaucracy was a splendid social invention in its time—the nineteenth century. In his deathless (and deadly) prose Weber first brought to the world's attention that the bureaucratic, machine model was the ideal for harnessing the manpower and resources of the Industrial Revolution. To this day, most organizations retain the macho, control-and-command mentality intrinsic to that increasingly threadbare model.[32]

When any organization is dominated by an hierarchical, top-down, *"macho, control-and-command mentality,"* management style has so dominated the leadership-management tension and continuum as to leave the organization struggling "in the starting blocks" while the world around it is in full stride for the finish line!

It is the *macho-control* dynamic of management that has been identified as the core of the problem in several significant studies, for example in Zaleznik's *The Managerial Mystique*, and James M. Kouzes and Barry Z. Posner's, *The Leadership Challenge*.[33] Much traditional management style, characterized by a bureaucratic control mindset which has been encrusted by its many formal layers of management, is unable to move rapidly enough to adjust to the many demands for change currently being forced on managers or leaders by globalized and secularized society.

Management is inherently opposed, by the very nature of its conservative control dynamic, to rapid changes and the innovations demanded by those changes. Peter Drucker, in his 1992 work, *Managing for the Future*, comments on what he identified as a fundamental factor in future organizational success or failure. He observed:

> The greatest challenge to American business in the 90s, especially the large company, may well be its management people. And we are totally unprepared for it (that is, the calls for rapid change in the 90s, IAF). One reason why there will be a problem is the sharp turn in the structure of management. For 35 years...the trend ran toward more and more layers of management and more staff specialists.[34]

The traditional, hierarchical, bureaucratic structure that characterizes all authoritarian organizations, whether corporate business or non-profit, is simply too cumbersome or comfortable for the immediate or swift response demanded by rapid change. Somehow, business executives and heads of non-profit organizations must loosen up their organizations and free them from bureaucratic encrustation so that strategic planning, decision making, and delivery can move flexibly and freely along the leadership-management continuum as the exigencies of the occasion demand.

If organizations are to become effective and competitive in the new world of the twenty-first century with its rapidly developing new realities, more time must be spent at the leadership end of the continuum, as risky as this may seem to some. Good management must continue, but not at the expense of dominating creative leadership through management's penchant for control and preservation of the corporate *status quo*. It is almost impossible for creative leadership, and the necessary innovation demanded in dynamic organizational strategy, to exist today in a traditional bureaucratic culture.

ENTREPRENEURIAL LEADERSHIP

If leadership and management are two extremes on a continuum, then *entrepreneurship* falls off the continuum on the leadership end. More space will be given in a later chapter to defining management and leadership in detail, but it is appropriate at this point to clarify what we mean by the term *entrepreneurial leadership*. Drucker explained the term and its pivotal role in the discussion of management:

> I turn now to crucial issues for managers in the knowledge society: innovation and entrepreneurship. It is not a coincidence that these necessary concepts are back in fashion. For a long period they were neglected, to the point where for all intents and purposes they vanished from the list of corporate concerns. Only in the last 15-20 years have these two practices...come to the fore again.[35]

It is not surprising, as Drucker indicated, that these concepts have not universally been part of the corporate mindset if the corporate culture has been dominated for the past 50 or more years by a Weberian bureaucratic management mindset. By definition both innovation and entrepreneurship run counter to bureaucracy and the focus of fundamental management principles.

The term *entrepreneur* was coined approximately 200 years ago by a French economist, J. B. Say.[36] In Say's use the term meant "one who upsets and disorganizes."[37] The term has elsewhere been defined as "creative destruction." Drucker observed, "To get at the new and better, you have to throw out the old, outworn, obsolete, no longer productive...of the past."[38] Ingrained deeply, however, within the psyche of the managerial culture is the preservation of the *status quo*. It is no wonder, then, that traditional bureaucratic management has been uncomfortable with innovation and entrepreneurship, for innovation means abandonment of the old. This mindset has profound implications and challenges for church leaders in a conservative movement in which roots, heritage, and the history of the movement are extremely significant.

The relationship between entrepreneurial leadership and change was emphasized by Drucker:

> In *Innovation and Entrepreneurship* (1985) I wrote that "systematic innovation...consists in the purposeful and organized search for changes, and in the systematic analysis of the opportunities such change might offer for economic or social innovation." I want to identify seven sources to look out for as signs and sources of a chance to innovate...They are basically symptoms of change.[39]

Entrepreneurial leadership is an effective tool by which organizations can introduce, confront, or manage change, especially when the change presents itself in demographic, sociological, and economic forms. Traditional management philosophy with its authoritarian control model is unable by its very nature to adjust rapidly to and manage such change.

Entrepreneurial leadership neither demands nor necessitates that all of the past be discarded. It does mean, however, that leadership cannot remain locked into its past, that leadership must face the future with confidence, knowing that the past gives stability and direction, and can form the basis of the necessary adjustments to the changes of the present as well as the future.

This is especially important to church leaders whose community is as much an organization challenged by calls for change as is the business corporation. Conservative[40] church leaders often find change difficult to accept, since most church leaders in traditional churches today tend to come from the more traditionally minded and civic oriented G.I. generation who are by nature uncomfortable with change.

Many conservative church leaders, unfortunately, tend to interpret sociologically motivated calls for *organizational* or *leadership style* change as calls for *theological* change, and therefore oppose change on two fronts: one, a generational discomfort with change, and two, a theological opposition to change that might threaten the organization's theological foundations. Mere mention of the term *innovation* in some church circles is liable to cause considerable uneasiness, discomfort, and resistance.

Sociological, demographic, economic, and other changes facing the church in the twenty-first century are a serious call to church leaders to explore innovative changes, and, without abandoning fundamental biblical foundations to faith, to be entrepreneurial leaders rather than control managers. The contemporary postmodern world in which, and to whom, the church must minister simply will not stand still and wait for a church that refuses to address and successfully manage change. The status quo of the past now finds itself constantly faced by a state of flux. Church leaders cannot, therefore, ignore calls for change and comfortably canonize the past. To do so is to alienate a major segment of society, namely, the "Boomer, Generation X, and Millennial" cohorts.

BEWARE THE E MYTH!

Michael E. Gerber warns that leaders should beware of what he describes as "the E Myth" in which leaders place excessive emphasis on entrepreneurship, not realizing that while entrepreneurial leadership is a necessary ingredient in the successful organization, other factors are equally important.

Gerber asks the question, "What does the successful business person know that the unsuccessful business person doesn't?" In Gerber's mind the answer does not lie simply in entrepreneurship, but in the "*insatiable need to know.*" Gerber observes:

...the problem with most failing businesses I've encountered is not that the owners don't know enough about finance, about marketing, about management, about operations—they don't, but those things are easy to learn. The problem is that *they think they know enough*. And so they spend their time defending what they know, rather than discovering what they don't.[41]

Three elements are essential in the dynamic of successful business, according to Gerber. Unfortunately these three are often locked in a three-way battle, a battle that no one can win. The three elements are the Entrepreneur, the Manager, and the Technician.

The Entrepreneur wakes you with a vision. The Manager screams, "Oh, no!" And while the two are battling it out, the Technician seizes the opportunity to go into business himself—not to pursue the entrepreneurial dream, however, *but to finally wrest control of his work from the other two.*[42]

As Gerber defines the situation, the Entrepreneur lives in the future and thrives on change, the Manager lives in the past and is committed to maintaining the status quo and resisting change, while the Technician lives in the present and is concerned with getting the job done. "To the Manager, then, the Technician becomes a problem to be managed. To the Technician, the Manager becomes a meddler to be avoided. To both of them, the Entrepreneur is one who got them into trouble in the first place!"[43]

In the framework of the leadership-management continuum, Gerber's observations regarding either excessive entrepreneurship or management are timely. Successful leaders have an insatiable desire to know all there is regarding their enterprise, and as the occasion demands, to be capable of moving along the leadership-management continuum without being locked into any fixed position or strategy.

The similarity to the situation described by Gerber and that encountered in many churches today is interesting. The entrepreneurs, represented by Christians, many of them from the younger and newer generations, call for change. The managers, represented by older, conservative elders comfortable with the past or status quo, resist the calls for change. The technician, represented by the average member, wants to get on with the job of ministering to the community and is frustrated by the traumatized leadership who seem unable to provide the aggressive and creative leadership necessary for real growth.

Gerber's warning regarding excessive entrepreneurial leadership adds an appropriate conclusion to this brief discussion of the leadership-management continuum. In every organization, whether it be a corporate business dedicated to financial growth and profit, or a non-profit organization, as in the case of the church, the goal should be a healthy balance between entrepreneurial leadership and responsible management.

Unfortunately, given their conservative heritage, many church leaders have most often favored the safe haven of a traditional status quo rather than the uncertain future of change, new horizons, and a participative leadership model.

We conclude this brief introduction to the leadership-management continuum by stressing that effective leadership within the parameters of biblical commitments and the new realities in which church leaders operate must be informed and flexible enough to move effectively and swiftly along the leadership-management continuum. Several concerns or interests will naturally determine how far or how rapidly leadership will move. These concerns, or parameters, include biblical commitments, the nature of the problem or situation, and not least in emphasis, the people involved in the process or decisions.

CHAPTER 6

PRIMARY INGREDIENTS OF EFFECTIVE LEADERSHIP

——✺——

There are absolutes for leadership: namely, integrity, information, innovation, and incisiveness.

PHILIP CROSBY, *TQM in Higher Education*, JUNE 1993

...integrity is consistency between what a manager believes, how a manager acts, and a manager's aspiration for his or her organization...But certain beliefs, actions, and aspirations are much more likely than others to lead to outstanding results...The concept of integrity is a nexus of ideas and guidelines that is central to business leadership...Integrity lies at the very heart of understanding what leadership is.

BADARACCO AND ELLSWORTH, LEADERSHIP AND THE QUEST FOR INTEGRITY, 1989

Correct principles are like compasses....Principles apply in all places. They surface in the form of values, ideas, norms, and teachings that uplift, ennoble, fulfill, empower, and inspire people.

STEPHEN R. COVEY, PRINCIPLED CENTERED LEADERSHIP, 1991

WHAT IS LEADERSHIP?

In this chapter we will draw on the vast research attempting to define this elusive quality and identify certain key leadership characteristics. We will use as our base for this portion of our study the *relational* dynamic of leadership,[44] and by examining some of these relational characteristics, surface leadership qualities that are typical of many successful leaders.

We should observe at this point that our primary concerns are not necessarily those of the managerial pole of the leadership-management continuum. In giving primary attention to the dynamic of leadership we will stress the conviction that the fundamental difference between managerial and leadership style is significantly one of context, emphasis, primary focus, and priority. It is our conviction that given the present environment of dramatic sociological change; generational, gender, and ethnic segmentation; and the contemporary erosion of confidence in institutional authority, that a flexible, relational, visionary, values-driven participative style will be more productive than a control-oriented, hierarchical, authoritarian management model.

Although aware of the point so well expressed by Bennis and Nanus that leadership, like love, is something everyone knows exists but few can define, we present the following leadership characteristics in some order of priority of importance, recognizing the subjective nature of the task.

LEADERSHIP IS INTEGRITY

Kouzes and Posner point to integrity as the most often identified characteristic admired in, or necessary to, effective leaders. They write:

> To begin the investigation, along with professor Warren Schmidt we surveyed nearly 1,500 managers from around the country in a study sponsored by the American Management Association. We asked the open-ended question: "What values (personal traits or characteristics) do you look for and admire in your superiors?" More than 250 different values, traits, and characteristics were identified. Subsequent content analysis by several independent judges reduced these items into fifteen categories. The most frequent responses, in order of mention, were (1) integrity (is truthful, is trustworthy, has character, has convictions), (2) competence (is capable, is productive, is efficient), and (3) leadership (is inspiring, is decisive, provides direction).[45]

In several similar studies, Kouzes and Posner likewise found that honesty and credibility ranked high in the list of essential characteristics to leadership. They conclude with the following comment: "Leaders without integrity are only putting on an act. The believability and credibility so essential for leadership are earned when your behavior is consistent with your beliefs."[46]

Several comments from Badaracco and Ellsworth confirm the profound role integrity plays in effective leadership:

> Undergirding our entire argument is a single, powerful, but complex idea that is encapsulated in the seemingly familiar notion of integrity....The concept of integrity is a nexus of ideas and guidelines that is central to business

leadership....Integrity lies at the very heart of understanding what leadership is. The word "integrity" suggests wholeness and coherence. It also suggests rightness, a sense of moral soundness....Leadership in a world of dilemmas is not, fundamentally, a matter of style, charisma, or professional technique. It is the difficult daily quest for integrity....In the final analysis, the power of executive leadership rests not so much on the personality of the individual as on the power of ideas, purposes, and values he or she represents.[47]

In spite of the complexity of the concept of integrity, it is possible to identify certain qualities that form the "grid" through which we "sift" integrity. Personal values such as honesty, sincerity, fairness, trust, loyalty, consistency in thought and behavior, a well-identified ethical system, a consistent standard of morality, sincere desire for the well-being of others, and a lack of malice and manipulation, seem to be those qualities that surface most when integrity is discussed.

LEADERSHIP IS BUILDING RELATIONSHIPS

Vance Packard has stated that "Leadership appears to be the art of getting others to want to do something that you are convinced should be done."[48] Edwin Locke defines leadership as "the process of inducing others to take action toward a common goal." He stresses that "Leadership is a *relational* concept. Leadership exists only in relation to others—namely followers... Leadership requires *inducing* others to action."[49] Driving this point home, Philip B. Cosby observes that "Relationships are where it all comes together or comes apart. Nothing else can be made to happen if relationships do not exist."[50] Max DePree likewise expresses this succinctly: "Leadership is an art, something to be learned over time, not simply by reading books. Leadership is more tribal than scientific, more a weaving of relationships than an amassing of information...."[51]

Perhaps it is James MacGregor Burns, distinguished political scientist and historian of the presidency, who expresses this aspect of leadership in the most decisive manner.

> We recognize, I believe, that leadership is interpersonal, that leaders cannot be seen in isolation from others, that linkage between the two embraces the dynamics of wants and needs and other motivations, that leadership is largely a teaching process beginning with the parental nurture of children, that creative leadership is closely related to conflict and crisis or at least to debate and dialogue, and that—above all—transforming leadership carries grave but not always recognized moral implications.[52]

In summary, then, leadership is a matter of developing relationships with others through which the leader is able, by personal example and interpersonal skill, to influence them to work toward a commonly shared goal. Emphasizing the difference between leadership and management, H. Ross Perot correctly maintained that "People cannot be managed. Inventories can be managed, but people must be led."[53]

Zaleznik[54] discusses the relational aspect of leadership under the concept of a *leadership compact* "that binds those who lead and those who follow into the same moral, intellectual, and emotional commitment." It is the leadership compact rather than structure or process that should be the tie that binds men and women in organizations, rather than the "narrow self-interest" that normally binds them together at the professional and managerial levels.

A key ingredient to building lasting relationships is trust or trustworthiness. Covey makes trust and trustworthiness two of the fundamental components of his program of Principle-Centered Leadership. He correctly observes, "Trust—or the lack of it—is at the root of success or failure in relationships and in the bottom-line results of business, industry, education, and government."[55]

It has been our experience in conducting leadership seminars across the nation that a lack of trust on the part of church leaders, as well as on the part of church members, has been a major factor inhibiting church life. This lack of trust most often is seen in the "we–they" mindset that is common in authoritarian, hierarchical models of church life. A common expression might be, "Well, *they've* decided to do.... Now I wonder how *they* are going to pay for it!" When conducting discussion groups among both elders and deacons, it is not uncommon for elders to observe that they would like to share some of the decisions and leadership with the deacons and members, but their experience in the past when doing this had too often been unfortunate. Those entrusted with the responsibility of leadership had failed, had not followed through, or had not been mature enough for the task, creating more problems than necessary. Likewise, deacons often express the concern that elders made decisions to share leadership, but never followed through on them. In many instances the deacons found their decisions to be "second-guessed" or interfered with, often even overturned without the deacons being informed. When any group perceives that it is being manipulated, mistrust is inevitable, and meaningful relationships break down.

It also seems endemic in conservative groups, especially those that have a high regard for "form over function" or for whom "sound doctrine" takes precedence over all other considerations, that they develop a lack of trust in one another. Evidence for this claim is replete in the literature of conservative groups. A specific case in point can be found in the sad controversy surrounding events in the Southern Baptist Convention with the takeover of the Convention by the ultra-fundamentalist group.

Similar trends, many of which can be traced to a lack of trust on both sides, can be identified among Churches of Christ.

Trust is in many ways similar to a bank account. Deposits are made over a period of time. One cannot purchase trust, it has to be deliberately built up or progressively earned. It is the fruit of experience, not propaganda. Trust results when individuals work consistently in building relationships; it rarely "just happens." It is the product of individuals manifesting integrity and trustworthiness in relationships. It is not a serendipitous by-product to life. It follows when individuals work to ensure that they place the interests of others, especially their followers, before their own interests.

Trust breaks down when individuals feel they are being manipulated, or when they suspect, often based on experience, that the other person is inconsistent or not evenhanded in their relationship, or is motivated by selfish interests. When personal integrity is under question, mistrust can lead to distrust which in turn eventually unfolds in anger and rebellion.

Research from a number of disciplines investigating the workplace and man-agement-leadership dichotomy indicates that supportive relationships are critically important to maintaining organizational vitality. Kouzes and Posner maintain that "Extraordinary accomplishments are not achieved without everyone—leader and follower alike—getting personally involved with the task and with the people."[56]

It is absolutely crucial that leaders recognize that organizations are comprised of people, not structures, goals, tasks, and the mysterious "bottom line" that managers prefer to cite. These managerial concerns are essential to responsible management. Organizations, however, are more than objective tasks or goals. They are comprised of groups of people who have formed a "relational compact" or "contract" with the organization. As members they are focused and effectively motivated by the values and vision of the organization. In building an effective organization, relationships—or an awareness of people as individuals—are fundamental to its health. This is especially true in the case of churches which are profoundly involved in the "people business."

It is our conviction, therefore, based on our research in the field of leadership, and on our experience in a wide range of leadership seminars, that developing relationships in which trust and trustworthiness are at the core is a fundamental key to effective church leadership. Building relationships is, furthermore, directly and inextricably linked to personal and organizational integrity.

If church leaders do not trust (or have confidence in) their church members, especially their deacons, or if church members and deacons do not trust their church leaders, churches will be plagued by apathy, negative feelings, little effective ministry, and most likely the departure of some of their most competent workers.

Leadership Is Vision

Vision is another essential ingredient to effective leadership. Strong relationships, in one crucial sense, are the product of shared values and vision. All Americans who experienced the tumultuous 1960s remember clearly the rallying call of Martin Luther King, Jr. The visionary call, "I have a dream!" reverberated around the world and revolutionized race relations in America. His cry to a nation struggling to find direction galvanized his people with a sense of purpose and gave them hope. A meaningful vision, well articulated and communicated, cements relationships and becomes a platform for effective and purposeful action. Robert L. Swiggett, Chairperson, Kollmorgen Corporation, observes, "The leader's job is to create vision."[57]

We consider *vision* to be a primary component of leadership since this characteristic is so definitive of the fundamental character of the leader. The visionary leader's refusal to be limited by the "system" or status quo, and the visionary leader's passion for expanding the organization's horizons, stands in striking contrast to the structural control characteristic of the manager. Kouzes and Posner state, however, that vision has not until recently been part of the manager's vocabulary. Managers were more comfortable with *purpose*, but scholarly research in the field of leadership "has made us aware of the importance of leadership vision"[58] in addition to, or in place of, purpose.

Commenting on the increasing role given to vision in leadership discussion, Gardner observes:

> Of the popularly expressed requirements for leadership, one of the most common is that leaders have vision, which can mean a variety of things: that they think longer-term; that they see where their system fits in a larger context; that they can describe the outlines of the future that lifts and moves people; or that they discern, in the clutter and confusion of the present, the elements that determine what is to come.[59]

Edwin Locke adds that "vision should be the primary guiding force of all organizational activity." "Without vision, the motives, traits, knowledge, skills, and abilities" of leaders will ultimately not matter."[60] Max DePree observes that "A leader must have vision...be a person who is primarily future-oriented....the first duty of a leader is to define reality."[61] Roger Smith, former Chairman and CEO of General Motors, succinctly summarized this discussion on vision:

> The art of management begins with vision, a quality that has never been so crucial as it is today.... Competitiveness—and for some companies, survival itself—depends on the manager's ability to envision new things...to organize and reorganize operations...and to imagine how, and by what kind of intervention, the course of events might be changed...."[62]

It is imperative to realize that vision is not simply a "pie in the sky dream." Vision and intuition are based on the hard facts and experiences of life. Both vision and intuition refer to one's ability to see things clearly from a firm vantage point. Ross Perot defines intuition as "knowing your business. It means being able to bring to bear on a situation everything you've seen, felt, tasted, and experienced in an industry."[63] Likewise, vision is the ability to integrate knowledge, experience, and one's creative and innovative senses into a strategy that will lift one above and beyond the present. Visionary thinking must proceed from the very best, up-to-date information, the clearest thinking, and tested experience in the field in which the leader proposes to lead his organization.

Vision is the ability of leadership to see beyond and not be bound by existing horizons. Vision enables the leadership to conceptualize what the organization could be, where it could go, and what it could do if certain circumstances were to prevail. It is vision that creates the possibility of leadership, and it is the communicating and sharing of the vision that causes followers to form a relationship with one another and with their leader, and to follow that leader to new heights or horizons.

Corporate or organizational vision must be a clearly articulated mental image of what and where the organization will be in the future. It should be expressed in clear, precise frames of reference which can be easily understood and grasped by all involved. Vision statements that are arcane, abstruse, and mysterious tend only to confuse. Vision statements should be meaningful, brief, concise, clear, and challenging. Both Martin Luther King Jr.'s visionary statement, "I have a dream!" and Douglas MacArthur's statement, "I shall return!" are classical formulations of brief, meaningful, and challenging vision statements.

Well-defined vision statements provide an organization with a focal point, direction, purpose, value, goals, standards of excellence, uniqueness, imagination, and momentum. Vision statements are intended to move an organization from the limitations of the status quo and present horizons to a future that goes beyond the immediate.

Vision, once it has been formulated, must be communicated to all involved in the organization. This should be done positively and in an upbeat manner. The intention is to excite people within and without the organization to buy into the vision and bring the future into being. The implementation of the vision may involve corporate renewal, restructuring the organization and corporate culture, training and empowering managers and workers, building team spirit and self-confidence in the management team and workers, motivating, and managing accountability. Each of these features will be addressed in due course, but suffice it to say at this juncture of our study that without vision all of these ingredients of leadership are meaningless and without purpose.

LEADERSHIP IS PURPOSE AND MISSION

Somewhat akin to vision are purpose and mission. Whereas vision is more specific and detailed, purpose and mission are expressed in broad terms. *Purpose* addresses the *identity* of the organization, or in broad terms *why* it exists. *Mission* defines the *function* of the organization, or more specifically *how* it carries out its purpose. *Vision* speaks to the *direction* of the organization, or *where* or *what* it intends to be in the future.

Perhaps the most effective manner of demonstrating the precise nuances of these terms is to express them through case studies or models of purpose, mission, and vision statements. For the purpose of this study we will make brief reference to sample purpose, mission, and vision statements for a church.

Purpose statement: The purpose of the Tenth Avenue Church is to bring glory to God through Christ Jesus and his church.

Mission statement: The mission of the Tenth Avenue Church is to be with God in heaven and to take as many people with us as possible. We plan to do this by making positive efforts to meet the needs of people through evangelism, fellowship, worship, and benevolence.

Vision statement: The vision of the Tenth Avenue Church is to be a community of Christians who are friendly and family oriented, with a passion for people who are hurting, being sensitive to people's needs, and reaching out to all of God's creation in a commitment to world evangelism.

LEADERSHIP IS VALUES

Every organization has certain *values* that shape its *culture* and provide its *operational parameters*. It is the responsibility of leadership to guide the organization into a definition, clarification, and appreciation of the value system by which it will live. We emphasize the "symbiotic" nature of values, organizational character, and operational parameters.

Recognition of this symbiotic relationship between organizational character and key values is of profound significance to church leaders, especially those of a conservative conviction for whom "doctrine" is essential to defining congregational identity. Constant, careful, and critical study of the principal values of the organization is critical to the life of the church. This has both positive and negative implications. Obviously, conservative church leaders will give careful consideration to their doctrinal values, but it is not beyond possibility that doctrinal values are sometimes shaped by cultural considerations. Furthermore, such matters as the nature and role of church buildings, the formal structure and "culture" of worship services, and the educational programs of the church must constantly be evaluated in the light of the changing sociological scene. Each of the factors mentioned above falls into the category we are considering here, namely, values.

James E. Burke argues for the need of a strong value system when leading an organization:

> Leadership means shaping an organization so that its values, norms, and ideals appeal strongly to its individual members while at the same time making the company a stronger company. When this occurs, outstanding performance follows. Values are one thing you should not be flexible on. We do not temporize about morality with our people.[64]

It is unfortunate that Burke limits values to such qualities as morality. Although doctrinal, moral, and ethical considerations are of profound importance to a value system, there are other values to organizational life that need constant evaluation in view of the shifting sociological scene in which organizations must function.

Emphasizing the significance of executive values, Peter Drucker observes:

> What executives do, what they believe and value, what they reward and whom, are watched, seen, and minutely interpreted throughout the whole organization. And nothing is noticed more quickly—and considered more significantly—than a discrepancy between what executives preach and what they expect their associates to practice.[65]

Discussing the difference between American and Japanese corporate culture, Drucker concludes:

> The Japanese recognize that there are really only two demands of leadership. One is to accept that rank does not confer privileges; it entails responsibility. The other is to acknowledge that leaders in an organization need to impose on themselves that congruence between deeds and words, between behavior and professed beliefs and values, that we call "personal integrity."[66]

Kouzes and Posner draw attention to the importance of values by observing that "a leader needs a philosophy, a set of high standards by which the organization is measured, a set of values about how employees, colleagues, and customers ought to be treated, a set of principles that make the organization unique and distinct."[67]

Values are of enormous importance to how an organization manages change and the organizational transformation necessitated by such change. All too often the inability to manage change is the specific cause for organizational failure. A specific, sound, clearly articulated, and meaningful value system is of vital importance to the health, vitality, and survival of all organizations, especially during times which demand traumatic change.

Two fundamental methods can be adopted by an organization when determining its value system. These methods are primarily determined by two basic leadership philosophies. The organization may choose to be a *hierarchical*, "from-the-top-down" organization, or it may choose to be driven "from-the-bottom-up" in a *participative* fashion. In one sense, decisions in regard to the style or philosophy of leadership to be adopted by the organization are the choice of the organizational leadership or management. This choice of leadership style will have a profound and fundamental influence in shaping the corporate culture of the organization. Suffice it to say at this point that whether the leadership adopts a hierarchical model or whether it chooses a participative, "from below" model, leadership must provide the parameters and process by which the values are determined and communicated to the organization. Given the pluralistic nature of contemporary society—and this pluralism is apparent even in conservative churches—a hierarchical model will not prove as effective in most cases as a participative model.

When an organization adopts a hierarchical culture, then the leadership inevitably determines the values for the organization and communicates them in clear concise terms which can be easily understood and implemented by the management and working teams. This procedure fits better in an organization in which management and control are the priorities. The process is quick and efficient, and works well in a short-term culture.

On the other hand, should the organization adopt a participative model of corporate culture, the leadership guides the organization through the process of surfacing the values that will be significant to the life and future of the organization. The process is slow, less efficient, yet more effective in the long term. In this procedure the leadership initiates the process and provides focus, direction, and guidance to the organization as it works slowly in a consensus model of decision making toward determining its value system. The leadership periodically summarizes and articulates the values and returns them to the organization for feedback, evaluation, and final acceptance.

Attention will be given later to the primary philosophical leadership alternatives available to organizations, and to their impact on organizational culture and effectiveness. Regardless, however, of the process by which an organization chooses its value system, it is imperative that the organization strive for a value system that will by nature provide character, direction, and purpose to the organization. In management-driven cultures the fundamental value tends to be the "bottom line" expressed most often in terms of profits. In leadership-driven cultures the primary values will be expressed in terms of people, service, matters of integrity, and *primary principles*.

Stephen R. Covey, author of the bestselling book *The 7 Habits of Highly Effective People*, proposes four *primary principles* that he believes should undergird all other values.[68] They compose four levels of principle-centered leadership that together form the solid foundation necessary for all effective corporate cultures. Covey outlines *first*, a level of personal relationships built on trust, personal integrity and character; *second*, a level of interpersonal relationships based on trustworthiness; *third*, a level of managerial relationships driven by empowerment and delegation; and *fourth*, an organizational level guided by trust and commitment which leads to extreme organizational flexibility. Covey argues effectively for a value system that goes beyond the superficial "bottom line" mentality of many goal-or task-driven organizations.

In similar fashion, Badaracco and Ellsworth present a forceful case for *leadership by integrity* in which they stress personal values, relationships, ethics, belief in others, trust, loyalty, open communication, fairness, and substance as the ideal values, in contrast to many corporate values such as meeting the schedule, maintaining or improving "the bottom line," the system, and the process.[69]

Values form the ethical glue that hold an organization together, the compass that gives it direction, the integrity that gives it respectability, and the parameters that give it stability. Values provide the culture, the spirit, and fiber of the organization that controls the organization. Values also shape the fundamental principles that give the organization its meaning and purpose.

CHAPTER 7

RELATIONSHIPS DON'T JUST HAPPEN!

—⁕—

*Extraordinary accomplishments are not achieved without everyone—
leader and follower alike—getting personally involved with the task and
with the people.*

KOUZES AND POSNER, *The Leadership Challenge,*
1987

*Relationships are where it all comes together or comes apart. Nothing else
can be made to happen if relationships do not exist.*

PHILIP B. COSBY, *Leading,* 1990

RELATIONSHIPS DON'T JUST HAPPEN!

In the previous chapter we examined several primary leadership elements, observing that these qualities, all similar in nature in that they relate directly to relationships, are fundamental to the dynamic necessary to developing leadership. Among them we discussed the symbiotic role that integrity, honesty, vision, purpose, mission, and values play in leadership. We observed that each of these can be summarized in, or are inextricably related to, the *relational leadership* frame that is seen by many to be in need of serious attention at this juncture of the American sociological scene.

The purpose of this chapter will be to develop still further the acute need for a prominent relational dimension in effective leadership. Kouzes and Posner observe that:

Researchers investigating the workplace have long recognized that supportive relationships at work are critically important to maintaining personal and organizational vitality. Many managers have a difficult time with personal relationships. Traditional managerial wisdom has asserted, "Don't get too close to your people, or they will take advantage of you."

Investigations from a wide variety of disciplines consistently demonstrate that social support—that quality of interpersonal relationships—serves to enhance not only productivity but also psychological well-being and physical health.[70]

The process of developing effective relationships includes a number of related elements that correlate directly with the character of the leader as well as with his or her relationships with the followers. We are reminded of the discussion of the previous chapter in which personal integrity and values were argued to be primary and foundational qualities to effective leadership.

But more than "integrity, honor, and tradition" are involved in building effective relationships. One of the most dramatic demonstrations of the failure to build relationships and develop effective leadership from a traditional frame of management is portrayed in the movie *Dead Poets Society*. In the plot of the movie a traditional, hierarchical, autocratic, management paradigm of leadership, depicted through a private academy and one parent, is contrasted with a relational style of leadership seen in an English literature teacher, Mr. Keating. The suicide of one of the lead characters, a schoolboy, led one viewer of the movie to comment, "What a tragic waste of a life!" Whatever valuable leadership lessons may be gleaned from this movie, it is apparent even to the casual viewer that the primary reason for the "tragic loss of life" was the failure of those working solely out of an inflexible paradigm, in which "integrity, honor, and tradition" were rigidly followed, to establish meaningful relationships with the young schoolboys.

Building relationships, however, is a "two-way street." It involves both leaders and followers. Kouzes and Posner explain:

> But it works both ways. Extraordinary accomplishments are not achieved without everyone—leader and follower alike—getting personally involved with the task and with the people. Some leaders liken the emotional attachment to being in a chorus. Others say it's like a feeling of family...Our personal best cases were filled with the importance of building genuine personal relationships between the members of the team and the leader.[71]

If, as Kouzes and Posner claim, building relationships must work both ways, then considerably more attention must be given to the dynamic of being an effective follower than is presently taking place in the discussion of leadership. We will address this key element in the effective leadership dynamic later in this chapter. Suffice it to be pointed out here that the dynamic of being an effective follower is critical to effective leadership.

The relational elements that we will develop in this chapter are factors that all leaders must take seriously when transforming a traditional organization, driven by

Zaleznik's "Managerial Mystique," into a "learning organization" capable of meeting the challenges confronted in a rapidly changing socioeconomic culture. Although some of these elements may in some respects seem to be secondary, they relate directly to the leader's or the organization's ability to develop and sustain those meaningful *relationships* that are critical to the *process* of leadership.

TRUST

A vital ingredient to building relationships in an effective leader-follower dynamic is that of trust. Gardner observes:

> In this fast-moving market environment filled with shrewd manipulators, a high value is placed on trust, keeping commitments, and returning favors punctiliously. Machiavellian principles defeat themselves: unscrupulous members tend to be isolated....It is not possible to overstate the value of steadiness in leadership. Individuals and groups who wish to align themselves with a leader find it hard to do so if the leader shifts position erratically....A good community nurtures its members and fosters an atmosphere of trust.[72]

Gardner's comments are particularly germane in the context of churches whose business is primarily people oriented and relational. Relationships involving trust do not necessarily mean that the followers will always agree with the leader, or that the leader is always correct, although this would be felicitous! Such trust relationships simply mean that followers and leaders are involved in a reciprocal relationship of mutual respect for the character and integrity of the other.

The importance of trust in building relationships in an effective leadership dynamic is emphasized by Peter Drucker, under a sub-heading entitled "Earning Trust Is a Must." Drucker astutely introduces the subject by observing that "the final requirement of effective leadership is to earn trust." He continues:

> To trust a leader, it is not necessary to like him. Nor is it necessary to agree with him. Trust is the conviction that the leader means what he says. It is a belief in something very old—fashioned, called "integrity." A leader's actions and a leader's professed beliefs must be congruent, or at least compatible. Effective leadership-and again this is very old wisdom—is not based on being clever; it is based primarily on being consistent.[73]

In any environment embroiled in change, mistrust is one of the first symptoms to surface. Questions are frequently asked indicating that manipulation is often suspected to be lurking in the wings. Building and establishing trust, therefore, becomes a prime requirement in the leadership dynamic and in the success of organizational restructuring or adjustment. It is simply impossible for an organization surrounded by change to survive successfully without a heavy commitment to trust. Bennis and Nanus note that in view of the fact that "this is an era marked with rapid and spastic change" with "too many ironies, polarities, dichotomies, dualities, ambivalences, paradoxes, confusions, contradictions, contraries, and messes for an organization to understand and deal with," leaders must create and instill an environment of mutual trust between the leadership and their followers if they are to effectively navigate the complexity and contradictions of the contemporary environment.[74]

Kouzes and Posner stress that the responsibility of creating mutual trust lies fundamentally with the leadership. "Leaders must demonstrate their willingness to trust the members of their teams *first*, before the team members can wholeheartedly put their fate into the leader's hands."[75] Nanus adds, "All leaders require trust as a basis for their legitimacy and as the mortar that binds leader to follower."[76]

In Covey's system of principle-centered leadership, trust and trustworthiness are axiomatic principles. In his scheme, principles are the central core and foundation to the whole process without which successful community life and personal emotional health are impossible. Principles are "like a compass to the map, the map tells one where they may go, but principles inform on how to get there." Trust is for Covey one of those foundational principles. He observes, "Trust—or the lack of it-is at the root of success or failure in relationships and in the bottom—line results of business, industry, education, and government."[77]

With special relevance to non-profit organizations such as institutes of higher education and the church, Drucker observes:

> Organizations are based on trust. Trust means that you know what to expect of people. Trust is mutual understanding. Not mutual love, not even mutual respect. Predictability. This is far more important in the non-profit organization, because typically it has to depend on the work of volunteers and on people whom it does not control.[78]

One would expect that in the church, where love for one another is fundamental to the Christian faith, that mutual respect and trust would be axiomatic, but Drucker is correct in pointing out that *trust is separate from, and must transcend even love and respect*. It is possible to love a person with Christian love in the sense of desiring the best for him or her, yet not to trust the person because the person has not yet responded to love and earned the right to be trusted. Trust must be earned! Love is by grace and is free and undeserved!

Trust is especially significant in situations of stress or at times when dissent leads to conflict and confrontation. Contrary to common opinion, confrontation is not a disease that should be avoided at all costs. Neither is confrontation unhealthy or undesirable in leadership relationships. Confrontation, handled correctly, builds mutual respect and emotional stability among team members. Drucker correctly observes that we should:

> Look upon dissent as a means of creating understanding and mutual respect.
>
> Emotions always run high over any decision in which the organization is at risk if that decision fails, or is one that is not easily reversible. The smart thing to do is to treat this as constructive dissent and as a key to mutual understanding.
>
> If you can bring dissent and disagreement to a common understanding of what the discussion is all about, you create unity and commitment. There is a very old saying—it goes back all the way to Aristotle and later became an axiom of the early Christian Church: In essentials unity, in action freedom, and *in all things trust*. And trust requires that dissent come out in the open, and that it be seen as honest disagreement (italics added).[79]

Primary trust in the leader can contribute to mutual trust among followers. Gardner observes: "A leader capable of inspiring trust is especially valuable in bringing about collaboration among mutually suspicious elements in the constituency. The trust the contending groups have for such a leader can hold them together until they begin to trust one another."[80]

Building trust, therefore, must become a prime concern to leadership, and trust begins with the personal character of the leaders. Without personal integrity, honesty, consistency, dependability, clarity of purpose, competence and knowledge of the task, trust will not develop. Trust is not a natural gift, nor a *charisma*; it is a reflection on life-style that has to be developed and earned. In one sense, trust is like a savings account; one makes deposits into and withdrawals from one's "trust" account. Too many or haphazard, unplanned withdrawals without constant careful deposits will eventually bankrupt the account!

Several elements are essential to building up a "trust" savings account. *First*, leaders should be aware that building trust takes time and careful planning, and that trust is not simply inherent in an "office." Bennis and Nanus observe: "We are not arguing that a two-day exercise is all that is needed for a leader to build trust in an organization. Obviously, trust is built up over a long period of time in a multitude of circumstances."[81] It is a common fallacy in some church contexts for leaders, both elders and ministers, to assume that since they have been appointed to an "office" (which itself is a faulty interpretation, as will be defined later in this study) or ministry, that trust is something *owed* them in view of their office. This false perception is unfortunately too common in conservative churches in which an authoritarian mindset prevails.

Second, building trust involves an *element of risk*. There is no guarantee that followers will not manifest human fallibility and fall short of expectation. But without venturing out in faith in the integrity of the followers, leaders will never generate competence among workers, which itself is an essential element of trust. The ability to demonstrate trust in followers enables followers to develop first self-confidence, and then confidence in the organization, the team, or the leader. Planting the seeds of trust, as in agricultural planting, necessitates some risk, but the fruits of the planting far outweigh the risks. The only way to develop trust is to first be trustworthy, and second, to trust others. New relationships, new vision, new ventures into the future, always contain an element of uncertainty and risk, but without risk, no growth is possible. Effective leaders always find risk-taking worth the investment; control managers are reluctant to take the risk. We should point out, however, that risk-taking trust is not blind. It is based on the skill and experience of the leader and previous effort, nurturing, discipling, instruction, and training. In a real sense, the only people ultimately to be blamed for the failure of the team are the leaders responsible for building and developing the team.

Third, trust involves the old maxim of *"going first."* Without the leader first manifesting trustworthiness and being willing to trust the followers, followers will resist trusting the leadership. Simply put, "If you do not trust me, do not expect me to trust you!" The trustworthiness of the leader is foundational to building trust in the leader and the organization. For Covey, trustworthiness relates directly to the integrity of the leader. He observes that "trustworthiness is based on *character*, what you are as a person...."[82] Kouzes and Posner add:

> One of the clearest advantages of trusting others comes from the way people respond to trusting individuals. Trusting people are regarded by others as trust-*worthy*. Managers who fail to demonstrate that they trust their subordinates are perceived by those subordinates as less deserving of trust. Our perception of how trustworthy others are also effects our relationships with others.[83]

Fourth, trust involves *sensitivity* to the needs and interests of others. If followers sense that the leadership does not have their personal needs and interests in mind, they will feel they are being manipulated out of ulterior motives. Genuineness and perceived sincerity are fundamental to trust.

Fifth, the ability to *listen* to others is crucial to building trust. Followers need to feel keenly that their opinion is valued if they are to trust the process being negotiated. An inability or failure to listen carefully and actively to followers is a prime reason for failure to generate trust.

Sixth, being *open* with followers and others about one's *intentions* is essential to build trust. Followers need to feel that they have all the facts, and that there are no hidden agendas or ulterior motives operating behind the leadership. In keeping with this concern, failure to follow up on the input or opinion of the team contributes to a fear of insincerity and manipulation.

Seventh, open and regular communication is needed to build trust. Nothing builds suspicion and destroys trust faster than followers not having all the relevant information and being left to guess what is transpiring. Once again, fear of being manipulated can destroy trust that has taken years to build. Regular and meaningful communication and feedback is a vital and key element in the process of establishing trust.

Eighth, a final element in building trust is *sensitive accountability*. We do not have in mind a reversion to an authoritarian, control-oriented accountability, but rather a nurturing relationship that is perceived by the followers or team to be in their interests. In this relationship the leader strives to establish an environment where accountability is also a two-way street, so that, although the team is accountable to the leader and the organization, the leader is likewise accountable to the team and the organization.

Teamwork

Building a spirit of teamwork is a vital ingredient to organizational success, especially in the case of non-profit cultures. In the context of the church, teamwork is emphasized in considerable detail by the Apostle Paul in Ephesians 4:1-16. In this key leadership passage Paul develops themes stressing *unity*, the church as a *corporate body*, and the essential role of leadership in *equipping* the members for ministry.

Effective church leaders in the context of growing churches in America today recognize the vital role of small cell group teams in revitalizing the church and leading it in an effective outreach ministry. The development of "lay leaders" who lead these ministry teams or cell groups is a common ingredient mentioned by church growth specialists. Elmer L. Towns in his description of the ten most innovative and growing churches in America today[84] frequently cites this phenomenon as a feature in these growing churches. Developing teams and focusing on teamwork applies not only to the marketplace, but is a primary component of effective non-profit organizations such as the church.

Drucker argues forcibly for teamwork as a key to successful growth. With particular reference to developing teams in non-profit organizations such as hospitals, churches, and institutions of higher education, Drucker observes:

> The more successful an organization becomes, the more it needs to build teams. In fact, non-profit organizations most often fumble and lose their way despite great ability at the top and a dedicated staff because they fail to build teams....A common mistake is to believe that because individuals are all on the same team, they will all think alike and act alike. Not so. The purpose of

a team is to make the strengths of each person effective, and his or her weakness irrelevant.[85]

Undergirding the concept of team is the awareness that team members need the strengths that each brings to the task and that as they pool their abilities and energies they become stronger and more effective. This is the very argument developed by the Apostle Paul in Ephesians 4, with every member being knit together and each individual member supplying to the body the strength of his or her own unique function.

While discussing the diversity of leadership roles, and the rise of women and minorities in every sector of society, Marjorie Blanchard, president of Blanchard Training & Development, observes:

> The masculine hierarchical structure of yesterday is giving way to more feminine, web-like networks. Within the new culture, we see the rise of interactive and multidisciplinary leadership teams. Creativity and communication can flow easily and rapidly throughout these networks and teams, making organizations better equipped to respond to their customers.[86]

The need for teamwork, however, is not unique to the non-profit organization. Drucker lays much of the blame for the failure of the American automobile industry in the 1980s on their failure to understand the value of small, site-based development teams. He charges:

> The socioeconomic bent of the American automobile industry also explains in large measure its long lead times in developing new models and in reacting to market changes. Instead of being divided into autonomous market-segment divisions, the Japanese companies are decentralized into powerful, autonomous company-wide functions, such as engineering, manufacturing, and marketing. It is easy for them to form company-wide teams to work on designs outside the existing product scope. In Detroit, however, where market-segment divisions dominate, people who work on such teams risk being considered traitors by the division on whose payroll they are.[87]

While fully in support of teamwork, Bolman and Deal point out that successful teams do not always look alike. Teams need to be designed and developed with specific purposes and contexts in mind. They argue that "The right team structure depends on what the team is trying to do....Even within the same organization, team structure may shift according to changes in the task."[88] Although we are not at this point in our study considering team *structure*, Bolman and Deal's point is germane. Flexibility in team structure must be a major concern of leaders responsible for team building and designing teamwork procedures.

Research in the field of leadership reveals that the essential elements of teamwork are *trust, common vision, purpose, mission, communication, and strategy*. It is the task of leadership to so integrate these elements into the organizational culture that the organization functions as a corporate body. It is noteworthy that the Apostle Paul began his treatise on teamwork in Ephesians 4 with the primary need for commitment to *unity*. Building on that unity, church leadership (apostles, prophets, evangelists, and pastors and teachers) equip members by *training* them, *bonding* them, and *motivating* them.

Gardner concludes our discussion on the need for building a spirit of teamwork in any organization by emphasizing (Gardner's own italics): *"Skill in the building and rebuilding of community is not just another of the innumerable requirements of contemporary leadership. It is one of the highest and most essential skills a leader can command."*[89]

One additional yet vital element in building team spirit or *esprit de corps* is the matter of reward. In non-profit organizations reward is somewhat limited or restricted in comparison to the profit-oriented culture of the business corporation where the team shares in the profits. Nevertheless, rewards in the form of positive affirmation, sharing the results of success, and the significant role of every individual on the team, are a powerful force in nurturing and enriching team spirit and encouraging growth. Perhaps the most significant reward provided in a participative, teamwork oriented, non-profit organization is the sense of "ownership" in the team function, purpose, and goals. The negative factors, or "we–they" attitude of the top-down, autocratic culture, are replaced by the positive rewards of the "we–us" mindset of the participative team culture. In non-profit organizations in particular, successfully reaching the desired goal, and knowing that one is a valued member of the "winning" team is perhaps the most significant reward factor. Research indicates that this phenomenon applies with equal force in profit-driven organizations.

COMMUNICATION

A critical ingredient for teamwork in the life of an organization is effective communication. Communication must be positive, well articulated, upbeat, realistic, frequent, and truthful. Communication must be available to every member of the team. New leaders in any organization stressing the significance of teamwork must ask more questions, listen attentively and empathetically, be open to and solicit new ideas, and openly share information. A major factor in the disintegration of teamwork is a breakdown in open, informative, complete, and effective communication. Team members immediately feel unwanted, detached from the process, and unappreciated when they detect that they have been left out of the communication loop. Suspicions of manipulation surface, and any effective team dynamic is destroyed.

Leaders should take advantage of every medium of communication available to them. For example, communication is the key ingredient of "management by walking around." Leaders should realize early the power of personal contact with team members on both the formal and informal level. Communication in the form of bulletin reports, posters, displays, and any other medium is critical to the life and dynamic of team spirit. Communication through ceremony, ritual, and celebration must become a vital ingredient in effective leadership.

Effective communication is, moreover, a two-way process. Leaders must both share information and listen in a manner that leaves the clear and unmistakable impression that they respect the team and are willing to be influenced by the team members.

Gardner observes that the need for effective two-way communication is critical to developing both teamwork and a leader-follower relationship.

> It is a point that corporations have emphasized increasingly in recent years. There must be not only easy communication from leaders to constituents but also ample return communication, including dissent. Leaders, to be effective, must pick up the signals coming from constituents....Wise leaders are continuously finding ways to say to their constituents, "I hear you."[90]

Gardner's observation underscores a profound element in effective teamwork and communication: the critical need for leaders to listen empathetically and seriously to dissenting voices. In authoritarian organizations or communities the leader may ignore or take lightly voices raised in dissatisfaction or disagreement, but in today's pluralistic society which stresses the need for teamwork and networking, leaders do so at great risk to the health, vitality, and survival of their organization. This is especially true in the case of non-profit voluntary organizations such as the church. In today's climate members will vote with their feet. Any form of membership exodus should be taken seriously by leaders as a sign of breakdown in communication, teamwork, vision, and leadership style.

Leaders should pay attention to keeping the purpose, mission, and vision of the organization constantly before the members or team. Feedback, both positive and negative, must be frequent and meaningful. It is crucial to growth that team members know the successes and failures of their efforts. Only by knowing the failures can they take steps to correct the weaknesses apparent in their efforts. In many ways the leader must be one who enjoys working with people and sharing with them the value of their labor. Leaders must "beat the drum" of success for their team as part of the leader's role in building *esprit de corps*. If the leader is not able to do this, then the leader should find and train someone who can. Regular communication and feedback are essential to the team culture of an organization.

COMMUNICATING THE VISION

Without clear vision the organization has little to challenge it, little opportunity for growth, little to be excited about, and little challenge to communicate. The warning of the ancient Hebrew wise man remains true: "Without a vision, the people will perish!" (Prov 29:18).

Unfortunately, for a number of reasons, many organizations spend little or inadequate time developing a clear strategic vision for the organization, forming that vision into a meaningful and definitive strategy for the organization, and communicating that vision to the organization's personnel in clear, concise, and meaningful terms. In many instances vision is little more than wishful thinking about the future, and when some effort is made to communicate the vague vision of the future, it is often communicated in a haphazard and careless manner.

Once a creative and dynamic strategic vision has been developed time and effort must be given to the process of integrating the vision into the life and structure of the organization. Because the day-to-day life of an organization can be a pressure-stressed experience in which urgent concerns demand immediate attention, communication and integration of vision may be relegated to some form of printed memo-communication or an annual corporate event. The result is that organizations tend, under the pressures of day-to-day survival, to neglect such vital yet less demanding elements as the development, nurture, and communication of strategic vision that are so crucial to their very survival. Benjamin Tregoe and those associated in the strategic planning organization, Kepner-Tregoe, Inc., maintain that "Vision needs nurturing....Operational pressures are just too intense. They easily overwhelm strategic vision."[91]

A concise statement of strategic vision provides an organization with a clear self-definition, with direction, with a powerful driving force, with focus, with a sense of cohesiveness, and with a clearly identified standard against which to measure its success.

FLEXIBILITY

Survival in the contemporary environment of constant, sometimes frenetic change, demands that leadership and organizational teams be able to adjust rapidly and easily to these shifting challenges. Tom Peters describes the dynamic necessary in today's culture as "Thriving on Chaos."[92] The ability to adjust rapidly and sometimes radically to the demands of the organization's environment depends on well established relationships within the organization. A major weakness of bureaucratic organizations is the many levels of management through which a decision has to pass before it can be ratified and implemented. Corporate or organizational tradition is very often a factor inhibiting change. Without rejecting their traditional foundation, heritage, or past upon which the organization has built its present structure, successful organizations must possess a fairly high degree of flexibility. Peters observes:

> The rate of change demanded by the prescriptions in this book and the boldness of the goals suggested will be unfailingly new—and frightening....It challenges everything we thought we knew about managing, and often challenges over a hundred years of American tradition. Most fundamentally, the times demand that flexibility and love for change replace our long-standing penchant for mass production and mass markets....[93]

A major criticism of both corporate and church leaders of the traditional university or seminary is that these organizations are tied too securely to a traditional bureaucratic structure, and thus are consequently unable to react rapidly enough to the demands of their market. Facing the challenges of the contemporary needs of corporate America, the rapid shifts in the makeup of American culture, the rapidly inflating cost of a university education, and the pluralism and consumerism of their constituencies, the traditional university will need to restructure its faculty-dominated, degree-oriented, ivory tower mentality if it is to flourish as a significant and major leader of American and global society.

Flexibility, and the consequent ability to adjust to a rapidly changing environment, will be a key factor to the success of all organizations as they attempt to stay abreast of the confusing contemporary kaleidoscope of change. Likewise, the participative nature of effective teamwork demands that flexibility and tolerance become foundational to building a vibrant, successful organization in today's changing environment.

This will be especially true in the context of church leadership. Churches, whose culture is often shaped by an older and consequently more traditionally oriented generation, experience considerable difficulty in accepting the essential ingredients of flexibility and tolerance to change which are such a natural part of the younger Boomer generation's psyche.

We must stress that flexibility and tolerance do not necessarily imply that churches surrender essential or primary values. Within the parameters of cherished values, many of these being biblical principles that shape the church, there is always room for flexibility and tolerance in the practice of faith. We stress again that this discussion of tolerance and flexibility is in the context of style, not biblical conviction.

The following observation by Marjorie Blanchard draws the need for flexibility and tolerance to change in leadership style into sharp relief, and brings this discussion to some point of closure. Blanchard observes, "New leadership models are definitely needed for the changing times. Leaders everywhere will need to develop greater tolerance and flexibility."[94]

We conclude by observing that flexibility, tolerance, and an open mind in regard to change, without surrendering primary values, are essential elements to effective church leadership in this age of *new realities.*

BEING AN EFFECTIVE FOLLOWER

Many studies on leadership say little about the need for careful attention to being an effective follower, yet this point should be axiomatic. It is impossible to have effective leadership without sensitive "followership." Much attention is given in leadership seminars to being effective leaders, leaving the impression that leaders bear the sole responsibility for providing the environment necessary to success in organizations.

Gardner prefers to call followers "constituents," stressing that the term "followers" often carries a pejorative connotation of "passivity." Nevertheless, being an effective follower is as much a frame of mind as being an effective leader. It is only when leadership and followership are forced into a hierarchical structure that the term absorbs the less desirable characteristics of passivity. When placed in an appropriate leadership continuum, or in a networking, organic structure such as the Apostle Paul's model of the human body (1 Cor 12 and Eph 4) in which the leader and followers are equal members of the team with different functions rather than status, the pejorative connotation and passivity of being a follower are diminished.

Max Weber's observation that charismatic leaders normally surface during times of distress in which followers exhibit "a devotion born of distress,"[95] is amply demonstrated in the charismatic leadership of Martin Luther King, Jr., Winston Churchill, Mahatma Gandhi, and Theodore Roosevelt. Gardner observes that "the state of mind of followers is a powerful ingredient in explaining the emergence of the charismatic leader."[96]

The frame of mind of constituents shaped by a shared vision and understanding of purpose and mission will have a profound impact on building teamwork and those relationships necessary for growth in today's culture. Followers must be caught up in the significance of the vision, understand the dynamic of "co-ownership" in the organization and its purpose, and be willing to participate not only in the process of decision making but also in the responsibility of providing the expertise and function in their possession. In a critical sense all followers in successful organizations are leaders in their special areas of expertise and function. Successful organizations and leaders see leadership and "followership" as functional roles, not as definitions of personal superiority or as a power base implying inferiority.

The relationship of followers to leaders in this new paradigm of leadership in which "followership" is seen as symbiotic or almost synonymous with leadership is difficult for many Americans to grasp. Being a leader is more highly praised than being a follower. The traditional model of leadership in an older generation remains an authoritarian one in which the leader is placed above, rather than alongside, the follower. With its radical stress on individuality and personal freedoms, the American psyche since the 1960s has most often demonstrated reluctance for acceptance of any form of leadership. Furthermore, the American psyche has traditionally experienced difficulty accepting a "win-win" mentality, preferring rather the "win-lose" mindset. Gardner addresses this: "Most young people in professional and executive ranks have had a long training—literally since elementary school—in individual performance. They learn that it is how they perform as individuals that counts, not how they relate to others."[97]

We conclude this point by stressing once more that submission to a leader need not imply inferiority, lower status, or less significance. Submission should be a frame of mind that interprets submission in functional ways rather than in authoritarian terms. It is only when leaders and followers understand this participative principle that effective team building and lasting relationships within an organization are possible. Jesus understood this concept and made it a cardinal principle in his teaching on the kingdom. Jesus stressed that the one who is the greatest in the kingdom is the one who serves (Matt 20:26).

CELEBRATION, CEREMONY, AND RITUAL

This chapter has explored a number of factors that contribute to building meaningful relationships. It is appropriate in closing this section on the relational dimension of leadership that we discuss three factors often overlooked, yet vital in developing and maintaining meaningful relationships.

Celebration, ceremony, and ritual form part of what Bolman and Deal refer to as the "symbolic frame" of organizational restructuring. The symbolic frame of organizational life represents those non-rational elements of life that are seen most clearly in "religious" contexts and in the emotional side of human experience. Bolman and Deal observe:

> Historically, all human cultures have used ritual and ceremony to create order, clarity, and predictability, particularly in dealing with issues or problems that are too complex, mysterious, or random to be controlled in any other way. Indian rain dances and the Thanksgiving celebration of the pilgrims both represent efforts to invoke supernatural assistance in the critical but unpredictable process of raising crops. Baptisms, bar mitzvahs, graduations, weddings, and anniversaries all serve to give meaning and direction to our lives.[98]

Church leaders readily recognize the powerful role that worship assemblies, singing, praying together, and celebrating the Eucharist or communion play in bonding the congregation and providing the church with a common center. Universities resort to a number of ceremonial convocations and commencements as the high points in academic life. Fraternities, sororities, and a host of service organizations incorporate ceremonies and rituals in their culture as a means of uniting and motivating their members. Young children in schools across the nation cement the fiber of American democracy and freedom through the regular recital of the Pledge of Allegiance.

Ceremony, celebration, and rituals in the form of awards and banquets honoring workers and those who have achieved unusual goals in life play a profound role in building and maintaining strong relationships. Creative leaders, especially church and non-profit organization leaders who depend heavily on volunteer workers, should design rituals and ceremonies that celebrate the unique nature of their organization. These may be in the form of annual functions, quarterly banquets, and ad hoc awards ceremonies, but all play a significant role in the relational life of their organization.

CHAPTER 8

STRATEGIC LEADERSHIP

—◌◌◌—

The Driving Force is the central hook for strategic vision. It is your organization's most fundamental building block upon which you develop consistent, coherent answers.... The Driving Force is the primary determiner of your organization's future strategic vision.

TREGO, ZIMMERMAN, SMITH, AND TOBIA,
Vision in Action, 1989

In addition to the relational factors identified above as primary leadership qualities, a number of other strategic leadership concerns vital to successful organizational strategy must be explored. Although not directly related to leadership in the same manner as the personal qualities of the leader examined in previous chapters, each of the following strategic leadership concerns is integral to successful strategic planning and thus to our discussion of leadership. Leaders must be sensitive to these strategic concepts if they are to successfully lead their team or organization in today's shifting cultural context.

STRATEGIC ADVANTAGE

Unless one is dealing with a "start up" program, any organization should by its very existence have some reason for its being; some form of successful history or identity. The very existence of the organization becomes in one sense, therefore, a form of organizational or "strategic advantage." Strategic advantage refers to that unique quality or service that the organization is able to offer. The very reason given by an organization for continuing its business may be considered part of its strategic advantage.

Strategic advantage analysis and diagnosis is the process by which the strategists examine the firm's marketing and distribution, research and development, production and operations, corporate resources and personnel, and finance and accounting factors to determine where the firm has significant competencies so it can most effectively exploit the opportunities and meet the threats the environment is presenting.[99]

Several factors are involved in the identification of an organization's strategic advantage. A detailed analysis of the organization's major strengths and weaknesses is a fundamental beginning point. Furthermore, the organization may seek to identify those unique qualities or characteristics that shape the nature or culture of the organization. In this analysis a number of factors should be considered. The organization's corporate history, traditional heritage, and operational successes play profound roles in determining strategic advantage. Furthermore, an appreciation of the organization's health, the expertise of its personnel, the condition of its physical plant, the market demand for its "product," the proximity and availability of necessary resources, and the clarity and acceptance of its vision all contribute to understanding and articulating the strategic advantage.

Another vital component in understanding strategic advantage is identifying the uniqueness or perceived uniqueness of the organization. Leadership should strive to identify and analyze carefully those factors that cause the organization to stand out or above other similar enterprises in order to be able to identify, clearly articulate, and communicate concisely these advantages to the organization's market, constituents, leadership team, and personnel.

Glueck and Jauch identify several factors that influence an organization's strategic advantage. The following are an adaptation of Glueck and Jauch's list which we include as typical of some strategic advantages that may be helpful: "corporate image and prestige, effective organization structure and climate, company size in relation to industry, strategic management system, effective staff support systems, effective management information and computer systems, high quality employees, and effective relations."[100]

Accenture, a global consulting and outsourcing corporation, includes the following strategic advantage factors as a vital component of their mission statement: "The best people, knowledge capital, partnering, best clients, and an ability to deliver value."

Without a clear understanding of strategic advantage an organization is unable to build on or play to its strengths. Although organizational weakness must be addressed in strategic planning, organizations are often successful simply because they have identified the unique advantages they possess. Growing organizations understand clearly their particular or unique niche, and consequently build their strategy around that strength. Peter Drucker has stated that unless an organization identifies and plays to its strengths it will exhaust its vital energy on matters or areas over which it might have little control and which make little contribution to its success.[101]

Concern for strategic advantage is vital to organizations such as institutions of higher education and churches simply because they operate in markets already overpopulated in today's environment. Universities, especially private institutions, must be able to identify their reason for existence, and know how to play up to this, if they are to survive in a climate of escalating costs. Unless they can identify a *unique* and *necessary* reason for existence—something that state universities cannot or do not offer—they will not survive in the demanding arena of an overpopulated higher education market. Identifying such an advantage is, nevertheless, only the beginning of strategic institutional planning. The market strategy must address clearly and maximize its advantage in public relations releases and recruitment, and it should allocate resources and personnel in a way that will enable the institution to maximize this advantage.

Churches, like all organizations, have a strategic advantage which in most cases is directly related to the *church culture*. In common terms, church culture involves those factors that make the congregation unique or "make it tick." Church leaders must be sensitive to the unique culture of their congregation. Although churches are often established with a common doctrinal base, the very nature and composition of its membership will shape the character or culture of the congregation. The location, the generational and socioeconomic character, and the maturity of a congregation should be carefully considered when seeking to understand a congregation's culture and consequent strategic advantage.

Each of the cultural components integral to the character and strategic advantage of a congregation, therefore, should consequently impact its plans to minister to its constituents. The character of churches, although significantly shaped by doctrinal concerns, is most often, however, shaped by the personality factors giving the congregation its unique identity. The strategic advantage of church culture should become the "selling point" of a congregation's ministry to its community.

DRIVING FORCE

It is fundamental to the success of an organization that it understands those factors that shape and drive the organization. Various forces might be considered significant to the shaping of the organization, but an organization should seek to be driven by one or two related forces lest it find its energy being dissipated or fragmented by attempting to address more situations than its resources and interests can support.

An organization may be driven by the nature of its constituency, by the nature of its product, or by the needs and demands of its market. For instance, it may exist to serve a particular group or constituency such as a religious organization or the Boy Scouts. Or, as in the case of a university, it may be driven by its ability to produce a particular product such as an academic degree. Likewise, an organization may choose to be more market-oriented by seeking to identify the product or service a particular group or market either desires or needs. In any case, a clear understanding of the factors driving the organization should become part of the organizational strategy.

In the case of a church, the congregation should understand clearly its identity and the purpose for which it exists. This "driving force" may be its unique ability to serve a military base or to reach out to a specific community. Another driving force may be the congregation's commitment to world evangelism or to family ministry. In some cases, congregations are driven by their concern to preserve some doctrinal commitment. Whatever the case, church leaders should identify their congregation's unique driving force or ability to offer certain services or ministries. In view of the fact that not all congregations are equal in locality or ability, church leaders should resist the temptation to copy what may be working well for another congregation. It is imperative that church leaders seek to determine and understand the unique potential of their own congregation and make this its driving force.

ORGANIZATIONAL ENVIRONMENT

Related to both strategic advantage and driving force is the environment in which the organization operates. Every organization operates within two specific environments, both of which profoundly impact the ability of the organization to function effectively.

External Environment. The external environment of an organization may be defined as the larger world market in which the organization functions. A number of factors contribute to this external environment. Leaders and strategists must consider the socioeconomic and geopolitical environments of the organization. A sensitive understanding of the sociological and demographic shifts, generational and ethnic segmentation, pluralistic worldviews, and similar factors in which the organization functions all have profound implications for the life and future success of an organization.

Globalization in place of nationalism has become an environmental reality that all organizations must take seriously in strategic planning. Dramatic urbanization, population movements, international travel, and international business are now well established components of our worldview and lifestyle. Although we live in a world whose problems remain complex and often confusing, the boundaries of our "corporate environment," whether we be engaged in the corporate world or in a non-profit organization such as the university or the church, have enlarged dramatically.

The world "out there," which was for many of us in our childhood a wondrously mysterious and exotic place, has become a commonplace yet fundamental part of our "immediate" environment. What was at one time distantly external has now become immediately familiar. What was at one time only the subject of our dreams has become an everyday reality. What had been a foreign world has now become our backyard.

A vacation in the Pacific Islands of Hawaii, a trip into the Heart of Darkness of Africa, or a journey into the past in the majestic halls of Westminster Abbey or the Tower of London were in my childhood only wishful thinking, yet for my seven- and nine-year-old grandchildren such dreams were little more than a spring break vacation. Our world has shrunk so dramatically in our lifetime that we have witnessed the formation of a new vocabulary to describe the phenomenon—"globalization." A 1974 dictionary in my office does not even include the word globalization, yet the term falls off our lips today with such ease that we are not even aware of its newness.

Recall that Peter Drucker and others have argued that our age passed through a profound divide in the mid-1970s into the next century and a host of new realities which would impact our lives in dramatic and challenging forms. Terms such as "globalization," "Internet," and "cyberspace" were completely alien to our vocabulary in the 1970s. They are now commonplace, not only in the corporate dialogue of the marketplace, but also in the mundane discussions of our homes.

Environmental factors relating to globalization and the shifts in the macro world in which an organization functions must become fundamental concerns in all organizational strategic planning and leadership. Organizations such as universities that have often operated in security within the safe harbor of the "hallowed halls and ivory towers of academia" must take seriously the impact of a much larger and rapidly shifting global external environment. Satellite and computer technology have expanded not only the knowledge and informational base of the university far beyond the quiet halls of the institutional library; they have expanded the walls of the classroom with class instruction now available on a daily basis in the home through the convenience of satellite, cable television, and computer networks.

Churches that in the past focused their attention on the parochial church building, often with the secure "cathedral" mentality of a holy sanctuary, must now live in the fast moving, mobile, and flexible world of travel and technology. Churches that were at one time "centripetal," focusing on bringing members into the sanctuary, must now become "centrifugal," carrying their message and ministry out into the world. The concept of foreign missions in a far away land, at one time the challenge of only the brave or intrepid missionary, is now the spring or summer vacation challenge of our children. Famine and hunger in Somalia, at one time the responsibility of the international community, is now the soul-wrenching concern of the teenage class who not only prays about the matter, but who now also conducts food drives for the world community. Freshman college students today expand the learning experience of the classroom and the church into the practical experiences of the ghettos of inner city ministries and global campaigns.

The new realities of globalization have thrust organizations into dimensions that a generation ago were of little concern to organizational strategists and leaders. Sober strategic planning must take seriously the expanding and challenging nature of the external macro world in which we now live and operate.

Internal Environment. In times of past opulence little attention was traditionally given in some non-profit organizations to careful analysis of internal environments such as budgets. For example, in the 1980s, a small rural church turned to a church leadership consultant for advice in developing a church budget. The church had never before in its fifty-year history needed a budget. Adequate funds had always been available. The 1970s energy collapse in West Texas dramatically changed this.

Universities across the nation are being challenged to carefully study their internal operational environments and to maximize their strategic advantage. Economic and demographic considerations are challenging academia to restudy the organizational culture of their institutions. New paradigms for higher education are springing up all over the nation as universities seek new "markets." Universities not willing to take seriously the socioeconomic and geopolitical changes in the 1990s will be hard pressed to stay in business in the twenty-first century.

Careful analysis of organizational culture, market orientation, driving force, leadership style, personnel, economic structure, and financial base must become the daily concern of organizational leadership in the contemporary world of new realities. Organizations, especially non-profit organizations such as the university and the church, must be sensitive, flexible, and open enough to meet the challenges and rapid changes demanded by both their external and internal environments. Organizations embedded in a culture resistant to change will find competition and survival in the twenty-first century extremely difficult, if not impossible.

Conservative churches must learn to adjust to the shifting moods of their environment, both externally and internally, without surrendering their God-given role to be salt to the world. Without surrendering the essential need for Christians and churches to be different from the world in which they live and minister, church leaders must be able to feel the pulse of both the external environment to which they minister and the internal environment which enables them to minister.

PLURALISM

A final, yet essential, ingredient to effective leadership in the world of the new realities under which our contemporary society operates is a clear understanding of the pluralism[102] in which we now live and work. With the erosion of confidence in institutions, in government, and in objective authority in general, leaders cannot simply function under the assumption that because they are leaders others will follow. Understanding the pluralism of the contemporary society which shapes the minds of many today, even of church members, is critical to effective leadership.

We live today in a generation of multiple choices. No longer are choices made with a view to lifelong commitments. Marriage to one spouse, which was for many the only choice, is no longer the standard view of marriage. Like any other usable commodity, marriage to a spouse is considered a pragmatic matter. While the marriage works, the relationship is continued. If the marriage is not working, you simply take another spouse more to your liking—much like buying an automobile! When it wears out, you choose another!

Children today learn much of their vocabulary and gain much of their information and knowledge from the television set. If they do not like the station or the information they are receiving, they merely click the remote to make another selection. The choices in every direction of life are multiple and readily available. In the mind of contemporary society one source of authority is as good as another. You simply choose the authority that fits your presuppositions. The global society in which we now live, the rapid mobility available to all, the enormous amount of information so readily available, the breakup of the family unit, the stress on individuality, the freedom of choice all contribute to a rampant pluralism of choices and centers to life.

The extent of pluralism and its implications leave many confused, frustrated, and threatened. Traditional organizations such as the church and the university, which are by nature either resistant to or slow to change, are threatened more than most by the specter of pluralism looming on their horizons. But if such traditional organizations are not able to manage and capitalize on the new reality of rampant pluralism, they will be unable to survive in the new century.

In the context of church life, pluralism need not necessarily demand the surrender of the unique authority of God, or Scripture, or trusted doctrinal values which most Christians accept as primary to faith. But in regard to choices in the "church culture," ranging from the ministries available, to the classes provided, to the songs sung, to the style or structure of the worship, church leaders must understand that flexibility, a willingness to listen and, in some cases, even compromise when the choices are of equal value will go a long way in addressing the needs, and sometimes the demands, of their generationally segmented congregation.

In the midst of pluralism, contemporary society nevertheless craves security, stability, and a center of meaning. The church and other similar traditional organizations can provide such a center of stability and meaning. They will be able to do so, however, only if they learn to adjust to the demands for change and to the pluralism of the people they are attempting to lead. Traditionalists find it extremely difficult to conceive how acceptance of change and pluralism can be achieved without surrendering those fundamental values that give them their sense of identity and essential character. In most cases, however, the changes called for are not in the area of "doctrine," but in leadership style, worship style, and in "church culture." How these demands for change are managed is the challenge of leadership in the age of new realities. These are the essentials of creative and effective leadership demanded by those already familiar in their corporate life with the new realities.

ENTREPRENEURSHIP

Innovation and entrepreneurial leadership are terms synonymous with the challenges being ushered in by the rapid change and flux of contemporary society. Unless organizations can disengage with the past rapidly enough they simply will not be able to survive long in the coming decade as we move into the twenty-first century. By definition, both innovation and entrepreneurship have to do with "organized abandonment" and "creative destruction."

The term *entrepreneur* was coined 200 years ago by a French economist, and was used in the sense of someone "who upsets and disorganizes." Later it was developed further into the modern economic concept of "creative destruction." Drucker observes that entrepreneurship can best be understood as the process by which one gets to the new and better by discarding the old, the outworn, the obsolete, the no-longer-productive, as well as the mistakes, the failures, and the misdirections of the past.[103]

Applied to the context of corporate leadership, entrepreneurial leadership implies the ability to disengage from those policies and procedures that may have been successful in the past, but which in the face of contemporary challenges restrict the organization in its ability to adjust to the challenges. Entrepreneurial leadership means a willingness to take well-informed risks, to be innovative in the face of uncertainty, to be driven by a vision of what might be, or what could be, and to adjust the corporate culture rapidly enough to address the rapid changes and needs of the future that are already shaping the present.

With the many changes taking place on a global scale, there will be a number of outstanding opportunities opening every year to church leaders. Through a vision of a man from Macedonia indicating that God had opened a door to him (Acts 16:6-10, 2 Cor 2:12, 13), the Apostle Paul was made keenly aware of the fact that new opportunities were opening in Gentile Europe (Macedonia). Although the doors opening to us today are not announced as dramatically as were Paul's, we nevertheless are keenly aware of striking new opportunities God is ever placing before his church.

Moving out through some of these doors will call on an entrepreneurial spirit among church leaders, or in terms perhaps more familiar, a true pioneer spirit. In these days the call is not simply, "Go west, young man," but far more diverse and challenging. Perhaps the most challenging call faced by church leaders is the call to be true disciples of Jesus and to "go into all the world" and "make disciples of all nations." Perhaps another way of phrasing this today for contemporary American churches is, "Go into the cities and suburbs of your own nation where the gospel message is not heard."

Church leaders will need to be bold and flexible enough to examine their leadership style and their organizational structure in order to effectively meet the new challenges and realities of contemporary society. In today's world, for the church to become an enclave dedicated to preserving its heritage and identity, is for the church to fail in its God-given responsibility to the world. Such changes as the demographic realignment that has taken place in American society (for example, we have in mind the gender, generational, and ethnic segmentation of society), the economic changes in the marketplace forced on us by the dramatic infusion of technology into both our corporate and home life, and the pluralism and decay of our monolithic cultural authority base will continue at an unrelenting pace to raise profound challenges for the church.

Again we must emphasize that this does not mean that churches should surrender their biblical doctrinal commitments. But it does mean they will need to seriously determine what is doctrinal and what is traditional, and be willing to change where change is both called for and appropriate. What is doctrinal must be treasured; what is traditional may need reinterpreting in terms of a more modern environment and culture. In order to be placed at a better advantage to reach that changing environment and culture, church leaders simply must know *how* and *where* to be flexible.

Some churches are already seeing the need to adjust their programs to be more specifically relevant to their local environment. This calls for courage, for change is never uniformly accepted or pleasing. Traditionalists will be uncomfortable and feel left out of the circle of concern. Some of the younger generation will feel that changes are not being made rapidly enough. Whatever re-evaluation of the *status quo* takes place must be carefully thought through, well prepared, and widely discussed before dramatic changes are made.

Areas being examined by many churches include the formalism and structure of worship assembly, the traditional model of education in the church through Bible school programs, the time and nature of congregational assemblies, evangelistic "seeker" services, and small cell group meetings. A word of warning is appropriate! Change should not be contemplated merely because some are calling for change, or because change is the latest "buzz word." Change should take place only because church leaders have carefully studied their external and internal environments and have determined that change is necessary for the growth and outreach of the congregation.

The point we wish to make here is that growth and the negotiation of change call for an entrepreneurial spirit. The remaking of an organization to meet the kaleidoscopic challenges of contemporary society will also necessitate significant paradigm shifts. An entrepreneurial spirit and paradigm shifts will involve risk. The risks of paradigm shifts must be carefully evaluated, but to inhibit an entrepreneurial spirit in the midst of the opportunities presenting themselves to church leaders today is tantamount to retreating into our shells and permitting significant opportunities for world and local evangelism to escape us.

We should be reminded that leadership involves taking people where they have never gone before, where they may not necessarily like to go, but where they must go if they are to be successful. Abraham (Heb 11:8) is a prime example of a biblical entrepreneurial leader. "By faith Abraham obeyed when he was called to go out to a place which he was to receive as an inheritance; and he went out, not knowing where he was to go."

CHAPTER 9

LEADERSHIP MODELS

—◇◇◇—

In the literature discussing leadership, several attempts are made to identify the various leadership models or styles available. This chapter will explore several of these in an attempt to identify the strengths and weaknesses of the options in the development of leadership style.

Joseph Badaracco and Richard Ellsworth identify three basic philosophies that dominate management style.[104] They maintain that each philosophy begins with a different view of human nature or worldview. Badaracco and Ellsworth argue that each philosophy has merit and will produce positive results under specific conditions. They caution, however, that without certain fundamental principles or "prejudices" undergirding each of these philosophies, inherent problems will surface that inhibit the effectiveness of the model chosen.

The aim of the discussion at this point, however, is not to discuss in detail the relevant merits of such models, but merely to identify them for the purpose of general discussion. The factors that characterize and drive each of them will be discussed later in greater detail. The three leadership philosophies or models identified by Badaracco and Ellsworth are:

1. Political leadership
2. Directive leadership
3. Values-driven leadership

Edgar H. Schein, working with an organizational psychology paradigm, also developed three similar primary models.[105] Schein maintains that

> any definition of "good leadership" usually reflects the historical, social, or cultural context in which the analysis is conducted. What we consider "good" leadership not only reflects our concepts of human nature as outlined in the previous chapters but is likely to be heavily colored by the political ideology and the socioeconomic circumstances in which the behavior takes place.[106]

Schein's research identifies the following three basic organizational types:

1. The coercive type
2. The utilitarian type
3. The normative type [107]

Although the "fit" between Badaracco, Ellsworth, and Schein is not exact, their three categories do agree in broad principle. Badaracco and Ellsworth's "political" model is similar to Schein's "utilitarian" type. Their "directive" model parallels Schein's "coercive" type, and Badaracco and Ellsworth's "values-driven" model is analogous to Schein's "normative" type.

Departing somewhat from Badaracco, Ellsworth, and Schein's trichotomous model of leadership type, Kenneth Blanchard proposes "four basic leadership styles."[108] His leadership styles are:

1. The directing style
2. The coaching style
3. The supporting style
4. The delegating style

Close examination of Blanchard's four categories of leadership style reveal that they closely parallel the three models identified by Badaracco, Ellsworth, and Schein. Blanchard's "directing" style is basically the same as the "directive" and "coercive" models of Badaracco, Ellsworth, and Schein; his "delegating" style is similar to the "values-driven" and "normative" models; and his "coaching" and "supportive" styles track closely with the "political" and "utilitarian" models.

Influenced by the trichotomous model of Badaracco, Ellsworth, and Schein, we propose to identify three primary models or styles available to leaders and their organizations. These will be defined under the following categories:

1. Directive (delegating/coercive)
2. Democratic (political/utilitarian)
3. Participative (values-driven/normative)

We will also work under the presuppositions developed by Badaracco, Ellsworth, and Schein that leadership style is fundamentally determined by political, philosophical, and socioeconomic concerns. In fact, it will be a major presupposition or "prejudice" of this study that leadership *style* is primarily a *sociological* phenomenon.

In keeping with Badaracco, Ellsworth, Schein, and Blanchard, we will maintain that leadership *style* is never an either/or selection of one of the above models, but that leadership style must be determined by the shifting conditions under which leadership is taking place. By this we mean that leadership style moves constantly along a leadership continuum between directive leadership on the one extreme and participative leadership on the other, with democratic leadership possible somewhere in between.

It will also be a major presupposition of this study that leadership style must be flexible, and should be determined by the circumstances and maturity of the organization. Blanchard's work is particularly helpful in this regard.[109] Blanchard speaks of the "situational leader" who is able to "match the leadership style to the development level." In this regard, leadership is somewhat analogous to parenting. As the family grows and matures, so the parenting-leadership style adjusts from a more authoritarian (management) style to a more participative style.

We are reminded of the leadership-management continuum discussed in an earlier chapter. In a healthy organization, leadership style and decision making move constantly with flexibility along this continuum. There will be occasions where a more directive, authoritarian style may be more appropriate, and other occasions where a participative style will function more effectively.

The remainder of this chapter will discuss the three leadership models identified above and will apply them in developing leadership style, especially in the context of the church.

The Directive Model

Directive leadership style operates mostly under the traditional hierarchical model of leadership which assumes that the interests or expertise of the leader or leadership team is greater, or more necessary to the health of the organization, than the ability, knowledge, or interests of the remainder of the organization. In some situations this may well be the case! In newly formed organizations, or organizations with little natural leadership among the members, the knowledge and ability of the leaders, coupled with the immaturity of the followers, may necessitate a more directive style than in other situations.

Badaracco and Ellsworth suggest that the directive leadership model works under three basic assumptions[110]:

1. That people derive self-satisfaction from performance, and that in order to maximize performance and "reach their potential" they need to be "pressed, stretched, and inspired to meet even higher standards."

2. Organizations need strong directive leadership in order to counteract confusion through a lack of direction, goals, and coherence. Organizations without strong leadership to keep them focused often drift from their purpose with the result that they lose impetus. Badaracco and Ellsworth are aware

that on some occasions aggressive leadership may be necessary. For instance, they observe that in the case of extreme political maneuvering aggressive intervention may be necessary. "Through forceful, vigilant action and strong example, managers can attack and subdue the political maneuvering that frustrates internal cooperation and diverts time and resources from the central task of building a sustainable competitive advantage."[111]

3. People produce best when motivated by substance: ideas and values create a more effective working environment. It takes strong and decisive leadership to provide the concise substance of ideas necessary to effective productivity. It is the task of directive leadership to determine vision, direction and goals. Articulating and communicating such goals is the responsibility of directive leadership.

Directive leadership operates under the assumption that the most important factors in producing results are situations in which workers are motivated by facts, goals, and clear, concise knowledge of tasks. Pure management, with its emphasis on tasks and goals which need to be met, finds a comfortable home in the directive model. Whereas pure leadership, which stresses relationships and people rather than tasks and goals, tends to shy away from control-oriented directive leadership. Directive leadership demands the direct, active, personal involvement of the leader. A statement by Ralph Bailey, former chairman of Conoco, summarizes this mindset: "The way to lead an organization is to be a tire kicker. You need to get out there where the field commanders are and find out what is going on. I want to know not only what we are doing, why we are doing it, and how we are doing it, but even more important, who is doing it."[112]

There will be times in the life of every organization when directive leadership becomes a necessity to the well-being of the organization. It is my opinion, however, that extended directive leadership in a mature organization will have a negative impact on the health and vitality of the organization. Mature people most often react negatively to excessive directive leadership.

Directive leadership has the tendency to create a love–hate dichotomy among followers. Some, with a definite need for structure and control in their lives, join an organization because of its strong directive leadership. Others with a strong self-image and resentment to external structure and intrusion leave because of the frustration created by what is perceived to be the excessive control of directive leadership.

In the twenty-first century a directive leadership style simply will not blend well with the new generations that are now coming to the fore to share in leadership responsibility. The rampant pluralism of contemporary society, the decline of confidence in institutional authority, and the increasing educational and professional sophistication of the Boomer, Buster and Millennial generations makes the directive leadership style a tenuous model, and one not always capable of producing the best results.

Excessive directive or authoritarian leadership can result in organizational frustration, resentment, lethargy, apathy, and a "we–they" mindset that deprives the organization of much of the vitality and giftedness of its workers. This should not be interpreted to mean that there is no place or role for directive leadership style. It simply means that leaders should be extremely sensitive in their decision to employ this style.

Leaders should adopt a directive leadership style only after carefully analyzing the situation and determining that the directive leadership style is the only or best option under the circumstances. Leaders adopting a directive leadership style in the contemporary environment should preface this with proactive communication regarding the urgent reasons for such action, and be prepared to follow the decision with considerable conflict resolution and damage control.

Since most church leaders become leaders primarily by reason of age or gender,[113] directive leadership style is often interpreted as an excessive autocratic, male-dominated attitude, and can lead to congregational apathy or worker frustration especially on the part of extremely well-prepared deacons. There will be times and situations in the life of a congregation, as in the life of a maturing family, when a directive disposition may be necessary. It is our opinion, however, that as the church family matures such directive leadership style should be avoided as much as possible.

THE DEMOCRATIC MODEL

What will be described under the descriptive designation of democratic leadership might, under some circumstances, be described as political leadership. Both are characterized by keen negotiating ability whereby an organization is led toward consensus through the political process of compromise. Although compromise and political maneuvering are in popular usage somewhat derogatory concepts, they speak of the process of a group coming to an agreement on an issue through negotiation. There are times in the life of every group when compromise is a perfectly suitable means of arriving at a decision. When primary principles are not involved, compromise and political sensitivity may be the most effective means of achieving a solution to a problem.

In the context of normal political procedure through democratic government, the political process initially describes the *mechanism* whereby the state or the community selects those who will lead them. At a later stage the democratic process describes the *manner* in which the leadership body defines the principles that will govern the people.

The English word "democratic" derives from the Greek word *demos*, meaning *people*. The democratic process, therefore, is the process whereby the *people* choose their own leaders and govern themselves. It is a process of "government of the people, by the people, for the people." It stands in opposition to a hierarchical, monarchial, dictatorial leadership style. Democratic leadership style is characterized by freedom, choice, negotiation, and compromise.

By transposing the term democratic to the management or leadership context, we most often use the concept to describe situations lacking a strong individual leadership presence, or situations where the leadership is not operating from an obvious position of strength. The term applies well to non-profit or community service organizations which operate primarily with a volunteer workforce. The concept of democratic or political leadership style can also apply in some managerial situations in which the manager has little empowerment by virtue of office.

Democratic leadership style is characterized by openness, flexibility, pragmatism, negotiation, compromise, consensus decision making, and a slow process of change. Badaracco and Ellsworth observe that the political or democratic process is "one of fragmentation and interruption. The trivial jostles the important in an endless series of meetings, memos, questions, and problems."[114]

Unfortunately, the process often becomes the field of self-interest, personal competition, and power struggles. Furthermore, in new or young organizations not blessed with an abundance of maturity and experience, the uninformed or less mature often have the power to overrule the experienced. Much unnecessary time and energy, therefore, must be expended on damage control and conflict resolution in the process of democratic leadership style.

Discussing the "realities of contemporary organizational life" and the slow process of democratic or political leadership style, Badaracco and Ellsworth observe:

> To be effective, a leader must be a pragmatic realist who understands the degenerative forces and has the skills to modify and shape them in ways that motivate people to act in the interest of the company as a whole. Thus we come to the central tenet of political leadership: strong business leaders must be adept at moving forward in small, incremental steps and at orchestrating astutely from behind the scenes.[115]

From the above observations we notice that democratic or political leadership style does not simply apply to new or young organizations that have not yet matured to the point where they can operate under a different style, or to non-profit or service organizations operating with a volunteer workforce. There are situations within every organization when the context of the situation demands a democratic or political style.

The above observations again reinforce the opinion of this study that leadership style must be flexible enough to move along a leadership continuum between the two poles of directive and participative style. In keeping with Blanchard's situational leadership views, effective leaders will adopt a situational leadership style adapted to both the situation and the personnel involved in the endeavor. Missionary churches, or newly established churches that have not yet developed mature leadership, operate effectively under the democratic model. This style may on occasions be more directive, while on other occasions the style may be more democratic or participative.

Most missionaries who have learned the political skills of leading the congregation toward consensus realize, however, that this democratic period in the life of a congregation is best replaced by a more mature form of shepherding and leadership.

There is a narrow line separating democratic leadership style and participative leadership style. As we shall shortly note, the participative style assumes a strong leadership core, whereas the democratic style relates more to situations where no effective leadership core exists. In the case of churches where a strong leadership core exists in the eldership, the elders may lead the group through a democratic *process* toward a solution once certain parameters have been laid down. This process should not be confused with a pure democratic leadership style.

THE PARTICIPATIVE MODEL

In organizations in which there is no obvious major differential between the expertise of the leaders and that of the workers, where the followers are in many cases as well informed and prepared as the leaders, a participative model of leadership may be more effective in leading toward shared goals and vision. This situation would be clearly different from the organization described above in the directive leadership model, where there would be a fairly distinct differential between the leaders' ability and that of the followers, or in organizations in which the leaders and workers are equally inexperienced or under qualified, with no apparent leaders stepping forward.

Participative leadership functions best in organizations in which the level of competence and experience of the workers or followers is as mature as, or at least as high as, that of the leaders. Here leaders share goals and vision with the workers who work together with the leadership as a team whose purpose and mission is the realization of the shared goals. Leaders initiate the process of decision making or organizational life by communicating the values of the organization, or by communicating the parameters under which the process will take place. Leaders, having confidence in the competence of their followers, empower their followers to work freely within the established values and organizational parameters.

Participative leadership calls for decisive leadership through example and creative initiative without the leadership having to resort to a domineering spirit.

Lorne C. Plunkett and Robert Fournier define participative leadership as "a philosophy that demands that organizational decision making be made in such a way that *input* and *responsibility* are extended to the lowest level appropriate to the decision being made."

The purpose of participative management is to ensure that effective decisions are made by the right people. Empowerment is a means to achieve participative management. It is the mechanism by which responsibility is vested in teams or individuals. Involvement, on the other hand, is the mechanism for ensuring appropriate input to decision making. Thus, empowerment and involvement become the building blocks for a participative management philosophy.[116]

Plunkett and Fournier surface several salient leadership factors: an emphasis on shared decision making, on different levels of decisions needing to be made, on the empowerment of workers to make decisions, on worker involvement, and on the strength of working in teams.

With the above introductory observations on the nature of participative leadership, we will now explore in greater detail the character and function of such leadership. We will seek to understand the real character of participative leadership, and comment on its strengths and weaknesses. We will also discuss those situations in which participative leadership will provide the most effective results. We will conclude with specific application of participative leadership in the church.

EFFECTIVE OR EFFICIENT?
We begin by observing that participative leadership is not the most *efficient* leadership style. By this we mean that if efficiency is defined as the quickest way to reach a decision, then participative leadership is not efficient. The participative leadership method takes time. It is a process, not a program.[117]

In most instances it is more efficient and much simpler for a small top-level team, or one top-level executive, to make a decision than it is to pass the decision down to "lower levels" of management for participative action. Team decisions and action at "lower levels" in the organization demand time for the process of dialogue and decision to mature into a consensus. *Efficiency* may work in short-term strategy, but it is inferior to *effectiveness* in long-term strategy.

Confusing efficiency with effectiveness is a fallacy often made in autocratic organizations in which management is primary. What is under normal conditions the most efficient route for an organization to follow is not always the most effective route to the desired goal. If goals or tasks are the primary consideration, then efficiency sounds impressive. However, if people and relationships are the primary consideration, then efficiency may not be the most effective route.

Not only does the process of participative leadership take time for dialogue and decision to "gel," but the participative process itself demands time for the effective maturation of the process. Plunkett and Fournier observe:

> Participative management must have at least a three-year plan that clearly identifies a transference of authority, accountability, access to necessary information, and skills to those people who will make the operating decisions of the future. Participative management is about changing structures, reward systems, procedures, and relationships.[118]

Participative leadership style is not a model that can be installed simply through a "top down" process. It is a process that requires time for maturation.

METHOD VERSUS PROCESS

We must stress the distinction we are making between method and process. Method may be introduced in short-time strategy, but process needs the "space" for maturation provided in long-term strategy. Organizational personnel must be brought along gradually to where the decision to operate in a participative model is a team decision; one in which the team has some investment. Plunkett and Fournier add that

> a business decision involving participative management requires attitudinal and behavioral responses that cannot be executed in immediate and automatic methods. A key step is that senior management must conceptually acknowledge a need to change. However, awareness is only the first step in a long journey to effective process.[119]

VALUES-DRIVEN LEADERSHIP

The terminology preferred by Badaracco and Ellsworth in place of what we are referring to as participative leadership is "values-driven leadership."[120] Values should be a fundamental issue in any model of leadership but are especially critical to the participative leadership model. In fact, the whole process of participative leadership hinges on how well the values of an organization have been delineated and communicated. Without a clearly defined and well-articulated value system any organization is without character and unable to establish criteria by which it will function.

Stephen Covey sees values as a vital ingredient of what he identifies as "principle-centered leadership."[121] Covey observes:

> Correct principles are like compasses: they are always pointing the way.... Principles are self-evident....They provide "true north" direction to our lives... Principles apply at all times in all places. They surface in the form of values,

ideas, norms...At the root of societal declines are foolish practices that represent violations of correct principles.[122]

In our discussion of participative leadership the term *values* will be used in the sense applied by Covey to principles. The fundamental difference is that Covey sees principles as being "self-evident and self-validating natural laws,"[123] whereas this study understands values as those principles chosen by the organization to become the shaping force of the "corporate culture." Values are, therefore, the primary principles that control the organization and, like a compass, give it direction. With Covey, we agree that principles and values should be self evident and self-validating. However, they should be identified as those values that are fundamental to shaping the culture and character of the organization.

Values not only define the character and direction of the organization, but also serve the valuable role of providing meaning to the members of the organization as they identify their efforts with the organizational values. Badaracco and Ellsworth cite James MacGregor Burns's discussion of "transformational leadership" as an example in which values provide the distinct difference between "transactional leadership" (that style characteristic of directional leadership or management) and "transformational leadership." Burns observes that the "moral" nature of leadership, in which moral issues are synonymous with values-driven leadership or "principle-centered leadership" is where

> [transforming] leadership occurs...in such a way that leaders and followers raise one another to higher levels of motivation and morality....Transforming leadership ultimately becomes moral in that it raises the level of human conduct and ethical aspirations of both leaders and led, and thus has a transforming effect on both....[124]

Institutionalized values, therefore, provide a definitive and powerful impact on organizational life and performance. They transfer the emphasis in an organization from tasks and goals to people, provide the parameters for organizational culture, life, and direction, and focus the members' commitment, enthusiasm, and sense of fulfillment. They play a vital role in determining the driving force of the organization and become a fundamental factor in strategic planning.

Since shared values are essential to participative leadership, so every organization must devote significant time, thought, and energy to clearly defining and articulating its values. Highlighting one of the profound differences between leadership and management, Badaracco and Ellsworth maintain that

> what separates a leader from a competent professional manager is the ability to build an organization that is a source of self-fulfillment and personal integrity for its members....This is not a new observation. Philip Selznick, a

pioneer in the study of leadership, has described a leader as "primarily an expert in the promotion and projection of values." He describes the leader's task in this way: "to infuse [an organization] with value beyond the technical requirements of the task at hand."

Badaracco and Ellsworth continue by implying that "focus, energy, commitment, and creativity...come from appeals to deeper values" and that dynamic leadership plays a pivotal role in shaping these values.[125]

A primary responsibility, therefore, of participative leadership (or values-driven leadership), when building a participative organizational culture, is leading the organization into determining and understanding its values. Badaracco and Ellsworth stress the role played by "norms, values, loyalties, aspirations and unwritten laws.... values are critical to channeling behavior."[126] Values form the primary and fundamental parameters for the participative organization.

BUILDING TEAM AWARENESS

In addition to the primary role that determining and communicating values plays in developing a successful participative culture, several other factors are essential to participative leadership. Team awareness and team building are also vital. Providing the initiative and direction for leading the organization in the development of working teams is a prime responsibility of organizational leadership.

This is especially true in the case of church leadership, with special reference to the elders. Organizing the congregation into teams built around ministry needs and "equipping" those teams for "the work of ministry," according to Paul, is a primary function of the elders (Eph 4:11ff.). Elders do this by *leading* (teaching, role modeling, and mentoring) the teams (in many instances, deacons as special servants may provide the core of the leadership teams) into determining, understanding, and building on the values chosen by the congregation as critical to congregational identity. These values may be biblical or doctrinal issues or they may be a particular focus for ministry chosen by the congregation because of its unique internal environment or giftedness. Whatever these values are, or however they have become the prime values of the congregation, it is the responsibility of the leadership to facilitate the building of team unity and cohesiveness around these values.

Once the ministry teams are built and equipped upon a sound understanding of the congregational values, the deacons and ministry teams should be freed (empowered) to carry out their specific ministry charge. At a later stage of the study we will comment on values and ministry accountability since both are equally essential to participative ministry or leadership. At this point we are merely stressing the need for values articulation in the building, equipping, and empowering of ministry teams.

PARTICIPATIVE TEAM LEADERSHIP

In a perceptive study of participative leadership and team building, John H. Zenger and associates demonstrate graphically the emerging role that teams are playing in successful contemporary organizations. They argue that, in contemporary society's new and developing environment, a shift from the traditional corporate pyramid model of leadership is essential to maintain vibrant growth in the coming decades. Given the enormous corpus of technological and business information with which contemporary corporations and institutions function, and the growing "corporate" knowledge and skill available to organizations in the contemporary workforce, a team approach to organizational leadership is the most effective solution to the challenges of global competition. Zenger and associates' publication, *Leading Teams: Mastering the New Role,*[127] argues effectively that building and leading effective teams will provide the "competitive advantage" necessary for survival in the coming decade.

The chart on the following page, adapted from Zenger and associates, graphically demonstrates the paradigmatic shift in leadership style they have proposed.

Zenger and associates' Team Leadership model is, in their mind, an advance over a pure participative style in which the leader is somewhat removed from the team. In their model the leader is an integral part of the team.

Plunkett and Fournier concur that teams and team building are perhaps the most essential element of participative management.

> Participative management is normally implemented through teams, groups, task forces, and other conglomerations of people. To participate means to interact, share in, take part in....The ultimate effectiveness of participative management often is determined not by how well an organization addresses its issues, but by how well the operational work groups make operational decisions, and identify and resolve their issues. Participative management is not necessarily restricted to teams; however, teams seem to be the dominant manifestation of participative management.

Since participative leadership is primarily related to focused behavior and people working together to achieve commonly shared goals, the concept of teamwork and team building flows naturally from a participative model of leadership. Careful attention must be given by organizational leadership to the dynamic of team building and team culture. Members of teams will come from different backgrounds with different characteristics. These characteristics must be blended into the dynamic of teamwork. It is only as the individual team members relate to and espouse the team values that any effective team dynamic can develop. It is the responsibility of leaders in a participative organization to shape the team within the parameters of the organization's values and to develop a team dynamic within the group.

Furthermore, teams must learn to interact with other teams within the organization. As the individual teams come to understand their unique nature and role in the life of the organization, how they relate to the goals of the organization, and how the diverse teams can reinforce one another in their efforts to reach their shared values and goals, they become integrated into an effective whole in a participative culture. It is the role of leadership to provide the environment and initiative for such integration into the corporate whole.[128] Values determination and team building are essential components to the internal environment or culture of the organization.

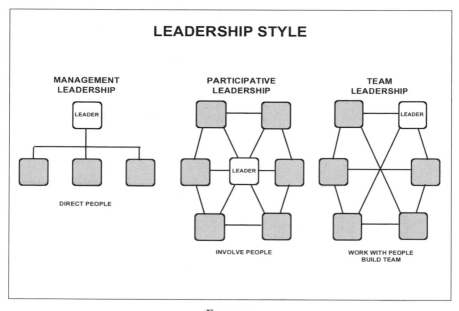

FIGURE 2

Several final observations are germane to the discussion of participative leadership. *First,* it is extremely unwise to dictate a model of participative leadership "from the top down." Participative leadership must of necessity be the decision of the group. Leadership will play a profound role in initiating and developing the participative leadership culture, but the final decision and shape of the leadership model must be that of the organization as a whole. Without organizational involvement in the process of installing a participative model, the group normally will interpret participative leadership as an attempt by the management to manipulate the group and to use the team concept as a subterfuge to conceal autocratic intentions. Ulterior motives can easily be attributed to sincere intentions!

Second, participative leadership is not something that can be legislated. It must be learned, and the "flat" learning curve for the process demands time. It is appropriate to stress once more that participative leadership is a *process* or *culture* that matures slowly along with the group. Whereas the directive model of leadership may at times seem *more efficient*, and the participative model may on occasions appear to be inefficient due to the time taken for the process to develop, participative leadership will, in the long-term, prove to be *more effective*. Participative leadership works best in organizations characterized by long-term planning and strategy as opposed to short-term planning and results.

Third, trust can be the ultimate determining factor in the success or failure of the participative leadership model. Trust is both a fundamental value to the process of participative leadership and an essential factor in the process of building and functioning as a team. Trust must function in every direction within the organization. The leadership must trust the team members, the members must trust the leadership, the teams and the team members must trust one another, and the organization as a whole must trust the process. Without careful attention to building trust within the organization and maintaining trust, participative leadership will be unable to function effectively.

CONCLUSION

In this chapter we have examined briefly three possible models for leadership: directive leadership, democratic leadership, and participative leadership. Each model has its merits and role in the life of an organization. We have noted, however, that each is related to the level of maturity of the organization and its leaders. In congregations with either young or immature leadership the directive or democratic models work more effectively. In congregations with a mature leadership and membership the participative model is the most effective, if not the most efficient.

PART THREE

The Church and Leadership Strategy

People and churches must sometimes let go of the past ... Just as individuals must be willing to say good-bye to attitudes or circumstances in their past in order to survive and prosper, congregations must free themselves from nonproductive historical practices in order to be effective.

Some congregations are dying today, for example, because they will not turn loose of an obsolete leadership style that is autocratic and dictatorial. This type of leadership might have made sense in the Army or the Marines during a time of war, but it is as out of place in the Lord's church today as a ring in a swine's snout. Church leaders who insist on running the church business from behind closed doors in a climate of secrecy are killing the church, no matter how good their intentions.

Some congregations are dying today because they will not say good-bye to methodologies of the 1930s, 1940s, and 1950s that do not fit the cultural patterns of urban America in the 1990s. I am confident that a part of the generation gap in Churches of Christ today stems from this fact: Young Christians who grew up in urban America feel that many of the church's methods today are foreign to the world they live in. These young people love the church, but seriously question the way the church performs its task.

Not only individuals, but congregations must learn to say good-bye to some things in order to be productive in the present and be prepared for the future. Congregations must not say good-bye to biblical truth ... However, they can be flexible in methodology.

HOWARD NORTON, EDITOR, *Christian Chronicle*,
DECEMBER 1993

CHAPTER 10

THE BIBLICAL MODEL FOR CHURCH LEADERSHIP

—◦◦◦—

Today the church as the kingdom of God, like God's kingdom through the ages, needs quality spiritual leadership. To be effective, modern church leadership, like that of Abraham, Moses, David, Elijah, and Nehemiah, must first be biblical and spiritual, then courageous, innovative, bold, and visionary. This leadership must spring naturally from a deeply spiritual living faith in God. It must be carefully nurtured through regular medita- tion on the will and purpose of God, through prayer, and by a deep and loving concern for the church as the people of God. The growth and matur- ing of the church in the twenty-first century, as always, will be in direct proportion to the quality and depth of its spiritual leadership.

LEADERSHIP IN THE NEW TESTAMENT

Several specific terms are used in the New Testament for the leaders of the church of God. Terms such as elder, bishop, shepherd, and pastor are used interchangeably on different occasions. Contrary to the contemporary practice of some, these are not dif- ferent "offices" in the church. We learn from the biblical use of these terms that they are *descriptive* terms used for the same leadership ministry in the church. Elders are the bishops, the shepherds, and the pastors in New Testament usage. They do not have reference to different *levels* of office. Each term defines a specific emphasis or *function* of ministry provided by the same leaders of the church.

The practice of using several terms to describe the same person is not uncom- mon. We often use different descriptive terms to define the many roles each of us plays in life. A man could fill the role of a husband, a father, a professor, an American, a Christian, and several other roles as well. Likewise a woman could be a wife, a mother, a lawyer, an American, a Christian, and possibly as many other roles as she chooses. We might merely be describing the range of roles that men and women play by the use of these different terms, but we could still be referring to the same man or woman. Likewise, a leader in the church may be described as an elder, a bishop, a pastor, or a shepherd while referring all the time to the same man. The terms merely describe the various roles or ministries the same person performs.

For example, in Acts 20, Paul called the leaders of the church in Ephesus to meet him at Miletus in order to charge them concerning their *ministry* responsibility. In his narrative report of these events, Luke referred to these leaders as *elders* (Acts 20:17, *presbuteros*). When Paul discussed their ministry in Acts 20:28 he charged them to be *overseers* (*bishops*) of the *flock*, to *care for* (*pastor*) them because *wolves* would *enter the flock* (thus to protect the flock). "Take heed (*care for*) to yourselves and to all the flock, in which the Holy Spirit has made you overseers (*bishops*), to care (*shepherd*) for the church of God which he obtained with the blood of his own Son." Hence, we learn from Paul's discussion of the elder's ministry, and his use of these descriptive pastoral terms, that an *elder* is an *overseer* of the church who as a *shepherd* cares for (*pastors*) his flock.

It is apparent from Ephesians 4:11ff; Acts 14:23, 15:1-35, 20:17-30; 1 Timothy 3:1-13; Titus 1:5-9; Philippians 1:1; James 5:14; and 1 Peter 5:1-4 that the church in the New Testament was served by several different categories of "ministers," namely, apostles, prophets, evangelists (preachers and ministers), elders (bishops, shepherds, pastors), deacons, and possibly some form of special servant identified vaguely as "deaconesses" (Rom 16:1, 1 Tim 5:9ff).[129] We will shortly consider each of these terms, emphasizing that each has reference to a unique aspect of ministry in the church.

TRADITIONAL PRACTICE AMONG CHURCHES OF CHRIST

For various reasons, however, some churches and church leaders today have an unclear or poorly defined understanding of the biblical role of the various ministries in the church, especially the ministry of elders and ministers. It is traditional among most Churches of Christ to use one term exclusively for congregational leaders. This term is *elder*. Little mention is made of other terms used in the New Testament for church leaders such as *bishops* and *shepherds* or *pastors*. Occasionally, one encounters the use of the term shepherd, but a survey of church bulletin title pages will reveal that this is rare. Obvious denominational connotations behind "bishop" have caused Churches of Christ to shy away from the term. Evangelical denominational use of the term *pastor* for the preacher has also caused Churches of Christ to shy away from this term.

Drawing on a long standing heritage in the American Restoration Movement, it has become the common practice among most Churches of Christ for church leaders to favor the term *elder* as opposed to *bishop*, and consequently to exclusively use this term in reference to officers governing the church on a church board. The paradigm upon which this perception of church leadership has been built derives more from a

Presbyterian form of church government than a biblical model. Many church members consequently see elders occupying an "office" at the top of a hierarchical structure of authoritarian decision makers, rather than as spiritual shepherds caring for the flock. A common prayer for elders among Churches of Christ is that the Lord will give the elders *wisdom* in order to *make the right decisions*. The tendency to use the term elder exclusively and to view them as a board of elders has biased church leadership in favor of an administrative ministry rather than a shepherding ministry.

We will notice at a later stage in this study that elders do have authority in the local church, and that they are significantly involved in the decision making process in the church. However, we will learn that authority in the New Testament is functional, related to ministry, rather than autocratic or authoritarian. Problems arise (especially in regard to 1 Pet 5:1-4) with the view that elders are the "rulers"[130] of the church who autocratically make all the decisions for the church. This "from above" authoritarian concept is unfortunately a misunderstanding of biblical authority or of how decisions were made in the New Testament church. By embracing the view of elders *autocratically ruling* the church, many Churches of Christ have unfortunately adopted a denominational model for church polity (governance) rather than a biblical model. They have merely shifted autocratic church rule from the diocese to the local congregation.

Because of an over-emphasis on authority as ruling in a hierarchical model of the church, many elders are troubled by what they fear as a challenge to their authority. Eldership authority is real, but as we will shortly demonstrate, it is more correctly defined and proscribed functionally by the ministry of shepherding and serving that God has designed for the elders. Biblical authority in the case of elders is, therefore, functional rather than absolute; it is located in ministry and not in an autocratic "position" or "office."

One of the major pressures faced by church leaders today is a call for change in *how* the church is run. Deacons especially, but also other capable Christians, are seeking a more active voice in the life of the congregation. Men and women who occupy responsible positions in the workplace feel they have much to offer the church in the realm of strategic planning and decision making. These cries for change, or for a greater role in the life of the church, are often unfortunately interpreted by some elders as challenges to their leadership, wisdom, or authority.

Furthermore, it is apparent from concerns often expressed by church leaders that they are uncertain how to meet these challenges, most of which arise out of the rapidly changing sociological and demographic environment. In many instances church leaders face these challenges and calls for change with trepidation and fear. In some cases elders merely refuse to pay attention to them. Pleas from deacons for an increased role in determining the direction of the congregation are seen as denominational inroads or creeping liberalism. Additionally, calls to integrate women into some form of leadership role in the church are also interpreted by some as feminist attempts to "usurp" authority.

With little exaggeration, it may be said that church leaders find themselves in the same plight as many contemporary corporate managers. They are challenged daily to understand calls for change. Their leadership style in the context of a rapidly shifting pluralistic socioeconomic environment is daily in need of review, development, and enrichment. Some elders, like their corporate colleagues, are both threatened and confused by this.

The natural tendency in such cases of uncertainty and fear is to retreat into a safe, traditional *office of the elder* in the name of biblical conservatism, rather than be challenged to search for biblical insights into leadership that might threaten the comfortable security of the traditional authoritarian *office of the elder*.

The demographic shifts of contemporary society naturally will pose many new challenges to church leaders. The steady movement of young people from rural to urban churches has significantly changed the vitality of many rural churches. The upward socioeconomic mobility of members in urban churches, especially among the Baby Boomers, Busters, and "Millenniums" has also added a fascinating ingredient to church life and church leadership. With the decline of trust in established authoritarian structures and institutions, young people, especially the Boomers, expect to play some participative leadership role in society, and especially in the church.

Faced with the challenges of a secularizing society and the demographic shifts in "downtown" churches, some church leaders are frustrated by the flight of their younger members to the suburban churches. In other cases they cling adamantly to their traditional authoritarian models, interpreting the concerns of the younger generation as either denominational or secular. As the church moves into the next decade of change with its fast moving and kaleidoscopic new realities, church leaders must return to their Bibles for ways in which to address these concerns. This book is an attempt to rethink leadership in light of these new realities, as well as in light of biblical emphases on ministry.

As never before, biblical models for leadership need to be explored in order to bring comfort to the older, established, more traditional church leaders and encouragement to the competent yet frustrated younger church members who have such enormous talent and giftedness and who expect, even demand, to be included in the future direction of the church. We should never forget that biblical faith is able to transcend all cultures and sociological structures. Without deserting their conservative, biblical roots, church leaders need to be encouraged to explore new avenues of church leadership that are in accord with their biblical mandate, yet are open enough to address the changing contemporary scene.

PAUL AND CHURCH LEADERSHIP

In Ephesians 4:11, Paul gives perhaps the most cogent argument for dynamic leadership in the church. He refers to *apostles, prophets, evangelists,* and *pastors and teachers* in a manner that draws attention to their vital role in the maturing process of the church. In this pivotal passage on leadership Paul articulates the primary function of leaders in the most insightful and meaningful manner. The leaders described by Paul in this text have the primary responsibility of *equipping* the saints for the work of *ministry* through their individual leadership roles.

Careful examination of the inherent ministry of each of the leaders described in Ephesians 4:11 reveals that theirs is fundamentally *a ministry of teaching.* These church leaders, through their *ministry of teaching,* are responsible for leading the congregation into a closer relationship with and deeper maturity in Christ. In this manner they *equip* their members for effective ministry. Furthermore, by leading their members into a closer relationship with Christ, they stimulate and sustain the growth of their followers.

Apostles. Paul begins his discussion of the church's equipping ministry with the *apostles.* The English word apostle is, in fact, merely the anglicized form of the Greek *apostolos. Apostolos* was a common word in the Greek vernacular of the day and simply meant "one sent out" or "one commissioned." From this basic sense, *apostolos* came to mean "one chosen and sent out on some form of mission, or a uniquely commissioned person."

The New Testament writers formalized and reserved the term for those chosen and commissioned by Christ to carry out his mission of establishing the church through preaching the Word to all nations (Mk 16:25, Matt 28:18-29, Lk 24:44-49). They became "the Apostles." The term "apostle" has inherent within it the authority for the bearer to function and develop the ministry commissioned by the sender, who in the Christian context was the Lord Jesus.

Certain qualities were required of those commissioned to be apostles of Jesus. They were to have personally witnessed Jesus' public ministry and to have been witnesses to his resurrection (Acts 1:21, 22). Paul, personally chosen by Jesus, to be an apostle according to God's will and purpose (Gal 1:1,15,16, Acts 9:15, 22:6-16, Rom 1:1, Col 1:1), was also witness to the resurrection of Jesus (1 Cor 15:8, Gal 1:16).

In a generic sense, anyone sent out or commissioned would be termed an apostle, but in the New Testament the term is used in a *unique* sense for those distinctive leaders personally chosen and commissioned by Jesus to inaugurate the public proclamation of the saving Word of God, and to whom was given the responsibility and authority to establish the church of Jesus.

It is apparent from Jesus' commission to the apostles as recorded in Matthew 28:16-18, that their ministry was to be one of inaugurating redemption among the nations in the name of Jesus. This was to be achieved through the preaching of Jesus' death, burial, and resurrection (Lk 24:44-49, Matt 28:18-20, Acts 2:14-42; 10:34-48). The apostles themselves left no question in regard to their understanding of their ministry, for in Acts 6:1-6 they emphasized that theirs was implicitly a ministry of preaching the Word and prayer.

When the church's ministers (in this case, the apostles) understand clearly their unique ministry and devote themselves to that ministry, great things happen. In Acts 6:7, Luke observed that the result of apostles and special servants (possibly "deacons") devoting themselves to their individual and unique ministries was that "the word of God increased; and the number of the disciples multiplied greatly in Jerusalem, and a great many of the priests were obedient to the faith."

By reason of the uniqueness of the apostles' qualifications, that is, having personally witnessed the ministry and resurrection of Christ, the church today is not served by living apostles. The witness of the original biblical apostles is, however, preserved in the inspired Word of God and remains firm; no further authenticating witness to the death, burial, and resurrection of Jesus is necessary.

Prophets. The next category of minister mentioned by Paul in Ephesians 4:11 was *prophets*. The prophets of the Bible have always been uniquely inspired spokespersons for God. From early Hebrew times prophets were considered to be "called by God" for the purpose of "speaking for God." Their calling was simply to proclaim his Word, to warn, to exhort, to comfort, and to teach. (The Greek term has similar implications.) Among a long list of faithful prophets were Elijah, Isaiah, Jeremiah, and Ezekiel. Isaiah 6:8, 9 clearly captures the spirit of the prophet. Speaking to Isaiah, God asks, "Whom shall I send...?" Isaiah answered, "Here am I! Send me...." God's response was, "Go, and say to the people...."

Ezekiel's commission adds to the dynamic of the prophet. God said to him, "Son of man, I send you to the people of Israel...and you shall say to them, 'Thus says the Lord God' and...they will know that there has been a prophet among them" (Ezek 2:3-5). Whether Israel listened to Ezekiel or not, he was to speak out boldly for God. God warned Ezekiel not to be rebellious like Israel, but to listen carefully to his words. He was to speak "with God's words to them... whether they hear or refuse to hear" (Ezek 2:8-3:11).

In the early church, prophets likewise served as God's commissioned and inspired spokespersons. They apparently functioned in worship services (1 Cor 14:23), exhorting, comforting, and edifying the church. They communicated knowledge and revealed the mysteries of God's will (1 Cor 14:2, 3). Prophets were included by Paul in the list of teachers responsible for equipping the saints (Eph 4:11).

In an age when the infant church was almost solely dependent on the apostles for their knowledge of God's will, prophets and other inspired teachers (2 Tim 2:2) filled in the gap between the apostles and the written Word. Uniquely qualified through the inspiration of the Holy Spirit, they could confirm the Word spoken by others and could themselves impart divinely inspired knowledge. Prophets provided vital leadership in communicating God's word to his people and in equipping them for maturity and ministry in Christ.

Evangelists. One cannot speak of the church in the New Testament without giving special attention to the ministry of evangelism. *Evangelists* were at the vanguard of missionary church life. They played a vital role in the maturing of the church. In Ephesians 4:11, when speaking of those ministries essential to the maturing of the church, Paul included evangelists in the same category as apostles and prophets, thus emphasizing the importance of this ministry.

The term *evangelist* (*euangelistes*) is derived from the same root as the term *gospel* (*euangelion*). Both speak of the *good news* being proclaimed in the person and work of Jesus. The *good news* was that sinners do not have to die for their sins. Through God's loving grace and mercy, Jesus' death on the cross and subsequent resurrection, and their faith in the saving message of the cross, sinners can be forgiven and live. As Paul so beautifully expresses it in Romans 8:1, "There is therefore now no condemnation for those who are in Christ Jesus. For the law of the Spirit of life in Christ Jesus has set me free from the law of sin and death." This was *good news*, and those proclaiming it were called *evangelists*.

As this message was announced in oral form by the pioneer evangelists during the first thirty to forty years following the cross and resurrection of Jesus, the good news began to solidify into traditions relating to the life of Jesus. Some developing oral traditions were, unfortunately, unrelated to the historical facts of Jesus' life, giving rise to the need for some reliable account of Jesus' life and ministry. The four written forms of this Jesus tradition that were finally accepted by the church became known as *gospels* (good news) since they presented in reliable form the gospel message of Jesus. The authors of these gospel accounts are commonly referred to today as "*the evangelists.*"

Evangelists in the early church were those who proclaimed to *both the church and the world* the *good news* of their salvation in Jesus. They formed a primary source of ministry in the growth and maturation of the church. Paul's closing exhortation to Timothy, his son in the gospel, was that he "should preach the word with urgency, do the work of an evangelist, and fulfill his ministry." It was for this good news that Paul, himself an evangelist, had "fought the good fight and had finished the race" (2 Tim 4:2-7). The ministry of preachers in the early church was *evangelism*, not church chaplaincy!

A vital lesson can be learned from Paul, Timothy, and the New Testament preaching of the gospel message. It is clear from Paul's use of the terms *evangelist* and *gospel* that the core of his preaching ministry, whether to Christians or those who had never heard the good news of Jesus, was "Jesus Christ and him crucified" (1 Cor 1:17-2:5). It was through the preaching of this *good news* that Paul believed all people could be brought to maturity in Christ. For this message Paul strove with all the might inspired in him by God (Col 2:28, 29). Christians need constantly to be reminded of, and challenged by, the good news of Jesus' saving grace. Evangelism is not some special ministry for those outside the church. Both the church and the world need daily to be reminded of this gospel.

It is no small wonder that *evangelists* are essential to the process of maturation within the church. It is only as ministers focus their ministry and message on the good news in Jesus, and preach the message of Jesus' cross to their congregations (whether from the pulpit, in Bible classes, or in small groups such as youth ministry) that Christians will mature in Christ. To the degree that preachers stray from the core of the gospel and get sidetracked into personal or sectarian hobbies, the people of God will struggle in their effectiveness in evangelizing the lost.

Although the terms *minister* and *preacher* do not appear in the Ephesians 4 passage regarding "equipping the saints for the work of ministry," the terms are common in Paul's vocabulary and are, to all effects and purposes, synonymous with the work of the evangelist. Since the establishing and maturing of Christian faith has always been so integrally related to the public proclamation of the Word, it is only to be expected that ministers and preachers are featured prominently in the New Testament (Acts 21:8; Eph 4:11; Col 1:7, 23, 25; 2 Tim 4:2-5). Similar to the Old Testament prophets, ministers and preachers were, and remain, God's special spokesmen to his people. Commissioned by the Word of God, and working through the message of the Word, they serve as the conscience of the church, exhorting, teaching, encouraging, equipping, maturing, and even rebuking the church (2 Tim 3:15-17; 2 Tim 4:1-5; Eph 4:11-16).

It is a fallacy, however, to differentiate between evangelists and ministers and preachers. Every minister and preacher should be an evangelist whose message is the saving grace in Jesus. The terms merely stress different aspects of their ministry. *Minister* emphasizes the fact that the minister is a *servant* for God to the people. The minister is in a special sense God's *suffering servant to the nations*. *Preacher* emphasizes the function of *proclaiming the Word of God* in this ministry. *Evangelist* draws attention to the content of the message, namely, the *cross of Jesus* as the good news and power of salvation.

Perhaps no passage brings this point into sharper focus than 2 Timothy 4:1-5. Here Paul instructs Timothy to "*preach* the word and to do the work of an *evangelist*." He is to "*fulfill his ministry*." It is a tragedy that too many ministers get entangled with church administration and the "power positions" this seemingly implies. By becoming overly involved in administration, ministers are drawn away from the real power of their ministry, namely, preaching and teaching the Word of God.

The leadership role intended by God for the *evangelist-minister* is leading people closer to Christ through the public and private proclamation of the message of the cross. The minister's power to lead is not through any office or through his erudition, education, or communication skills. Ministers effectively lead the church through their faithfulness to Christ, their own personal example in imitation of the suffering service of Christ, their faithfulness to the Word of God and to their ministry of bringing the congregation into contact with the dynamic power of God's Word (1 Tim 4:11-16).

Pastors and Teachers. Included in his list (Eph 4:11) of those "ministers" responsible for equipping the saints for ministry and leading God's people to maturity in Christ, Paul speaks of *pastors* and *teachers*. From the Greek grammatical construction of the expression "pastors and teachers" we learn that Paul considered them to be *teaching pastors*. A primary role of the elder as *pastor* is *teaching*.

In his discourse with the *elders* in Acts 20:17-35 Paul described the ministry of the *overseer/bishop* as *caring for* or *pastoring* the church.[131] The Greek term translated "to care for" in this passage (*poimaino*) is the same word translated *"tend the flock"* in 1 Peter 5:2. In Acts 20 and 1 Peter 5 the discussion of the ministry of the elder is set in the context of shepherding a flock. In Acts 20:17-35, we noticed above that the terms *elder* and *bishop* were brought together in one ministry that defined their function as *shepherding* or *pastoring*. Again, we stress that the term *pastor* in the New Testament was used descriptively to define the ministry of the *elder* or *bishop* (cf. 1 Pet. 5:1-4).

Unfortunately, years of denominational tradition have resulted in considerable confusion over these terms. In some evangelical traditions the terms *elder* and *pastor* have become separated into two different ministries, with the minister or preacher adopting the term pastor. In addition to this unfortunate misapplication, the term bishop is reserved in some Christian traditions for a single ecclesiastical officer who presides over a number of churches in some form of diocese or synod. Furthermore, the term elder has fallen completely from the vocabulary of many denominational traditions. Much of the simplicity of the New Testament pattern has been lost in this confusion.

Similar confusion is found among Churches of Christ where ministers have become church administrators and ceased to be evangelists. In many instances ministers who should be evangelists have become church "chaplains" or "pastors." Elders who should be the pastors have become congregational "business managers" or "budget comptrollers."

As we have already observed, in Ephesians 4:11 Paul couples *pastors* and *teachers* in an interesting grammatical relationship. This unique juxtapositioning of *teaching pastors* implies that a fundamental function of *elder/pastors* is that they *teach*. It is no small wonder that in 1 Timothy 3:2 and Titus 1:9 Paul emphasizes that the bishops or elders should be effective teachers, that they should be capable of "holding firm to the sure word as taught," being able to give "instruction in sound doctrine and confute those who contradicted it." In their ministry of *shepherding* their flock, *elders* or *bishops* are active leaders and overseers in the maturing process through their *teaching ministry*.

In their ministry as *teaching shepherds, elders* (bishops and pastors) are intended to be the spiritual leaders of God's people today just as the prophets and priests were intended by God to be the spiritual leaders of Israel. The future security of God's people depends in large measure on the spiritual quality of the leaders. Hebrews 13:7 reminds us that a primary role of these spiritual leaders is to bring God's message to his people. Their ministry of the Word, the quality of their lifestyle, and a faith directed by Jesus, who "is the same yesterday and today and forever," bring equilibrium into the lives of the new Israel as they struggle with the vicissitudes of daily living.

It seems most likely from the implication of the Scriptures in which the terms are found, that the model of elders, bishops, and pastors in the New Testament church was one of a plurality of such leaders. The wisdom of this plurality is obvious. Such is the magnitude of their task, and the responsibility of their ministry, that any sense of a monarchial bishopric or episcopate was unthinkable.

Deacons. Although not mentioned in Ephesians 4, nor as prominent in the New Testament as the bishops, *deacons* play a significant role in the ministry of the church. As *"special servants"* to the church, deacons perform a meaningful *spiritual* ministry. It is a mistake to limit the role of deacons purely to care for the *physical* matters of the church. It is doubtful whether the church in New Testament times owned property as is the practice today, or that it distinguished between physical and spiritual ministries.

If Acts 6:1-6 is a model for deacons, and there is solid ground for believing this to be the case,[132] then one could conclude that the work of the deacon is manifestly one of a spiritual ministry. In the delicate situation that had developed in the Jerusalem church between the widows (the Hellenists and the Hebrews), seven special servants were appointed to attend to matters of a profound interpersonal nature, namely, the friction between the Hellenist widows (Jews who had adopted Greek culture) and Hebrew widows (Jews who had preserved their Hebrew culture in Palestine). Although seemingly a simple physical problem regarding food, the implications of the problem had deep spiritual and religious overtones.

The contemporary concept that deacons take care of the physical needs of the congregation, such as the church building, etc., is misinformed on two counts. *First*, this model of service is not derived from New Testament practice since there is no record of churches in the New Testament owning church buildings, and *second*, because the dichotomy between physical and spiritual is ill-conceived and also not derived from New Testament practice.

The spiritual qualities identified by Paul as essential in the deacon (1 Tim 3:8-13) add further strength to the impression that *deacons* are intended by God to be *special servants* or *"ministers"*[133] intensely involved in maturing the church through developing interpersonal relationships. Deacons function along with elders and evangelists in the church as spiritual leaders in the congregation. They, too, should be deeply involved in equipping every member for the work of ministry. In a healthy vibrant congregation, deacons working alongside the leadership of elders are vital to the effective ministry of the body. They provide crucial leadership in a constructive process of developing both horizontal relationships with others (Acts 6) and vertical relationships with God and Christ.

One word remains to be said concerning *deacons*. The etymology of the word *diakonos* simply means *servant*. However, three words were available to the inspired writers of the New Testament for servant. One was simply the word *diakonos* or *servant*, another was *doulos*, or *slave*, the third was *pais*, which was normally rendered *child* or *youth*, but in certain circumstances was translated as *servant* (cf. Isa 37:35, Matt 12:18, Acts 4:25). In one sense, all Christians are *slaves* of God and Christ, having been bought with a price (1 Cor 6:19-20), but this term does not do justice to the true nature of Christian service. In contrast to slavery, the concept of the Christian servant in simple voluntary service stands out in striking a manner. Christians serve God and Christ out of deep love and personal commitment (2 Cor 5:14,15; 1 Cor 15:10), not merely out of duty, slavery, or obligation, however strong their sense of obligation may be.

In the context of service in the New Testament, the term *servant* (*diakonos*) speaks of a *quality* of service deriving from a devoted love for God and Christ. It is in this sense that the term is used in a generic application of all Christian servants. Every Christian is therefore a *servant minister*. In certain contexts, however, the term *diakonos/servant/minister* takes on additional specific meaning and significance; it refers to *special servants* with *unique spiritual qualifications*. The translators of the English Bible have chosen to coin the word *deacon* for one category of these *special servants*. This is a good practice since it clearly establishes that certain Christians were chosen by nature of their unique spiritual qualifications, and dedicated to *specific significant ministries*. The term is used in this special sense in 1 Timothy 3:8 and Philippians 1:1.

Some uncertainty remains in the minds of biblical scholars in regard to the existence of *deaconesses* in the early church, if this word is used in a sense parallel to the ministry of *deacon*. The uncertainty is complicated by the translation of the term *diakonos* in Romans 16:1. The Revised Standard Version (1971) translates this word *deaconess*. The King James Version, the New American Standard Version, and the New International Version translate the term as *servant*. We are faced with the challenging dilemma of determining from the context of the verse whether in this instance *diakonos* should be translated in the general sense of *servant* or the narrow specific sense of *deaconess*. Unfortunately, there is simply insufficient biblical or historical evidence to make a definitive decision. In similar fashion, there does not seem, to be adequate textual evidence to draw *firm dogmatic* conclusions in either direction in regard to this or any other passages in the New Testament that might support the existence of a designated group of ladies parallel to the deacons of the New Testament. Dr. J. W. Roberts, late professor of New Testament at Abilene Christian University, however, suggested the possibility of a special group of widows who could be designated as *deaconesses*.[134]

There may well have been some form of special servant role for widows as is reflected in 1 Timothy 5:9ff, but these widows are not specifically referred to in this passage as deaconesses. In spite of our desire to be open to discovering rewarding ministries for women in the church there simply is not sufficient textual evidence to be firm or dogmatic in regard to *deaconesses*. Many churches have solved this dilemma by appointing women as *"special servants"* in the church with *specific ministries*. In one sense, "deacons" are *designated servants*, and it may be appropriate to designate them as such rather than by the archaic, and in most cases, meaningless term deacon.

Leaders. Although not a Pauline text, Hebrews 13:7, 17, 24 introduces us to an additional dimension of leadership in a unique manner. The writer to the Hebrews uses the term *leader* three times in these texts. It is interesting to note that the term translated *leaders* in this passage (*hegoumenos*, from which we derive the English word "hegemony"), as in other similar passages in similar Christian contexts in the New Testament, appears in the context of one who *teaches*. In Hebrews 13:7 it is the leaders who *"spoke to them the word of God."* In Acts 14:12 Paul was called Hermes because he was the chief speaker (*hegoumenos*). In Acts 15:22 we are introduced to Judas and Silas, *"leading men"* (*hegoumenous*), who were entrusted with a letter and message from the Jerusalem church to the church in Antioch. The point being made here is that these "leaders" in the early church were designated leaders because of their *teaching role* in the church.

It is difficult to hold a firm position on this point, but some scholars identify the *leaders* of Hebrews 13:7, 17 as *elders*, since they "keep watch over the souls of their group and will have to give account for them." This does sound like a reference to the responsibility of the elder. If this is true, it impacts and intensifies the significance of the *pastor-elder-bishop* role in the teaching ministry of the church. The term could, however, refer to any teacher or minister whose responsibility is to teach and care for the church.

EQUIPPING SAINTS FOR THE WORK OF MINISTRY

The church will be effective in its special ministry and outreach only to the degree that its leaders are given to the task of *equipping* their members for fruitful ministry. As uniquely qualified leaders, the pastors (elders/bishops), deacons (special servants), and evangelists (preaching ministers) care for the church. They identify members who need help and special attention, and through their special gifts as teachers they work in the process of leading their members to a closer relationship with Christ, and so equip them for the work of ministry.

In an intriguing manner in Ephesians 4:11, Paul describes these unique, yet essential Christian ministries as *gifts* given to the church by the victorious Lord. In this, we have an intriguing insight into Paul's understanding of Christian ministry; it is a *gift of God's grace*. The purpose of these gifts, in addition to "equipping the saints for the work of ministry" (vs. 12), was to empower these *ministers* of the church "to build up the body of Christ," that is, to lead the church into a quality of maturity found only in Christ. Adopting an analogy from the human body which he had previously developed in 1 Corinthians 12, and in which he had argued that no one member of the body was more important to the body than any other member; that the hand was no more important than the foot, Paul explained that each member is inextricably attached to, and dependent on, the other members of the body for bodily growth. In this manner, Paul in 1 Corinthians 12 had developed an argument for unity similar to that which he now develops in the first verses of Ephesians 4. The ministers described by Paul (apostles, prophets, evangelists, and pastors and teachers) play a fundamental and vital role in the unity and maturity of the church as the body of Christ. In each case (apostle, prophet, evangelist, teaching pastor) the terms used by Paul for these ministries carry within them the descriptive nature and function of the ministry.

CONCLUSION

In this chapter we have briefly explored several salient New Testament ministry leadership terms used by the New Testament for the church's special ministry servants. Through this investigation we have explored a lucid and meaningful understanding of these ministries. We have noticed as the study has developed that each of the ministries examined provided an essential leadership dynamic, and that the term describing the ministry included and defined the *authority* to *function* in that ministry.

The need of God's people for spiritual maturity in the world in which they live and minister, from ancient times in Israel to the church in modern times, demands a certain *quality* of leadership. This leadership must be faithful to God, to his purpose, and to his people. It must be a spiritual leadership which boldly speaks out for God in a world running contrary to God's purpose. It must be a leadership that models by example the care, passion, and moral character of its chief shepherd, Christ. It must be a leadership that nurtures God's people and equips them for God's ministry of suffering service. The leadership and equipping ministry performed by elders, bishops, shepherds, deacons, evangelists, ministers, and preachers must be understood as a continuation of the redemptive ministry of God and Christ with its roots in the eternal purpose of God.

The history of God's people clearly establishes the need for strong, faithful, concerned, and spiritual leadership. In every age God has raised up such leaders for his people. The maturity and success of God's people has repeatedly been directly related to the spiritual and visionary quality of that leadership. Today, as never before, the need for bold, innovative, yet biblical leadership lies at the heart of the future of the Lord's church.

Church leaders must find meaningful and challenging ministry opportunities for all of their members, young and old, male and female, if they are to keep these bright young minds in their congregations active, and if they plan to keep the church in the forefront of dynamic church growth. Church leaders must be prepared to equip all of their members for some form of leadership role, or rewarding ministry. A primary function of leadership is *"equipping the saints for the work of ministry."* Failure to do so will result in apathy, dissatisfaction, and negative growth.

Elders, deacons, ministers, and committed Christians must explore the depths of their leadership ministry as the church faces a world changing and opening to new vistas of evangelism at a rate seldom before experienced. The same God who opened doors to the apostle Paul (Col 4:3) stands beside doors opening daily to his church. Are the church's leaders ready and equipped to accept such challenges and opportunities?

Christians should constantly remember that God's people have always prospered in direct relationship to the quality of leadership available to them. The challenging times before the church and the wonderful opportunities presented by the dramatic changes in the twenty-first century call for bold, innovative, visionary leadership. Because of our unique religious commitment, however, this leadership must maintain firm biblical foundations.

CHAPTER 11

THE CHURCH AND ITS CULTURAL HERITAGE

---~W~---

THE CHURCH AND CULTURE

Any Christian who has traveled abroad and worshiped with fellow Christians in "native" congregations has noticed with interest the differences of style in the worship services of the "native" churches. A trip to England, and a visit to congregations that have not been significantly influenced by the Churches of Christ in the American Bible Belt, will underscore this point. The more dissimilar the local culture and society are to that in America, the more profound the differences.

Africa provides an excellent case in point.[135] Most African churches meet only once on Sunday, and then without what is traditionally known in the United States as Bible class. African worship services often celebrate the Lord's Supper as many as three times in one service, have two or three sermons, several prayers, and little structure as it is known in the United States. In many instances in rural churches no contribution is taken up and an invitation song is often sung before the Lord's Supper but not after the sermon. Furthermore, few African rural churches meet on Wednesday night, or any other night, for a mid-week Bible class.

A major reason for churches meeting only once on Sunday and not on Wednesday night is that many African Christians do not own automobiles and do not have the luxury of the fine transportation systems enjoyed in the more developed nations. Furthermore, few African churches are served by a supported or paid minister. If a local congregation has a minister he is in most cases self-supported. Many African churches are served by a "circuit rider" minister.

Rural African churches often celebrate the Lord's Supper several times during the one worship service since their worship services are protracted "come and go" occasions. Members walk, often great distances, to the service, stay as long as they can, and then leave. Promptness in American terms is not an African "virtue" since rural

African time is often determined by the position of the sun. Wrist watches are worn by the privileged few as status symbols rather than timepieces! Services often begin when enough people are present, and end whenever everyone has left!

Foreign or "native" churches are as committed to the biblical principles of worship as their sister American churches, but the structure, expression, and form of church life and congregational worship are culturally and sociologically determined or shaped. All Christians, whether American, European, African, or Asian are so accustomed to the familiar that they sometimes are unable to differentiate between what is traditional, cultural, or sociological, and what is biblical. This is perfectly normal and creates no real problems until Christians in one culture or tradition begin to bind their form of Christianity on another significantly different culture. Problems also surface when a local culture undergoes profound paradigm shifts and when members of a particular segment of culture or tradition fail to, or are unwilling to, understand the shifts and pluralistic traditions present in their group.

The point we are making in this chapter is that much of what we do in church life is culturally or sociologically determined. Our culture or society has a number of different factors that shape us. Some are ethnic, some socioeconomic, some generational. Yet others are religious, traditional, or philosophic differences. We are all shaped by these influences. It is of vital importance, however, that we understand those forces driving our culture and church life.

In the context of this study it is necessary that we explore some of these influences in order to better understand how we "do" church in our church community. In one sense, members of Churches of Christ form a community of believers in a particular Scottish or American Restoration Tradition or Movement.[136] We will explore some of those influences shaping the cultural mindset of Churches of Christ in America, and in foreign cultures significantly influenced by the American Church of Christ Restoration Movement.

A DENOMINATIONAL HERITAGE

Churches of Christ as they are known in the United States and many parts of the world today are historically part of a religious awakening or movement which began in Scotland and America in the early nineteenth century. This awakening which was theologically deeply rooted in Scripture, began out of a reaction to denominationalism and as an attempt to restore the church as it could be identified in the New Testament. It was, in addition, an attempt to call Christian denominations back into the unity of the church described in Ephesians 4:1-6. This Restoration Movement, as it is now identified in American church history, was committed to a return to Scripture as the only definitive creed for the church. Churches of Christ today are proud of the achievements of their Scottish and American forebears in the Restoration Movement and of their Restoration heritage. They esteem highly all attempts to restore the New Testament church in the "unity of the Spirit in the bond of peace" (Eph 4:1-6). Although at times frustrated by sectarian spirits and divisions among Churches of Christ, the dream of a church established in unity along New Testament principles is both noble and worthy of serious attention.

In spite of the attempts of Restoration leaders in the nineteenth century to rid their faith and practice of all denominational spirits, they found it extremely difficult to escape the sociological characteristics of the churches in whose midst they functioned. For instance, Churches of Christ soon fell into the universal practice of acquiring church buildings, a sociological practice that has no New Testament foundation. Furthermore, the Sunday School movement among denominational churches was adopted as Bible School among Churches of Christ. Two services on Sunday and a prayer meeting on Wednesday night became the standard. There is absolutely nothing wrong with these practices[137] as long as they are considered optional and are not bound on other congregations or individuals.

Without often realizing it, Churches of Christ continue in many ways to be part of their Christian denominational, sociological environment, although rightly rejecting many denominational doctrines. Some of this denominational, sociological heritage has found its way into Church of Christ practice. There is nothing inherently wrong with this as long as it does not clash with biblical principles. We notice this tendency specifically in regard to church polity (or government). By this we have in mind how congregations are organized and operated.

The purpose of this chapter will be to briefly identify some areas of church polity in regard to several major denominational movements, and to show how these have impacted Church of Christ practice. Some of these practices have crept into Church of Christ practice and thinking through Bible translations, such as the King James Version, due to the theological convictions of the translators of those versions. Others have become part of Church of Christ life by association. What follows will not be a detailed examination of denominational church polity, but merely a sketch of church structure in order to trace developments significant to this study.

THE ROMAN CATHOLIC CHURCH

Along with their "protestant" neighbors, Churches of Christ have been particularly careful not to adopt Roman Catholic patterns of church polity. Fundamental to this rejection is a hierarchical structure and pontifical authority alien to Scripture. With a strong conviction that the churches of the New Testament were profoundly an autonomous fellowship of congregations, Churches of Christ reject the "universal" concept of a catholic church under one earthly head located in Rome. Churches of Christ find no precedent for Peter becoming the universal head of the church as Christ's regent on earth. In keeping with their commitment to congregational autonomy, Churches of Christ also reject any form of creed other than the Bible, and in particular the New Testament.[138]

Of particular relevance to this study, however, is the hierarchical system of church government practiced by the Catholic Church.[139] With the Pope in Rome serving in the place of Christ, and with Cardinals forming a council under the Pope, local dioceses are governed by bishops and local congregations by ordained priests. In this form of hierarchical government, authority is attached to an office and moves down a chain of authority from the top to the members at the bottom of the pyramid structure. Certain decisions may be made at lower levels, but the nature of the decision determines at which level of the hierarchical structure the decision will be made.

This hierarchical model, in which either some "papal figure" or certain councils and individuals are set in a pyramid structure with those at the top having higher authority than those below, creates problems for those working from within a biblical perspective. In most instances, those who view the church as a hierarchical structure understand leaders to speak almost "ex cathedra" (from above) for Christ.

Associated with the above pyramidal concept is the view that authority is somehow attached to an "office," and that one moves up the pyramid in a system of promotions. Those at the top are perceived to have more authority, and to be more important to the function of the body than those below them. No biblical support is found for any of these practices, with many being distinctly contrary to Scripture. This concept of certain persons of significance occupying an office in which authority is vested is often found even within churches professing to be profoundly "protestant" or "biblical." This discussion will be of considerable interest to this study at a later stage.

THE EPISCOPALIAN CHURCH

As an offshoot of the Roman Catholic Church, the Episcopalian Church retains the same hierarchical model and pyramid structure, with the exception of rejecting the universal authority of the Roman Pope. In place of the Pope, however, the Episcopalian Church has inserted the Archbishop of Canterbury as the head of the church. The major difference with the Roman view is that the Archbishop does not speak with the final authority of Christ. The church, nevertheless, operates in a similar pyramid structure under bishops, priests, and deacons.

Of vital interest to us in regard to church leadership is the fact that the translation of the King James Version was made under the "authority" of the Church of England, and for almost three centuries was viewed as the "authorized version" of the Church of England and most major English-speaking Protestant denominations. In almost every case, English-speaking denominational terminology has been significantly shaped by this translation.[140] The King James Version has profoundly influenced later translations such as the English Revised Version, the American Standard Version, the New American Standard Version, the Revised Standard Version, and the New Revised Standard Version. Each of these translations has over the last three centuries perpetuated not only much of the Episcopalian terminology of 1611, but also through its translation of doctrinal terms, a specific slant or definition of Christian doctrine. This impact is felt today in regard to church polity with striking impact in the interpretation and application of such texts as 1 Timothy 3:1ff, Titus 1:5f., 1 Thessalonians 5:12f., and 1 Timothy 5:17f.

With particular relevance to our discussion of church polity, we mention the Episcopalian or Roman Catholic concept of authority as vested in a clerical office. The King James translation of 1 Timothy 3:1, "If anyone aspires to the *office* of a bishop, he desires a noble task," has led to an unfortunate concept of a church "office" with authority. This view has dominated much Christian leadership vocabulary, as well as church doctrine and polity. The problem is heightened by the fact that the term *office* is simply not in the Greek text, and any attempts to insert this word into the translation as a result of the presence of the word *episcope* elsewhere in the New Testament cannot be sustained with any integrity.

This unfortunate situation is not limited to this one concept of "office." There are several other terms used in conjunction with the ministry of bishops and elders that have been significantly shaped by this tradition. Here we have in mind the terms "rule," "usurp authority," "bishop," and "ordain." More will be said to this point at a later stage of this study. Suffice it to say that the translation of the King James Version in the context of Episcopalian tradition and theology has had a profound influence, sometimes negatively so, on modern Protestant terminology and theology.

THE PRESBYTERIAN CHURCH

The roots of the Restoration Movement in the Presbyterian Church are well documented. Although several of the early leaders among those identifying themselves with this movement eschewed the synodal practices of the Presbyterian Church, they nevertheless perpetuated an extremely authoritarian view of elders. This mindset, perhaps a residue from their early Puritan heritage, would have lasting effect on Churches of Christ. The result of this influence, and some reaction to the Roman Catholic preference for the term *bishop*, was that the word *elder* became the nomenclature for church leaders most favored by Churches of Christ in the nineteenth and twentieth centuries, almost to the exclusion of the terms bishop and shepherd.

The Baptist Church

In some measures, exclusive of major doctrinal differences, there are a number of similarities between the Southern Baptist Church and Churches of Christ. This is not surprising, given the common origins of these two groups in America.

It is difficult to argue whether Churches of Christ have emphasized local church autonomy more than the Southern Baptist Church, or vice versa. Whatever one's views on this might be, local church autonomy is a fundamental tenet of Southern Baptists to the point where some Baptists argue that the concept of a universal church is completely alien to the New Testament. Although united in a Southern Baptist Convention, local Baptist churches vigorously defend their local autonomy.

It is argued, however, that the views of local church autonomy treasured by Churches of Christ are founded on views developed out of New Testament practice. This may be so, but this point is never one argued as a cardinal characteristic of the church by New Testament writers. The practice of congregational fellowship can be argued from the New Testament (Acts 14, 15) in a manner that may not fully support the strident autonomy argued by some non-cooperation Church of Christ leaders over the past five decades. Perhaps we are more indebted to Southern Baptist "landmark" autonomy views of the church than we realize! Perhaps considerable influence in this autonomous emphasis can also be found in the Congregational Church's views of congregational autonomy. In one respect, there is possibly as much reaction in the above mentioned Protestant churches to the Roman Catholic and Episcopal Church polity as there is a biblical concern for church autonomy. The point we are making here is that, even in regard to some views on "congregational autonomy," we are as much indebted to our religious cultural heritage and environment as we are to our New Testament roots.

One cannot escape the fact that much of the worship liturgy among Churches of Christ and the Baptist Church is very similar. Admittedly, Churches of Christ have resisted the intrusion of the musical instrument into congregational worship services, and in some measure the incorporation of a church choir (although it is a tradition among Churches of Christ to use a choir at weddings and funerals). Nevertheless, in many other instances the *practice* of faith in worship assemblies is very similar between these two churches in contrast to the differences between Churches of Christ and other mainline Protestant churches. Like the Baptists, Churches of Christ have chosen a "low church" liturgy rather than a "high church" liturgy. Without denying Church of Christ attempts to be biblically correct in the choices of *what* they do in worship, they owe much to their religious neighbors in *how* they express this worship. Merely observing the differences in worship liturgy among Churches of Christ in different ethnic and national contexts will emphasize that much of the *how* of worship is culturally shaped. For instance, an American Christian would feel far more at home or "comfortable" in a Baptist Church (with the exception of the instrument in worship) in regard to the *how* of worship than in a rural Zulu church in Africa.

CONCLUSION

The fact is that Churches of Christ are in many instances as much shaped by their cultural heritage as they are by their biblical roots. We are not at this point discussing *doctrinal* tenets of faith, but rather the *style* or *model* of *practicing* those doctrinal commitments. We have seen that this principle of influence from our past cultural and sociological heritage in both style and practice is particularly germane, either negatively or positively, in respect to some aspects of church polity, and particularly in reference to some terminology and attitudes. Because of this, Churches of Christ must constantly return to Scripture as they carefully examine their faith and practice. Church leaders should not fear such examination if they are sincere in their efforts to be biblically conservative rather than traditionally conservative.[141]

Churches of Christ are a Christian movement with a firm commitment to scriptural principles and a biblical foundation. *Theologically* speaking, Churches of Christ are a biblically conservative group; *practically* or *sociologically* speaking, however, Churches of Christ are profoundly shaped by their religious, sociological, and cultural environment. Churches of Christ must be careful, however, not to permit religious, cultural, or sociological factors in disagreement with biblical principles to determine their faith and practice.

The following is a brief attempt to identify some characteristics of church polity in which Churches of Christ have been most influenced by their religious, cultural, and sociological heritage. At this point of the study we merely list them as areas of concern to the vitality of our movement. We emphasize, however, that these factors may not necessarily in themselves be wrong or unscriptural, but may be detrimental if not clearly understood.

Areas of concern to this study:

1. The model of ministers becoming church "chaplains" where the emphasis on their ministry is focused inward on the congregation. In this sense ministers have become "pastors" of local churches. A paid clergy system has also diminished the importance of all Christians being "ministers," and influenced churches to see elders occupying an "office" rather than a ministry.

2. The hierarchical, pyramid model of the church in which decision making is moved up as high as possible from the base, and in which *more* authority is vested in *higher* offices

3. The view that elders hold an "office" which is vested with some form of absolute authority

4. The concept that elders "rule" the congregation in an autocratic manner

5. The extreme view of church autonomy that limits congregations from working effectively in a strategically planned process of ministry and outreach such as domestic or world evangelism

If these understandings are based more on tradition and denominational custom than Scripture, what are the alternatives? To begin answering this question, we turn to a discussion of the biblical understanding of the nature of leadership in God's kingdom.

Chapter 12

A Biblical Model for the Church

―⟋⟍―

A Traditional Model

In previous chapters we have discussed church polity and referred on several occasions to a hierarchical, pyramid model for the church in which Christ, as the head of the church, is at the apex of the pyramid. Just below Christ appear the elders with the deacons and ministers somewhere below the elders as they serve under the oversight of the elders. The members form the base of the pyramid.

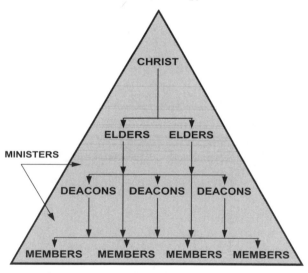

FIGURE 3

Among Churches of Christ there is some confusion as to where to place the ministers in this pyramid. They obviously serve under the elders, but are they placed above or below the deacons? We offer the following comment in a lighthearted manner, but with some truth in the humor. Churches of Christ have placed the ministers, being paid staff members, outside the pyramid, not sure whether the minister really is a member of the congregation or not. Church leaders move them in or out of the congregation on a regular basis.

One advantage of this hierarchical, pyramid model is that it is an efficient model. This model, however, is not a biblical one, but rather a Roman Catholic, Episcopalian, or corporate business model inherited from a management or administrative paradigm that is currently falling out of favor with corporate management theory.

The problem we have with this model is that there simply is no church administrative model in Scripture analogous to this pyramid structure. While it may have been efficient at one time in the corporate world, or may have appeal to the hierarchical mindset of the Roman Catholic Church, it sets up a structure of authoritarian dominance alien to Scripture. A fundamental problem for biblical thinking is that this paradigm sets biblical authority in the context of an "office" or an elevated position of rank, rather than in the context of ministry and service.

In this chapter we will explore a biblical model of the church, one that is drawn from Pauline use rather than a model inherited from a Catholic or corporate model. We will find that this model addresses every concern we might have in regard to the church serving under the headship of Christ and matters of authority in ministry. This model will provide a paradigm for understanding participative leadership and mutual ministry under the authority of Christ and Scripture.

THE CHURCH AS THE BODY OF CHRIST

We have an excellent analogy in Scripture for local church polity. **Figure 4** on the following page depicts this model. We find this model described in several passages, but 1 Corinthians 12:12-27 and Ephesians 4:16 will suffice to illustrate this. In these texts Paul argues that the church is the body of Christ and that Christians are all members of that one body. In both instances Paul's concern is congregational unity. 1 Corinthians 12, in particular, is opposed to ranking certain Christians over others because of giftedness.

The beauty of this model is that it illustrates how all Christians are members of the one body of which Christ is the only head. We should observe that in these texts Paul is discussing relationships within local congregations. He draws several profound lessons from this analogy. The first is that no Christian is more important or essential to the health and vitality of the body of Christ than any other member; no ministry is more essential, more glorious, or more spiritual than any other ministry (1 Cor 12:13-31).

This point is driven home in 1 Corinthians 12 with profound implications for those who feel that their giftedness is greater than that of others, or that their "position"

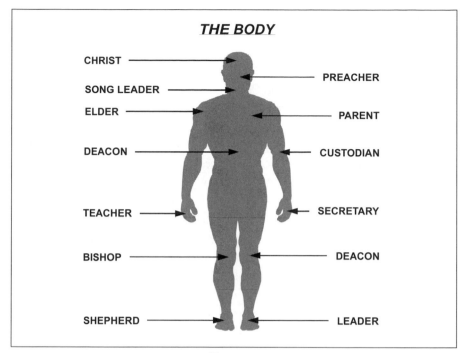

FIGURE 4

or role in the church is of greater value to the congregation than those of lesser gift-edness. Jesus had on several occasions reasoned with his disciples on this very same issue. Seeking self-fulfillment and importance through position is a worldly mindset not worthy of the kingdom of God (Matt 18:1ff, 20:20ff, Lk 22:27). Paul clearly makes application of this point in the context of Corinthian arguments on position, author-ity, and self-aggrandizement. It is not "position" or giftedness that is important to the body, but the willingness of every member of the body to function as gifted for the benefit of the body as a whole rather than for self-awareness.

Paul's argument in Ephesians 4:11-16 reinforces this view. In this context Paul is concerned for the unity of the body. He has already argued that this unity is one cre-ated by the Spirit (cf. also 1 Cor 12:12ff), and that Christians should strive to maintain that "unity of the Spirit in the bond of peace" (Eph 4:3). His final point is that in that spirit of unity every member of the body should be equipped for "the work of minis-try" so that every member can be knit together and supply whatever giftedness is nec-essary for the mutual upbuilding of the body. The body grows and functions properly only when every member is functioning appropriately. Paul stresses in this text that it is the primary ministry of "evangelists" (ministers) and "teaching pastors" (elders, bishops, and shepherds) to equip their members for meaningful ministry.

The conclusion we wish to make from this analogy of the church as a body is that, when giftedness is set in the context of mutual ministry rather than in the context of position or authority, the church prospers. When giftedness is viewed as a matter of position providing authority (and it should be stressed that being an elder, deacon, or minister is clearly both a gift from God and a matter of God-given giftedness), the church is hindered, and frustration and apathy emerge.

LEADERSHIP THROUGH RECIPROCAL MINISTRY

In the section in which we emphasized the biblical model of the church as the body of Christ, we noticed that Paul developed a concept of mutual or reciprocal ministry in which church members serve one another in building up the body toward maturity in Christ. This stresses a unique community dynamic in Christianity in which Christians are sincerely concerned for "one another." The New Testament makes much of this expression "one another." It appears at least 61 times in 54 verses in the Epistles of the Revised Standard Version in both positive and negative admonitions. A major emphasis is on "love one another" (Rom 12:10 *passim*). Christians are to "live in harmony with one another" (Rom 12:16), "not pass judgment on one another" (Rom 14:13), "welcome one another" (Rom 15:7), and have "no discord in the body, but...have the same care for one another" (1 Cor 12:25). Jesus himself said, "A new commandment I give to you, that you love one another; even as I have loved you, that you also love one

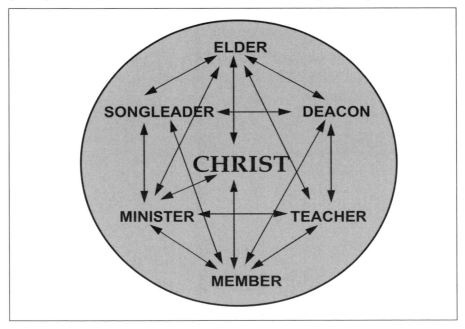

FIGURE 5

another. By this all men will know that you are my disciples, if you have love for one another" (Jn 13:34, 35). These are merely a few examples of reciprocity and mutual ministry through loving one another stressed in the Gospels and the Epistles.

Drawing attention to mutual ministry and reciprocity emphasizes the dynamic developed in a New Testament model of the church. The church in the New Testament does not have a hierarchical, pyramid structure in which members function at different levels of authority, but a flat model in which all members are equally important to the body in a mutual ministry. This model does not rule out the biblical fact that each ministry carries within itself the authority to function. It merely shifts the basis of authority from a hierarchical view on position and office to one of ministry function. More will be said to this point in a later chapter.

Participative Leadership Model in Acts

The New Testament book of Acts is unique in at least two respects. *First*, it is the only work written as a sequel to a Gospel in the New Testament.[142] The literary linkages between Luke 1:1-4 and Acts 1:1-5 are too remarkable to pass off as coincidental. It is this sequential aspect that contributes to the unique role that Acts plays in New Testament theology.

Second, it is the only book in the New Testament in which we can observe the New Testament church at work, doing what churches should do, namely, establishing community life in congregations and taking the gospel into all the world. It is called "Acts" due to the Greek title for the work, *Praxeis Apostolon*, which is translated into English as *The Acts of the Apostles*.[143] The book is better understood as the *praxis* of the church. Consequently, we see in Acts the early church *living* its faith and *practicing* its religion under the commission of Christ.

Several significant passages in Acts indicate that the church practiced a *participative* model of leadership or polity with certain leaders initiating and guiding the church through the process. The first is found in Acts 1:15-26 in the replacement of Judas as an apostle. The process is initiated by the Apostle Peter who invokes both the Holy Spirit and Scripture in support of the process he is initiating. Someone needed to be chosen to take Judas's place in the ministry of the apostles. Peter defined the parameters of the process, and then turned the process over to the gathered group which the context seems to imply included at least 120 people. Two names were proposed by the group. After prayer, in which the group prayed that the Lord would work through them in choosing the replacement, the group cast lots and Matthias was chosen and enrolled with the other eleven apostles.

Several factors stand out in this text. *First*, strong leadership was provided by the appropriate party—Peter acting on behalf of the apostles. *Second*, clear lines or parameters for the process were provided by Peter. *Third*, prayer, Scripture, and dependence on the Lord were fundamental ingredients in the process. And *fourth*, the whole group was involved in the process. What is surprising is that the decision being undertaken by the group was not some insignificant matter. The action of selecting a new apostle was a vital one to the life of the church of the future, and one that would have profound implications for the life of the church as a whole. Heretofore, this had been the responsibility of the Lord himself. But on this occasion the decision is not made by the apostles, as one would have suspected, in a closed meeting in the absence of the total group. *Participative* decision making should touch the heart of matters that will have significant implications for the *whole group*. Therefore, the decisions that are of significance to the whole group should be made by the whole group.

We learn several important lessons regarding the participative process from this text. *Strong decisive leadership* is necessary to *initiate* participative decision making. *Clear lines* or *parameters* are key to the success of the operation. Much *prayer* and guidance from *Scripture* and the *Lord* is involved. The participative process is not, as some imagine, the group wandering without leadership toward some conclusion.

The next instance of participative leadership in Acts is found in Acts 6:1-6. On this occasion difficulties had arisen between two groups of widows in the church, the Hellenists (probably Greek-speaking Jewish Christians from Galilee or the Diaspora) and the Hebrews (Aramaic-speaking Christians from Jerusalem and Judea). The problem arose in the daily distribution of food to these widows, yet went deeper than simply a matter regarding food, for it involved serious "ethnic" and religious overtones.

The apostles, realizing that their ministry was broader than the problem at hand and that their ministry would be seriously restricted if they had to take care of the problem, exercised creative initiative. The solution to the problem lay in the congregation itself, not in the ministry of the apostles. The twelve, therefore, instructed the congregation to choose seven wise men of good reputation who were full of the Holy Spirit, and to have these seven take care of the problem. The congregation chose seven such men who were installed in the new ministry with prayer and the laying on of hands.

The results were immediate and pleasing to the whole group. Dramatic growth following the division of ministry was impressive (Acts 6:7). In similar fashion to Acts 1:15-26 we encounter *creative initiative* and *leadership* by the apostles, *definite parameters* and *qualities* being defined, *participative involvement* on the part of the *whole congregation*, and *prayer*. This event provides an insightful example of participative leadership in the selection of ministry servants (possible deacons), and of participative ministry in a volatile and sensitive situation which could have had a severe negative impact on the life and welfare of the church, not only in Jerusalem, but on a much wider scale.

Perhaps the most striking and significant occasion of participative leadership and decision making in Acts is found in Acts 15:1-35; the "Jerusalem Council" or "Jerusalem Conference".[144] Acts 14 closes with Paul and Barnabas at Antioch, having returned from Galatia and Paul's first missionary journey, reporting the dramatic results of the gospel among the Gentiles in that area. Acts 15 opens with the report that certain men from Judea contested the gospel message preached by Paul and Barnabas, claiming that it was necessary to have the new converts circumcised according to the law of Moses. Paul and Barnabas strenuously opposed this view with the result that Paul, Barnabas, and others were appointed by the church to travel to Jerusalem from where the problem seemed to originate.

We should note that, even at this early stage of the life of the church in Acts, an *apostle* is appointed by the *church* to make the trip to Jerusalem. In matters of local church polity even an apostle falls under the care and leadership of the church. When Paul and others returned to Antioch as reported in Acts 15:30, they called the *congregation* together for a report of their meeting in Jerusalem.

When Paul and Barnabas arrived in Jerusalem they met with the apostles, elders, and the whole congregation in an assembly (Acts 15:6, 12, 22). Initially Peter spoke, followed by Barnabas, Paul, and James. Finally, the *whole church* sent Judas and Silas with Paul and Barnabas as they returned to Antioch with a letter for the church in that city.

The problem being addressed was one of major significance, involving serious implications for Paul's ministry. If his opponents succeeded in binding circumcision and the law on Paul's gospel, his message would have been destroyed.[145] One would have thought, given our views of apostolic authority, that Paul and Barnabas would have met with the apostles in Jerusalem, or at least with the elders. Surprisingly, however, they met with the *whole church*! This process of participative decision making must obviously have taken considerable time in such an unwieldy meeting. This drives home the point that in some circumstances *effectiveness* is far more important than *efficiency*!

In this passage we again see a *participative process* involving major doctrinal decisions. *Strong decisive leadership initiates* the process (Paul, Barnabas, Peter, James). *Clear parameters* are set by Peter and James (Acts 15:7, 14). The presence and will of the *Holy Spirit* are involved in the process. Time is given *for all who so desire* to comment and be involved in the decision. The *whole congregation* is involved. The results of a delicate decision were well received by the church because all had been heard and fear of manipulation was removed.

CONCLUSION

We began this chapter with a brief analysis of a traditional model for the church in which church leaders are arranged in a hierarchical pyramid model. The advantage of this model is one of efficiency. The disadvantage is that it is not a biblical model, and draws on corporate and Catholic bureaucratic roots. This tends to place greater emphasis on "office," position, and authority, than on participative mutual ministry.

In churches structured in this pyramid fashion, or in this hierarchical model emphasizing authority and position, a major concern among leaders often becomes one of others "usurping authority." Leaders tend to protect their position or authority and to interpret initiative, or pleas for a participative involvement in leadership, as "usurping authority." The net outcome of this model is often frustration on the part of deacons and ministers, and apathy on the part of members.

We do have a fine model provided in Paul's analogy of the church as a human body. It is one from which Paul draws on several occasions. The strength of this model is that Christ as head of the body is the one who gives direction to the church. All members, in varying degrees and ministries, function under that headship. Each ministry group, whether it be elders, deacons, ministers, Bible class teachers, parents, or others performing church ministry functions, does so under the sovereign leadership of Christ, and through the responsibility of their ministry with the necessary authority to perform that ministry. We will shortly develop the point in greater detail that biblical authority is related to ministry function, and not to an office or position.[146]

The great advantage of the analogy to the human body is, as Paul makes it abundantly clear, an emphasis on *mutual ministry* and *participative leadership* and *decision making*. The focus of this model, especially as Paul develops it, becomes one of *ministry* and the *mutual upbuilding* of the body. For Paul, this model which he has developed so carefully in Ephesians 4:1-16 becomes the foundation of his views on the teaching ministry of the church (apostles, prophets, evangelists, and pastors and teachers, namely, elders). In the context of the church in the twentieth century, elders, deacons, and ministers in this analogy provide a participative *equipping ministry* for the church.

CHAPTER 13

LEADERSHIP VERSUS MANAGEMENT IN THE CHURCH

—⁄⁄⁄—

This chapter will apply some of the significant leadership principles coming from recent research in the field of management and leadership style, notably in contrasting leadership with management. Traditional leadership models followed by many local congregations will be evaluated through careful reflection on the integration of leadership principles and biblical patterns of church leadership. Faithfulness to biblical principles will be a primary concern in this integration.

A WORD OF CAUTION

It is necessary at the outset of this chapter that we clarify one point in our discussion of the differences between management and leadership. We do not intend to construct a view in which management and leadership are set in opposition to one another. Neither do we intend a bifurcation of leadership and management styles in which management principles are disparaged, rejected, or denied. We will project management and leadership as two poles in a continuum of management-leadership. In this study we seek a better balance between leadership style and management through a sensitive emphasis on leadership principles. No organization can survive without management's attention to structure and process. This is especially true in the case of the church. Biblical principles in many instances call for responsible stewardship in leadership. Our concern, however, is that management style not become the driving force of the organization so that tasks, structure, and process take priority over people, content, and values.

Perhaps we should envision successful leadership as an ellipse with two centers rather than a circle with one epicenter. The two centers of the ellipse in this analogy would be leadership and management. The major problem, however, even with the analogy of an ellipse, is that it tends to make the two centers of equal importance. In successful times this might be a valid consideration, but in times demanding radical change, when growth has declined, when the environment is in constant flux, leadership with its unique penchant for creativity must prevail over management.

We will notice below that management and leadership reflect different mindsets, different worldviews. The fundamental mindset of management is to serve as conservator of the status quo, to administer more efficiently the resources of the organization. The mindset of leadership is that of the entrepreneur who is willing to press beyond the status quo and to develop new resources and envision new horizons.

DEFINITIONS

It has become common practice in some modern organizational theory to understand a clear distinction between leadership and management.[147] As a preliminary to understanding leadership, we draw attention to a fundamental point often made in management and leadership research. It is that management focuses on tasks, goals, and structure, while leadership is primarily concerned with people and building team relationships. This distinction is demonstrated in a stimulating article by Craig M. Watson, who argues that management concentrates more on the "hard" facets of organization such as *strategy, structures,* and *systems*, while leadership works with the "soft" elements such as *style, staff, skills,* and *shared goals*. Watson's perceptive article proceeds to illustrate how management style emphasizes organizational tasks and goals, while leadership is more concerned with human relationships.[148]

Abraham Zaleznik suggests that managers and leaders are basically two different kinds of people who operate with different "worldviews" and within different cultures. He maintains that managers relate to a "managerial culture" and that leaders prefer an "entrepreneurial culture." Furthermore, he contends managers see themselves as conservators and regulators of existing orders, while leaders strive to bring about change within those existing orders. Zaleznik suggests that managers direct and control existing organizations, while leaders explore new areas and opportunities.[149]

From the above discussion it should be apparent that the concerns of both management and leadership are essential to the success of effective or growing organizations. Tasks, strategy, and organization without values, mission, and purpose will lead to frustration and failure. Likewise, values, mission, and purpose without strategy and organization will eventually lead to confusion and failure. What is important, however, is the *balance* maintained between these two poles of organizational theory, and the correct emphasis given each at strategic or critical stages in the operation of the organization. At certain times structure and process need careful attention; at other times relationships and values should receive prime consideration.

Recent research in modern corporate business practice indicates, however, that the "hard" facts of organizational theory, such as management strategy and goals, are the most likely to receive attention. Careful attention to the "soft" aspects of values and relationships will be overlooked under the pressure of management needs. Unfortunately, Zaleznik argues, management principles of control will not produce the highest yield in today's society.[150] In fact, Zaleznik maintains that an overemphasis on management, with its natural inclinitation toward conservatism, will inhibit growth and development within an organization.[151]

Church leaders can learn much from Zaleznik's discussion of the mystique of management style in today's society. While no one will argue that careful stewardship and attention to tasks are not needed in the church, it may be that an over-concentration on control has led conservative leaders to overlook their role of providing dynamic leadership in the church.

James MacGregor Burns, noted political scientist, historian of the presidency, and distinguished author, observed in an interview published in *Psychology Today*, October 1978, that it is important that we no longer define leaders in terms of power structures. Burns argues that the success of leadership is in direct relation to *how* the leader responds to the wants and aspirations of his or her people. His point is that the source of leadership success, even that of the presidency, lies in a vast pool of human wants and collective expectations. The truly great, effective, and creative leaders arouse the hopes and mobilize the *higher* needs of their followers. Burns's point is that effective leadership draws more from relational structures than from organizational or managerial principles.

Managers tend to direct their energies toward strategies, goals, resources, and structures in an impersonal manner. Often the goals or structures of the organization are given priority over the people or personal relations within the organization. Church leaders may be giving more attention to the organizational structure *of* the church, namely its doctrine, than to the needs of the people who desperately need to hear *about* the church, namely, the lost. We stress once again that we are not recommending abandoning management control, but emphasizing the need for more dynamic creative leadership, especially in the church.

Managers provide direction through control, organizational structures, and the systematic development of rational processes. *They are primarily system problem solvers.* A manager's effectiveness is often minimized by an inability to see beyond system structure to the thinking processes and values inherent in the relations functioning within the organization. Managers focus on *procedure*, and therefore tend to *preserve* the *existing system* or organizational structure which they have personally or organizationally accepted. Managers consequently tend to be problem solvers *within the organizational structure*.[152]

Leaders, in contrast to managers, adopt an *interpersonal* attitude toward goals and values rather than an impersonal one. They focus on *relations* rather than on structural organization. Leaders choose to influence the *manner* in which people *think about the goals*, rather than the goals themselves. Managers see *structures* as the enabling process. Leaders see *relationships* and *values* as the enabling process.

We should recognize that leadership's tendency to pay less attention to control and more to creative change can create problems within an organization comfortable with well-defined parameters and structure. Leaders, therefore, must be prepared to take *calculated* risks, for it is only in risk taking that organizations produce growth.[153] Conservative management style is uncomfortable with risk. Entrepreneurial leadership thrives on risk.

Whereas managers tend to conserve structures, leaders develop new approaches and structures to suit the people and values within the organization. Managers seek to match people to organizational structure and organizational structure to goals, whereas leaders develop personal characteristics and shape the attitudes of individuals to the values of the organization. Managers, therefore, are *task oriented*; leaders *relational oriented*.

The real distinction between leadership and management is not that either is unaware of or insensitive to the opposing values. The difference is in the *primary emphasis* given to them. It has been our experience that many good churches are well managed, but often not well led.

Figure 6 on the next page illustrates the differing cultures and worldviews of leadership and management.

It is the consensus of modern organizational theory that in people-intensive organizations, leadership is the most effective driving principle. In task-intensive organizations, management is more efficient. The option in selecting a leadership or management style lies in the choice between long-term versus short-term results, and an emphasis on efficient "authoritarian" lines rather than the slower, yet more effective, "personal example" relational model.

THE CHURCH OF CHRIST AND LEADERSHIP TERMINOLOGY

The term most favored by Churches of Christ for their leaders has for generations been *elder*. The term as it has been traditionally used among Churches of Christ fits more naturally into the matrix of concepts defining *management* than it does *leadership*. Without fully realizing it, a heritage or church culture descending from a nineteenth-century Restoration Movement in frontier America had unconsciously become as much a factor in shaping Church of Christ attitudes regarding church government in the twentieth century as had Scripture. Heavily influenced by the Presbyterian

LEADERSHIP	MANAGEMENT
By Personal Example	By Authoritarian Control
Participative	Hierarchical
Anticipate Change	Resist Change
Build Relationships	Build Structures
Emphasize Values	Emphasize Goals
Visualize Concepts	Visualize Tasks
Interpersonal	Impersonal
Focus on the Individual	Focus on the Organization
Prize Effectiveness	Prize Efficiency
Growth	Stability

FIGURE 6

model of church polity, Churches of Christ in the eighteenth and nineteenth centuries adopted the elder paradigm for congregational government and modeled church leadership along *managerial control* lines with a heavy emphasis on a *hierarchical, authoritarian* model. Finding scriptural basis for the concept in Pauline usage, Churches of Christ have almost universally preferred the term elder to other scriptural terminology such as shepherd, which has more relational connotations.

As Churches of Christ in the twentieth century moved from a mostly patriarchal, agrarian, rural church to a corporate, urban-dominated church, its leaders tended to be drawn from the successful business or professional class. The rapid urbanization of the twentieth century, especially in the post–World War II era, precipitated the decay of the rural nuclear family and patriarchal system. Whereas in rural society *patriarchal nuclear family ties* predominated, the emerging corporate society of urban America presented a new *corporate managerial* system to church leaders. The model of church government in the new urban churches was consequently shaped by forces that are both similar, yet different from the rural patriarchal culture. In both the rural and urban cultures the patriarchal and corporate management styles of authority and control have predominated as the preferred leadership option. Church leadership style in the mid-twentieth century, therefore, was shaped more by the new reality of urban America, namely, the emerging corporate and technological global culture than by biblical models. Church leadership style accordingly shifted easily into the new managerial model of leadership more in line with corporate management style. It should be apparent that as we have moved into the twenty-first century with the rise of the Boomer, Buster, and Millennium cohorts, that leadership style will need serious consideration in order to be driven more by biblical models than corporate management or rural, agrarian, authoritarian models. Unfortunately, the traditional term *elder* with its traditional church implications fits more comfortably into the bureaucratic, hierarchical, managerial model than does the more passive and agrarian, yet biblical model of *shepherd* or *pastor*.

Looking further at terminological preferences and dislikes among Churches of Christ, it is not surprising that leaders who favor local congregational autonomy would look with some antipathy on the term *bishop*. Aversion to either the Roman Catholic or Episcopalian forms of government, which stress a universal centralized form of church polity, would naturally cause church leaders to turn away from the Episcopal/Catholic term *bishop*.

The term *shepherd/pastor*, although clouded by the denominational *pastor* concept, would fit comfortably into the more relational mindset of the fast growing Boomer, Buster, and Millennium generations. The term *shepherd* has consequently recently found favor among many, mostly urban Churches of Christ, although it is still a rarity to see the term *shepherd* listed on church bulletin covers or church letterheads. Perhaps one reason for the apparent aversion to the use of shepherd has been the denominational use of the term *pastor* for minister. Whatever the final reason, the term shepherd, which fits with greater ease into the leadership model, has been almost ignored or at least given only token acknowledgement by leaders among Churches of Christ. Regardless of the rural connotations of shepherd, we find in the new millennium of the twenty-first century that many church leaders are now favoring the term shepherd since it focuses more attention on the relational dimension of *people* rather than the formal *organization* of the church.

In a series of editorials in the *Firm Foundation* in 1972 addressed to elders in Churches of Christ, Reuel Lemmons challenged the authoritarian corporate model of leadership that prevailed at that time—and unfortunately still prevails in many instances today.[154] The series provoked considerable consternation and heated response among church leaders and ministers. Unfortunately the controversy produced little immediate change in leadership style among Churches of Christ. *But a seed was sown!*

BIBLICAL MODELS OF LEADERSHIP

As we attempt to examine current leadership style among Churches of Christ, we should be reminded that churches are primarily in the people business. Although mission goals, congregational tasks, and controlled organizational structure are important, the main resource with which churches work is people. Working with people, building relationships within the fellowship of the congregation, helping people mature in their relationship with Christ—these are the focus of the church. Organization and structure are servants of that primary purpose.

The primary functions of the church are to give glory to God through Jesus Christ, and to bring lost people into a healthy relationship with God through Jesus. Jesus clearly set the emphasis on ministry to people when he chastised his disciples for seeking positions of honor in his kingdom. He announced that in contrast to honor, "the Son of Man came not to be served, but to serve" (Matt 20:28), and that he himself was "one who served" (Lk 22:27).

Like their leader, Jesus, church leaders are in the people business, and consequently in the servant business. It is no wonder, then, that Scripture resorts to the analogy of shepherds for the leaders of God's people. With this clear emphasis on people, church leaders would be well advised to look to the paradigm of *leadership* rather than to that of *management* for models most helpful in leading God's people. It is not surprising today, however, in a world heavily influenced by corporate America, that many church leaders have chosen the corporate board management model as the one most suitable for the church.

One passage comes immediately to mind when emphasizing the model of *leadership* in local congregations rather than *management*. In keeping with modern theories of leadership and management, this passage intimates that style and personal example are fundamental to effective congregational polity. This passage implies, furthermore, that effective church leadership is essentially a matter of personal character, rather than one of organization, rule, or control. Consider 1 Peter 5:1-3 in which Peter adapts the analogy of shepherding to the ministry of being an elder. He suggests that the role of the church leader is one of tending (pastoring) the flock out of real concern for the flock. This shepherding is done by gently leading through *example*, rather than *ruling in a domineering, authoritarian manner*. The model for this leadership style is the loving *Chief Shepherd* who leads his sheep beside still waters, as in Psalm 23. By use of this analogy, Peter proposes a wonderful foundation for effective church leadership. Domineering management or authoritarian control is farthest from Peter's mind. It is obvious from this one passage that *leadership style* is a subject in which the Scriptures, and especially the New Testament, have considerable interest!

LEADERSHIP VERSUS MANAGEMENT IN THE CHURCH

That leadership through relationships is the intent of the organizational structure of the church is visible through the terms used to describe those designated by God to direct the church. It will be demonstrated later that certain ministry terms, namely, elder, bishop, shepherd, leader, deacon, minister, and evangelist are *functional* and *ministry related* rather than *authoritarian* or *hierarchical*. At this point suffice it to say that their function is *relational* rather than *task* oriented. These divinely designated ministries lead God's people as they teach his Word, as they minister to those in need, as they guard and shepherd the flock, and as they serve the congregation in a number of functions. They do not manage people or tasks. They minister to the people as servants after the model of their Lord (Jn 13:1-20; Matt 20:20-28; Lk 22:24-28). Like Jesus, they *lead through their suffering service.*

If modern organizational theories which emphasize leadership, relational concerns, and values are valid, and it is interesting to observe how biblical they sound, then running throughout church organizational theory, or church polity, leadership should receive prominent attention. This is obviously not always the case, hence the somewhat violent reaction to Reuel Lemmons's editorials. Leadership must take precedence over management theory in biblical paradigms of church polity. This does not necessarily imply that church leaders abandon good management principles. It does imply that management serve leadership and not vice versa.

Leadership through humble Christian service is clearly the model intended by Jesus in his penetrating reprimand of his disciples who sought greatness in the kingdom through position or office (Matt 16:21-26, 18:1-4, 20:20-28). Leaders in the kingdom must hear afresh these words of the Lord.

CHAPTER 14

BIBLICAL QUALITIES IN LEADERS

—◊—

Among Churches of Christ it has customarily been the practice when referring to those qualities desirable in church leaders to call them *qualifications*. Under normal circumstances, when these "qualifications" are considered, the texts most commonly referenced are 1 Timothy 3:1-7 and Titus 1:5-9. These two texts obviously have a profound impact on our understanding of the qualities necessary in church leaders.

A question that needs consideration is whether it is best to call these qualities *qualifications* or to understand them merely as qualities. It is my opinion that the term qualifications is a little too formal for what Paul had in mind when he wrote to Timothy and Titus. A major consideration in this regard will be the manner in which we understand the makeup of the Bible and how the Bible works.

The Bible is made up of a number of books or letters, each addressing a particular theological situation, setting, or occasion. For this reason we refer to the books of the Bible as "situational" or "contextual." It is extremely important when interpreting the Bible that one understand the historical, sociological, and theological contexts being addressed by the writer. It is only when interpretation is done within these contexts that one can determine the true meaning of the text.

First Timothy was a letter written in approximately AD 63 by Paul to Timothy who was at that time ministering to the church in Ephesus. The problem addressed by Paul was one of false teachers in Ephesus and Timothy's apparent reluctance to take a firm stand against them. It is important to understand the historical, sociological, and religious setting in Ephesus at that time in order to interpret this letter correctly.

Ephesus was the foremost city in the Roman province of Asia, a major seaport and center of Hellenistic and Roman culture. With the Temple of Artemis dominating the religious scene, the burgeoning Imperial cult running a close second in influence, and other popular local and mystery cults commonplace, Ephesus was teeming with various religious views. The Imperial cult was already becoming a major threat to the Jewish and Christian faiths. It seems also that some form of aberrant Jewish-gnostic teaching was making an inroad into the Christian viewpoint. The religious and philosophical tenor of the city was, therefore, posing a serious threat to the life of the church. Temple prostitution was a common part of Ephesian life, and a prominent house of prostitution was located in the central section of the city.

With this as a background, one can understand Paul's admonition to Timothy to pay more attention to and be more aggressive in response to false teaching.

> As I urged you when I was going to Macedonia, remain at Ephesus that you may charge certain persons not to teach any different doctrine....Certain persons by swerving from these have wandered away into vain discussion....This charge I commit to you, Timothy, my son...wage the good warfare....Have nothing to do with godless and silly myths...guard what has been entrusted to you.[155]

In the context of these admonitions Paul encouraged Timothy to see that the bishops of the church in Ephesus were men adequately prepared for their ministry, much of which would be a teaching ministry in which they would build up the faith of the church and defend Christian doctrine. It is possible that Timothy had not been careful in installing elders or bishops, for in the context of discussing Timothy's relations with the elders Paul warned him not to be "hasty in laying on of hands" (1 Tim 5:17-22).

Paul's discussion of false teachers and other related problems leads directly into his discussion of those qualities desirable in bishops. In order to lead the church, bishops needed to be *above reproach* in both the local church and the local community. Paul lists a number of concerns in this regard as *modifiers* to being "above reproach." In this chapter we will look briefly at the qualities stressed by Paul for these bishops and elders. We will first consider the specific needs and conditions in Ephesus (1 Tim 3:1ff) then those in Crete (Titus 1:5ff).

QUALIFICATIONS OR QUALITIES?
Our reason for proposing that it may be better to understand Paul's lists in 1 Timothy 3 and Titus 1 as qualities rather than qualifications is that the term *qualifications* has a sense of finality and exclusiveness. We have several reasons for concern.

First, there are other Scriptures that are as important to the "qualifications" of bishops as these two. Very often insufficient attention is given to these Scriptures. For instance, 1 Peter 5:1-4, Hebrews 13:7, and John 13:1-17 all speak directly to the *kind of person* the bishop should be and, therefore, should be of equal importance as 1 Timothy 3 and Titus 1. The tendency to consider 1 Timothy 3 and Titus 1 as qualifications almost invariably overlooks many equally important Scriptures relating to the qualities desired in church leaders.

Second, and perhaps of more import to our point, is that when Paul wrote his first letter to Timothy in Ephesus, Timothy presumably knew nothing of the letter to Titus. Likewise, Titus apparently knew nothing of 1 Timothy when he received his letter shortly after Timothy received 1 Timothy. In all likelihood, all Timothy had was 1 Timothy, and it was adequate for the situation at Ephesus; and all Titus had was his letter which was equally adequate for his situation in Crete. To add these two lists together into one comprehensive and all inclusive list of *qualifications* is not therefore sound exegetical or theological practice.

A close study of the two lists indicates several differences, as well as striking similarities, between the two. **Figures 7** and **8** demonstrate this.

Our chief concern with the practice among Churches of Christ to view these two lists as one composite list of qualifications is primarily that this does an injustice to biblical theology and what Paul is really saying in these letters, and that this practice tends to truncate the fuller view of those qualities necessary in bishops and elders.

1 Timothy 3:1–7

We will now consider in some detail Paul's discussion of those qualities he considered necessary for elders and bishops in Ephesus. His first requirement is that the *bishop* (*episkopos*—a bishop, an overseer, a guardian) should *aspire* to or have a passion for (*orego* or *oregomai*—to stretch, to reach out to, to aspire) the ministry of overseeing the congregation. We should be wary of translating *overseer* (bishop) in the context of a contemporary industrial factory understanding of *foreman* or *boss*. The word literally means "to see over, to watch over, or to watch out for." It is best understood as "one who cares for, watches over, or guards." One who aspires to this ministry *desires a noble task* (*epithumeo*—eagerly desires, longs for, has a passion for). This is a good work that demands more than duty or obligation. This ministry must be one that flows from the heart; it is a ministry of love. Peter adds that this work must not be done by constraint, nor for personal gain, but willingly (1 Pet 5:2).

With the expression "now a bishop *must be* above reproach," Paul gets to the heart of the matter of leadership. He prefaces this with the impersonal verb *dei*. This is a strong term carrying the weight of necessity or compulsion, *"for it is necessary, proper, or correct to be so."* The RSV translation "must be" is most appropriate for the occasion. *Above reproach* (*anepilemptos*—irreproachable conduct, blameless) does not imply sinlessness, or else this would rule out the possibility of anyone serving as a bishop! The expression refers to one who is well respected by both the local church community and the community at large. One cannot lead the church who is not held in high regard by society in general. This expression and the similar one in verse 7, "must be well thought of by outsiders, or he may fall into reproach and the snare of the devil," are

1 Timothy 3:1-7	Titus 1:5-9
bishop	for a bishop
must be above reproach	if any man is blameless
husband of one wife	husband of one wife
	elders
	as God's steward must be blameless
temperate	
sensible	master of himself
dignified	
hospitable	hospitable
no drunkard	not a drunkard
not violent	not violent
but gentle	
not quarrelsome	not quick tempered

FIGURE 7

in the form of a technical construction called an *inclusio*. An *inclusio* is a literary device that acts like parentheses—it contains whatever is between the two "bookends" in one thought. Although the term *reproach* (*oneidismos*—reproach, disgrace) in verse 7 is different from that in verse 2, the meaning is the same. The bishop must be above disgraceful behavior. His personal esteem in the community must be such that not only he but also the church will be respected with his appointment as a bishop. The *inclusio* of *respect* argues strongly that the bishop must be widely respected for his appointment as a bishop.

All of the statements following "above reproach" in verse 2, namely, *the husband of one wife* through *not be a recent convert* in verse 6, modify the initial expression *above reproach*. In other words, they explain *in what manner* the bishop should be above reproach. The construction of the paragraph is such that the central thought is that the bishop must be above reproach, and the statements following indicate how this should be understood. In the context of the Ephesian situation, the distinctive qualities stressed by Paul in regard to being above reproach have immediate and specific sociological and theological relevance. The use of the *inclusio* mentioned above reinforces this view.[156]

The first statement mentioned by Paul defining the quality *above reproach* is that the bishop should be *the husband of one wife* (*mias gunaikos andra*—literally, "a one-wife man"). This expression has been interpreted to mean "a one 'wifed' man" meaning that the man has been married only once. This is not a good translation of the expression. The term in no manner indicates whether the man has been previously married. Again, looking at the term literally (which in this case is not a sound reflection on how the term has been used in the Greek literature, but nevertheless is in response to a literalist's incorrect interpretation of the expression) indicates a *present situation*, not a past tense (in 1 Tim 5:9 in regard to widows, a similar expression is in the past tense). Literally, the best that could be said of the literalist interpretation, which I do not favor, is that *presently* the man must be the *husband of one wife*.[157]

Traditional interpretation of this term among Churches of Christ would imply that the man should not have had a previous marriage of any kind—one broken either by divorce or by the death of his wife. If the wife he now has is a second wife, then he, according to this interpretation, is no longer the husband of one wife. This raises all kinds of interesting situations. If his previous marriage resulted in a "scriptural divorce," how many wives does he now have? If this means he now has more than one wife, what is the church doing having fellowship with him if the wife he now has is not his legitimate wife (1 Cor 5:1-13)?

It should be obvious that the traditional literalist interpretation is simply not one which flows from within the text, but one made out of a contemporary cultural context (either a church culture or community cultural context). This comment should not be interpreted to mean that the Bible has nothing to say about divorce or that any marriage after divorce is legitimate. That is another discussion altogether. The comment here is simply meant to imply that some prejudice, either good or bad, has forced some interpreters into a particular literalist interpretation that is not found in the text.

1 Timothy 3:1-7	Titus 1:5-9
no lover of money	or greedy for gain
manage own household well	
keeping children submissive and respectful in every way	children are believers, not open to the charge of being profligate or insubordinate, well thought of by outsiders
not a recent convert	
	a lover of goodness
	upright
	holy
	self-controlled
an apt teacher	give instruction in sound doctrine

FIGURE 8

Setting the expression *the husband of one wife* (*mias gunaikos andra*) in the context of Greek literature of antiquity and common Greek usage, the term should be understood as "faithful to one's own wife." There are several instances in which the expression was used in this manner in the early literature. In the context of Ephesus, with its common practice of temple and other cult prostitution, the need for a bishop to be faithful to his wife would have profound import. The church in Ephesus, and elsewhere, could not have bishops who regularly frequented houses of prostitution or who flirted with women to where they were perceived as not being faithful to their wives. Bishops simply *must* be faithful to their wives if they are to be above reproach, especially in the community. There simply is no reference in this expression to how many times a man has been married. To read this into the original expression is to read contemporary concerns into the term, however valid these concerns may be. To adopt this practice may be convincing in some contemporary context of the interpreter, but to do so does the biblical text an injustice.

The understanding brought to the expression above does not necessarily mean that a man previously married and divorced should be a suitable candidate for bishop. Each case should be taken on its own merit, and each congregation should have the right to determine for itself whether it desires a man with a previous marriage to be a bishop. The guiding principle should always be the relationship of the candidate's marriage situation to his being "above reproach" in the congregation and community. If the congregation decides against a bishop in this regard, then the decision should not be made on the basis of the expression "the husband of one wife" meaning married only once, but on the feelings of the congregational culture regarding previous marriages. If the local congregation decides that it would not be in the best interests of the local church to have a previously married man serve as a bishop, especially if this in the mind of the community would be "reproachful or disgraceful," then the congregation should be free to make such a decision. The point remains, however, that this would be a decision made within the context of the community culture rather than out of the biblical expression "the husband of one wife."

The next concern Paul has regarding the bishop's behavior is that he be sober or careful in the use of wine. The RSV translates *nephalios* as *temperate*, which could be understood as "controlled" in the use of wine. This is followed by *sensible* (*sophronos*—moderate, self-controlled). It is imperative that the bishop be clear thinking, prudent, and able to control himself well under the pressures of his ministry. Perhaps the one term that speaks out most clearly regarding the bishop is that he be *dignified* (*kosmios*—respectful, honorable). The Greek word is built off the same root as the word *kosmos* which is often translated "world," but which also means "well put together, well organized, orderly." The bishop must be dignified, honorable, respected, "well put together" in his behavior.

It is important to the church's ministry to the world that the bishop be *hospitable* (*philoxenos*). The word is built of two Greek words (*philos*—friend, and *xenos*—stranger or foreigner) and literally means "one who loves strangers" or a "friend of strangers." No person should be a stranger to the church in which bishops are fulfilling their ministry.

The expression *apt to teach* (*didaktikos*—didactic, skillful in teaching) also gets to the heart of the ministry of the bishop or elder. Ephesians 4:11 and Hebrews 13:7 demonstrate that teaching is perhaps *the* primary responsibility of the elder/bishop/ shepherd. The bishop must be a capable teacher. He must know the "truth," be able to teach it, and be able to defend it when necessary. In Titus 1:9 Paul develops this more fully: "He must hold firm the sure word as taught, so that he may give instruction in sound doctrine and also confute those who contradict it." This does not mean that the bishop must teach in a class such as the traditional Church of Christ auditorium class, but it does mean that he is an active and willing teacher. Perhaps some of the best teaching that the bishop will do is "one on one" with a person or couple over a cup of coffee. *But teach he must!* In fact, bishops were most likely the primary source of teaching in congregations of the first century.

The bishop should not be a *drunkard* (*paroinos*—given to much wine, one who lingers around the wine, one addicted to wine). This is not the place for a detailed discussion on social drinking today. Suffice it to say that the New Testament does not in and of itself condemn social drinking. However, given the context of twentieth-century America and the dangers and injury caused by alcoholism, one would be hard-pressed today to defend social drinking. Perhaps one should set social drinking in the context of contemporary social decay in order to make sound decisions regarding social drinking. The point in question in the qualities desired in elders is that they should not be addicted to wine. *Drunkard* or *one given to wine* would be an appropriate translation of the Greek term.

An ability to get along with people and be a leader is important to the ministry of the bishop. He is, therefore, not to be *violent*, but *gentle*, and *not quarrelsome*. *Violent* (*plektes*—pugnacious, a bully) and *not quarrelsome* (*amachos*—peaceable, one who dislikes strife, not contentious) go together. The bishop should not be a person who is always involved in strife. He is a peacemaker. He does not manipulate or bully people. On the contrary, he is *gentle* (*epieikes*—gentle, gracious) and gracious in his dealings with people.

In addition, the bishop is not a *lover of money* (*aphilarguros*—not greedy). Paul in Titus 1:7 adds "not greedy for gain." Peter observes "not for shameful gain" (1 Pet 5:2). The bishop is not in this ministry for what he can personally gain out of the service he tenders. He does his ministry willingly and out of love for his people. It was a practice in the first-century church to support elders and bishops when necessary (1 Tim 5:17, 18). This would create a situation in which some might be looking for a salary or for payment for what they do as bishops. Paul is obviously not opposed to supporting bishops or ministers, but warns against the dangers of serving for mercenary gain.

In order to prove his ability to lead and *care for* (*epimeleomai*—care for) God's house, the church, the bishop must be able to *manage* (*prohistemi*—lead, direct, care for, give aid to) his own household. The Greek word *prohistemi* is used also in 1 Timothy 5:17 and 1 Thessalonians 5:12 in regard to elders and bishops. It also appears in Romans 12:8, but not in the context of elders. It is used in 1 Timothy 3:12 in regard to deacons, and in Titus 3:8 in regard to those who have believed in God. The word literally means "to stand in front of" or *to lead*. In Romans 12:8 it is translated in the RSV as "give aid." Here in 1 Timothy 3:4 and 12 it is translated as "manage." In Titus it appears as "be careful." 1 Thessalonians 5:12 renders it as "are over you" and 1 Timothy 5:17 as "rule." It is obvious that the term must gain its final meaning from its context, but should at the same time never lose its primary meaning of "lead, direct, manage, care for, and give aid to." Perhaps it is in this total sense that we should understand it in regard to bishops and elders. They are the responsible leaders of God's people—they direct, care for, and give aid to the church. To translate it simply as "rule" is to lose sight of the total picture of this ministry, and to translate the term more in the context of the hierarchical model of the Catholic and Episcopal churches than in the original pastoral sense.

In any case, as the head of their own homes, bishops are to *manage* (*prohistemi*—lead and provide for) their own families, "keeping their *children submissive* and respectful in every way." "Having submissive (*hupotage*—subjection, obedience, under control, submissive) children" is perhaps as good a translation of this clause as is possible. Because of their personal example, bishops cannot afford to have disobedient, uncontrolled, and unruly children. Some members of Churches of Christ have for years questioned the *number of children* requisite in order to meet this requirement. The statement in Titus 1:6, "*his children are believers*," has added to this concern. Does this mean the bishop must have a plurality of children, and does it mean that all his children are to be believers and in submission?

Perhaps it will help if we begin with the number of children involved. The word *children* (*tekna*—children) is plural, but is a term in which the plural can stand for the singular. We call this a generic plural. This use of the plural to include or stand for the singular is common in Scripture. We find it in Matthew 22:24, Mark 10:29, Ephesians 6:4, and 1 Timothy 5:4, to name a few occasions. In each of these instances the meaning includes one or more children. We understand the use of *tekna* in regard to the bishop in 1 Timothy 3:4 and Titus 1:6 in the classic generic plural sense to mean "one or more children." We will discuss the aspect of "believing children" below under Titus 1:6.

Due to the nature and responsibility of leading God's family, the church, the ministry of being a bishop is no place for a *recent convert* or neophyte (*neophutos*—

newly planted, newly converted). It takes time to grow and mature into a dignified and respected leader. New Christians should be given time and space in order to know from experience the difficulties of maturing as a Christian. Paul is well aware, as are many of us, of the danger of pushing people too far, too fast. Some new Christians respond to the gospel very quickly, yet if not permitted time to "be planted and rooted deeply," being neophytes (*neophutos*) they fall away very easily. They consequently *fall into the condemnation of the devil.*

Titus 1:5–9

The situation in Crete was similar to that in Ephesus. Paul had left Titus in Crete to take care of problems in the church by initiating the appointment of elders/bishops in every church. As in 1 Timothy 3 the list of desirable qualities in elders stressed by Paul is driven by the unique cultural nature and situation of the Cretan churches and community. Titus 1:10ff indicates that part of the problem was a group of false teachers, predominantly of a circumcision party and, therefore, presumably Jewish in origin. In addition, Cretans had the reputation of being liars whose word could not be relied on.

In this paragraph, Paul openly links the ministry of *elders* (*presbuteros*—an older person, an elder, a person of great dignity) and bishops (*episkopos*—a bishop, an overseer, a guardian) together in one person. Bishops, therefore, are elders. A reference to **Figures 7 and 8** earlier in this chapter will reveal that the lists in Timothy and Titus are similar, yet with minor differences. Sometimes the thought conveyed is the same but the terms differ or are synonymous. In one or two instances Paul has introduced a new concept. In this section of our study we will not comment on the synonymous terms and ideas in the two lists, but only on the new concepts presented in this list to Titus.

Paul stresses in Titus 1:6 that the elders' *children* (as we observed above, this is a generic plural) must be *believers* (*pistos*—trustworthy, faithful, dependable, believing). There is a question in the mind of some whether believing should be interpreted as a synonym for baptized member of the church or whether it should simply mean that the children believed in Jesus or were faithful to Jesus. In one form or another the expressions "those who believe, believer, or believers" occur at least 13 times in the Pauline writings in the RSV New Testament. In all but two it is clear that Paul has in mind "baptized members of the church." On two occasions it could merely have reference to one who simply believes. We should, therefore, prefer the meaning "baptized member of the church" for Titus 1:6. The elder must have proven ability to lead people to Christ since he has at least led his own children (or child) to Christ. Questions will still linger regarding whether this must be *all* of his children or *at least one* of his children. Reason should lead us to accept the fact that some might still be too young for baptism, but the bishop has already proven his ability if at least one is a baptized member and the others are "not profligate or insubordinate."

Profligate (*asotia*—debauchery, profligate) implies uncontrolled behavior. Debauchery is a good synonym and definition of profligate. *Insubordinate* (*anupotaktos*—undisciplined, disobedient, rebellious) merely adds to the nature of the conduct of the bishop's children. They must be well behaved, obedient, and respectful.

Furthermore, the bishop as God's *steward* (*oikonomos*—steward, manager, administrator, one who is responsible for) must not be *arrogant* (*authades*—self-willed, stubborn, arrogant) or *quick tempered* (*orgilos*—inclined to anger, quick tempered). He must be a *lover of goodness* (*philagathos*—loving what is good), *master of himself* (*sophron*—prudent, self-controlled, thoughtful), *upright* (*dikaios*—upright, just, honest, morally righteous), *holy* (*hosios*—devout, pious, pleasing to God, consecrated to God), and *self-controlled* (*egkrateia*—self-controlled in regard to sexual matters).

1 PETER 5:1–4

Peter addresses *elders* (*presbuteros*—elder, person of great dignity) as a fellow elder. He himself is also an apostle. The primary *ministry* of the elder and the apostle are the same—to teach, preach, and lead the church. The difference is that the apostle does this on a global scale, the elder within a local congregation. The elders are to *tend* (*poimaino*—herd, tend, pasture, lead, guide, protect, care for, nurture, shepherd) the flock of God *that is your charge* (*en humin*—in you, among you).[158] Peter resorts to the familiar analogy of God's people being God's flock and the leaders being shepherds. The flock in question is the one among whom they have been appointed as elders. This is one of the passages upon which Churches of Christ build the concept of local congregational autonomy. Elders are shepherds of the specific congregation that has appointed them to the ministry, not over a group of congregations or a diocese of congregations. Elders over the one congregation that appointed them have no leadership responsibility, jurisdiction, or charge over any other congregation, and no other eldership or congregation has any charge over them.

The elders accept their responsibility *willingly* (*hekousios*—willingly, deliberately, intentionally), not by *constraint* (*anagkastos*—by compulsion), not for *shameful gain* (*aischrokerdos*—fondness for dishonest gain), but *eagerly* (*prothumos*—willingly, eagerly, with great eagerness), not *domineering* (*katakupieuo*—to domineer, to become master over, to subdue, to be lord over, to rule) the congregation of *their charge* (*kleros*—lot, that which is assigned to you, portion, share), but by leading through personal *example* (*tupos*—pattern, model, example). Elders do this as servant shepherds following the example of the Chief Shepherd, Jesus (1 Pet 5:4, 2:25).

1 Peter 5:1-3 and the next passage we will examine, Hebrews 13:7, stress the point that much of the authority and effectiveness of the elder are derived, not from position or rank, but through personal example, quality of life, and faith.

HEBREWS 13:7, 17

Although it is not certain that Heb 13:7 and 17 actually refer to elders, the similarities in language and message indicate this possibility. In 13:7 the writer exhorts the readers to "remember your *leaders* (*hegeomai*—to lead or guide, to rule), those who *spoke to you the word of God*; consider the outcome of their life, imitate their faith." The use of the word *hegoumenos* in the New Testament in regard to church leaders is interesting. The word appears in this manner in this passage, Acts 14:12, and Acts 15:22. In Acts 14 it is translated "chief speaker" in reference to Paul, and in Acts 15 "leading men" in reference to Silas and Barsabbas, the two men from Jerusalem who accompany Paul and Barnabas back to Antioch after the Jerusalem "conference." From these passages we learn that the term *leader* in these contexts has reference to the leading ministry provided through *teaching* God's word. Note Hebrews 13:7, "those who *spoke* to you the word of God." The *leaders* were those who *taught* them and whose *life and faith* were *examples* to them. If this passage is understood in reference to elders, it reinforces the emphasis made elsewhere that elders are leaders through their teaching ministry. Whatever the case, the leading is done in this context through teaching God's word. However, teaching in any case or ministry in the absence of Christian example and faith is barren and hollow.

In Hebrews 13:17 readers are encouraged to "*obey* (*peitho*—obey, follow, be persuaded by someone, take someone's advice) your leaders and *submit* (*hupeiko*—to yield to or submit to someone) to them; for they are *keeping watch* (*agrupneo*—to keep watch over, to guard, to care for) over your souls, as men who will have to give account." To obey one's leaders in this context means to *be persuaded by* and *to follow* the leader's teaching. Christians do so because they recognize that their leaders are guarding their souls and caring for them. The leaders in turn do so diligently since they will be held accountable for the growth and security of their followers.

1 THESSALONIANS 5:12

Paul encourages the Thessalonians to "respect those who labor among you and *are over you* (*prohistemi*—lead, guide, care for, give aid) in the Lord and *admonish* (*noutheteo*—admonish, warn, instruct) you, and to esteem them very highly in love because of their work." It is difficult to know whether this is a reference to elders in that at the time of writing 1 Thessalonians the Thessalonian church was still a very young church. This does not, however, rule out the possibility of their having elders by this time. Whoever this has reference to obviously was caring for and leading the church in Thessalonica through a teaching and nurturing ministry. Once more we encounter *leadership* through a *teaching* ministry.

As in Hebrews 13:7 we learn that elders or leaders should be capable speakers and teachers who are able to nurture, admonish, and care for their followers in love, and who give aid when necessary.

1 TIMOTHY 5:17

"Let the elders who *rule* (*prohistemi*—to lead, guide, care for, give aid) well be considered worthy of double honor, especially those who labor in preaching and teaching...." Paul is actually encouraging the church in Ephesus to support those elders who are preaching and teaching. Again we encounter the interesting word *prohistemi*. The RSV for some strange reason translates this on this occasion as "rule." Elsewhere they have translated it "give aid" or "are over you" or "manage." The translation in this place is possibly determined by the Catholic and Episcopal hierarchical model rather than the biblical model of leadership. The term is better understood as "lead" or "care for" in this instance, since it is followed by emphasis on the teaching ministry of the elder. The net result is that the elders are involved again in a teaching or preaching ministry.

ACTS 20:17–30

Paul's exhortation to the Ephesian *elders* (*presbuteros*—elder, a person of great dignity) at Miletus in Acts 20:17-30 sets the ministry of elders squarely in the context of the pastoral metaphor. It is also one of possibly two instances in the New Testament where all three terms for congregational leaders (elder, 20:17; bishop or overseer, 20:28; and pastor, shepherd, 20:28) are brought together in one context. Expressions such as "take heed to yourselves and to all the *flock* (*poimen*—flock), in which the Holy Spirit has made you *overseers* (*episkopos*—bishop, overseer), *to care for* (*poimaino*—tend, care for, shepherd) the church of God...." emphasize that bishops must have the *spirit of a shepherd* if they are to lead and care for God's church. One of Paul's major concerns is that false teachers (wolves) would arise from within the Ephesian church who would lead some of the flock astray. For this reason Paul commends the elders to the gracious Word of God, laying stress once more on the fact that elders should know and teach the Word of God.

CONCLUSION

In this rather long and detailed chapter we have considered some of the *qualities* deemed necessary in elders and bishops. We have noticed that they are clustered around three areas. *First*, the elder is to be respected, dignified, and above reproach in both the local church and the community. *Second*, the elder must have established a life and faith worthy of imitation by his followers. In this regard he must have a proven ability to lead others to Christ and to lead the church. This proven ability can be seen in how effectively he has led his own family. *Third*, he must be a capable teacher of God's Word. This relates to his ability to pastor the flock, protecting and maturing them on sound doctrine.

We have also noticed that the lists of qualities stressed in 1 Timothy 3 and Titus 1 are related to the particular cultural, sociological, and theological needs of the local specific congregation. The qualities listed are examples of how the elder should be above reproach, how he should relate to the congregation, and how he is to mature and lead the congregation.

Whatever the qualities may be, they indicate that the elder is able to lead the church in the spirit of Christ *because he possesses the spirit of Christ*. Need we add that he is one who is led by the Spirit (Rom 8:5-9, Gal 5:16-24) and manifests in his life the gifts of the Spirit, especially, faith, hope, and love. He is simply an outstanding, mature, dignified Christian who has demonstrated through his ability to lead his own family to Christ that he can lead the church in to Christ.

CHAPTER 15

BIBLICAL AUTHORITY

—◦◦◦—

Churches of Christ have been a conservative biblical group since the beginning of the Restoration Movement. This has been one of their major strengths and one which should not be surrendered in any form or fashion if Churches of Christ are to remain true to their heritage of seeking to be the church described in the New Testament. One should not, however, confuse biblical conservatism with institutional conservatism or with traditional conservatism.

Biblical conservatism means that one wishes to remain biblical in everything that one does; that one wishes to remain true to what the Bible teaches since it is accepted as a fundamental truth that the Bible is God's inspired word. Biblical conservatism means that one does not wish to change what can be learned from Scripture, and that Scripture takes precedence over culture.

Institutional conservatism is a commitment to remain true to the institution without changing the institution in any manner. Likewise traditional conservatism is a desire to remain true to one's tradition without tampering in any way with that tradition. There is nothing wrong with either institutional or traditional conservatism as long as they are seen as guiding principles rather than absolute rules or laws.

Given the conservative nature of Churches of Christ, members should favor institutional and traditional conservatism as long as these guiding principles do not become the "rock bottom" conviction of their faith. Biblically committed Christians should have as their first commitment biblical conservatism, that is, remaining true to biblical principles. They should be willing to surrender their institutional and traditional conservative commitments to biblical truths.

There is one caveat to this proposition regarding biblical conservatism versus institutional and traditional conservatism. It is that Scripture must be correctly interpreted. Biblical interpretation is fundamental to the validity of biblical conservatism. It should be the commitment of every biblical conservative to return regularly to Scripture in order to understand it correctly, and when necessary to amend one's views in keeping with the truth of Scripture.

This was, in fact, the commitment of early Restoration leaders: to return to the old paths of Scripture and to surrender all personal presuppositions to scriptural pre-suppositions. Constantly returning to Scripture for one's faith and doctrine should be a primary commitment of members of Churches of Christ.

BIBLICAL AUTHORITY AND ITS PROBLEMS

Related to the conviction of Churches of Christ to return to Scripture and be truly bib-lical in one's faith is the question of biblical authority. Terms such as "biblical author-ity," "scriptural authority," and "usurping authority" stand out from the pages of Church of Christ literature. The concern for scriptural authority is without question one of the major strengths of Churches of Christ. At the same time, however, it has also been one of the most divisive factors among Churches of Christ. Divisions over congregational cooperation, orphan homes, Sunday Bible classes, eating in the church building, and one or more cups in the communion have racked Churches of Christ through the years. At the very source of these divisions has been the subject of bibli-cal authority.

Authority has also been a major concern in the stressful matter of the role of women in the church. Perhaps this is with some justification due to the pressures of a secular society which not only questions the subject of authority, but in fact stri-dently rejects it. The trend of contemporary society to either reject or distance itself from traditional institutional authority (one of the New Realities discussed in a pre-vious chapter) and move to a pluralistic self-centered authority system tends to make conservative persons suspicious of some secular demands. This is unfortunate since it is misinformed to simply interpret women's concerns for a larger role in the church in the context of "usurping authority" or a desire to "run the church." But the matter of authority looms large in the minds of those opposed to any changes in the role of women in the church. Perhaps it would be better to understand the women's con-cerns for an increased role in the church as a desire to be more committed and active in the life and ministry of the church without desiring to take over the church or "usurp authority."[159]

We close this brief introductory section on biblical authority with the comment that the plea for, and commitment to, biblical authority stands or falls with sound biblical interpretation. Every effort should be made to interpret Scripture within its own context, that is, within its historical and theological context, within its literary context, and within its linguistic context. The subject of biblical authority should be placed squarely within the context of the biblical text and biblical authority, and not in the context of ecclesiastical office or tradition, whether Catholic, Episcopalian, or Church of Christ.

Biblical Authority and Church Leadership

The subject before us in this chapter is a subdivision of general biblical authority, namely, the authority of elders, deacons, and ministers. The Greek word commonly translated "authority" in the New Testament is *exousia* (freedom, choice, right, power, authority, absolute authority, ruling power, official power). It can be seen from the brief list of options available that the term has a wide range of meaning. It is a term, however, that favors the sense of official or absolute power.

In the New Testament, *exousia* is often used in a secular sense of the official or ruling power of government officials (Lk 19:17; 20:20; Jn 19:10; Rev 17:12). It has reference to the general sense of power or right to do something (Lk 12:5; Jn 1:12; Acts 8:19). In addition it is used in reference to the sense of freedom to make choices or do something (1 Cor 9:12; 2 Thess 3:9).

In the religious sense of absolute authority, *exousia* is used in the New Testament of God, Christ, and the apostles. By inference, since Scripture is the Word of God and of Jesus, Scripture bears such absolute authority.

Although God is recognized as having all authority in the fullest cosmic sense, this is especially true in matters of religion. The authority of God is both axiomatic and absolute. He is "the Alpha and the Omega...the Almighty" (Rev 1:8). All heaven bows before his throne (Rev 4). He bestows authority on whom he pleases. God has granted absolute authority to his Son, Jesus (Matt 28:18; Jn 17:2) who through this authority will judge the world (Acts 17:30, 31). Jesus in turn has granted this authority to his apostles (2 Cor 10:8; 13:10). Whatever they bind on earth is bound in heaven.

From the above observations we note that *exousia* in the sense of *absolute authority* is reserved for God, Christ, the apostles, and Scripture. It does not reside in the church or any "official" of the church. Such views as held by the Roman Catholic Church which pass apostolic authority down through the Popes who supposedly speak *ex cathedra* for God are not sustainable from Scripture. In spite of this, many hold to the view, derived from the hierarchical model of the Catholic and Episcopal churches, that religious authority is vested in some form of church "office."

The "Office" of Bishop

It is not uncommon for church leaders to refer to their ministry as an "office." The background for this is 1 Timothy 3:1. The word "office," however, is simply not in the original Greek of 1 Timothy 3:1. One might ask how this term found its way into 1 Timothy 3:1? We must remember that most of our Bibles today, especially those which contain the word "office," are within the tradition of the King James Version of 1611, which in turn drew on a long and rich history of translation stretching back at least to William Tyndale's translations of 1525–1530.[160] Due to the fact that the King James Version and its predecessors were translated in the environment of the Episcopal or Catholic churches, it is not surprising that the word "office" would be used to express the work of the bishop. In the two dominant churches of the time, bishops had an "office," and vested in that "office" was "authority."

The term "office" is simply not part of, or within the sense of, the original Greek of 1 Timothy 3:1. A good translation would be, "If anyone aspires to be a bishop....," or perhaps, "If anyone aspires to the ministry or work of the bishop...."

Some have argued that the word "office" is inherent in the word *episcopos* since the word *episcope* is translated "office" in Acts 1:20. Again we must insist that the reason that *episcope* is translated "office" in Acts 1:20 is the same as for 1 Timothy 3:1. It was translated in the context of a church which believed that authority was vested in an office. Notice, however, that in the RSV, Acts 1:25 states "to take place in this *ministry* and apostleship." The *episcope* of Judas was not an office but a *ministry*. The NIV wisely translates *episcope* in Acts 1:20 as "leadership." This is a good translation, well in keeping with the sense of the context of the passage. To read "office" into *episcopos* simply because it is supposed to be included in *episcope* simply will not work!

Ministry as Authority

We will argue that, although *exousia* in the case of God, Christ, the apostles, and Scripture is absolute, authority in the case of elders, deacons, and ministers is functional or ministry related. We are stressing the point that elders, deacons, and ministers do have authority, only that their authority is different from that of God, Christ, and the apostles. The authority of elders, deacons, and ministers is limited to the ministry function God has assigned them. The following charts diagram effectively the point we will be developing in the remainder of this chapter.[161]

We will notice that the ministry function each servant receives as a gift of God's grace contains within it the definition or limit of the authority involved. It will be helpful

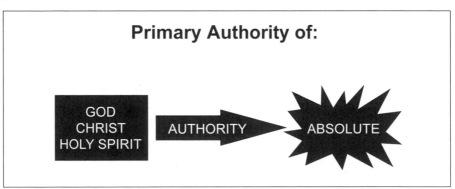

FIGURE 9: TYPES OF AUTHORITY—GOD

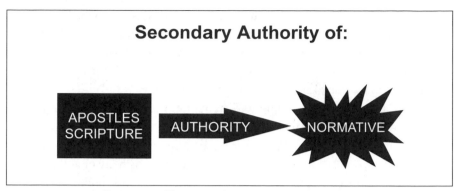

FIGURE 10: TYPES OF AUTHORITY—SCRIPTURE

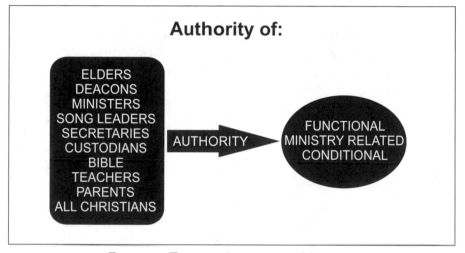

FIGURE 11: TYPES OF AUTHORITY—MINISTRY

to begin by emphasizing that God has assigned a number of servants specific tasks and in the very task is the description of their authority. For instance, in the above chart we have listed a number of special servants, each with a specific ministry. We might, for convenience and to illustrate a point, begin with the special servant class of *parent*. There are specific instructions in Scripture relating to the responsibility of parents. They are not exhaustive, but are adequate in defining the ministry God has in mind for parents. Briefly stated, fathers are raise their children in the discipline and instruction of the Lord, and not provoke them to anger (Eph 6:4, Col 3:21). One would assume from Paul's list of qualities for elders and bishops that fathers are to manage their families, lead them to Christ, and to teach them to be obedient. The authority of the parent is specifically related and limited to raising children. Consequently, the authority of parents is neither absolute nor universal. It is limited to their own family and to raising their family obediently in the Lord. We all recognize that the parents' authority changes as the children mature to the point where it is almost non-existent or at least limited in later years to the respect of their children. The parents' authority is consequently functional and ministry related.

Bible class teachers have authority. Their authority is to teach God's word. In the local congregational setting, the elders assign a class to the Bible class teacher. That responsibility does not make the teacher a parent *in absentia,* for the teacher does not assume the parents' responsibility. The teacher's responsibility or authority is to maintain order in the class and to teach God's word to the class, nothing more. The teacher does have authority; it is ministry related and functional. The same could be said regarding youth ministers and youth group leaders.

The secretary is an interesting illustration. Consider the following scenario. An elder calls the church office and asks to speak to the minister. The secretary tells the elder that the minister is in conference with someone. The elder responds that he knows this but still desires to speak to the minister. The secretary responds that this is not possible. She will ask the minister to return the call when he is through with the person with whom he is in conference. The secretary is exercising her authority. She has not "usurped authority," but is merely exercising the role given her by the elders and her ministry. She was hired by the elders with the strict instruction to protect the minister's time when he is in conference. Her authority is real, yet limited to her ministry role. It is functional, ministry related, and not absolute.

We conclude this section with the observation that elders, deacons, and ministers do have authority, but their authority, unlike that of God, Christ, the apostles, and Scripture, is not absolute but is limited to the function of their ministry role. It is imperative, therefore, that we spend some time exploring the ministry role of elders, deacons, and ministers in order to better understand their function and authority.

MINISTRY TERMS AND FUNCTIONS

We will learn from the following study that each ministry term is descriptive of the ministry or function performed by the person being described. This should not be surprising since in biblical times names on many occasions were changed to describe the personality involved. Abram's name (Abram—exalted father) was changed to Abraham (father of many nations), and Jacob's name became Israel because he strove with God, illustrating the point that names and ministry terms describe the function and character of the person.

Elder. As we have already learned, the Greek term for elder is *presbuteros.* This term has several uses. It can refer to an older person, and it is sometimes so used in

the New Testament (Acts 2:17, "... and your old men shall see dreams"). More pertinent to our study are the references to positions of leadership in some body or group
of people. There were city elders in local communities, elders in the Sanhedrin (Matt
16:21, Acts 6:12), and elders in the early church (Acts 11:30).[162]

In this special capacity as dignitaries in some organization the term was synonymous with leader. One became a leader in the community because one was recognized by the community as a leader and a *person of great dignity*. Elders, therefore, were
appointed as *leaders* in their communities because they were highly respected as persons of character and virtue, and because they possessed dignity in the conduct of
their lives. They would be people that the community could respect and follow. The
emphasis would be on their leadership capacity through personal example.

So what did elders do? They served the community as leaders with dignity and
virtue. In the church community, because of their recognized dignity and leadership,
they would serve as servant shepherds after the role model of their leader, Jesus. But
they would do this in the dignity of their personal lives and character and their example, not in a domineering manner.

Bishop. The Greek term for bishop is *episkopos* (overseer, one who cares for, super-
intends, and guards those in his charge). It was used of God in Greek antiquity, the
Septuagint, the Pseudepigrapha, the Apocrypha, and the Patristic Fathers (1 Clem
59:3). In the New Testament it is used in a unique manner of Christ (1 Pet 2:25, "the
Shepherd and Guardian of your souls").

In the church the term *episkopos* is used as a synonym for the elders as leaders
of the church. Acts 20:17-30 is an excellent example of this. Paul is addressing the
elders when he refers to them as *episkopoi* (overseers) who are to "care for the church
of God." The responsibility of bishops as leaders is to care for and guard God's people,
the church. In doing this they also superintend the activities of the church.

Shepherds. Both Paul and Peter adopt the pastoral metaphor in referring to the church
as the "flock of God" (Acts 20:28, 1 Pet 5:2). To refer to the leaders of God's people as *shepherds (poimen*—a shepherd, sheep-herder, a pastor) was not uncommon in Scripture (Ezek
34:1ff, Jer 2:8, the Hebrew uses "shepherd" here translated in the RSV as "rulers," and
Jer 3:15). Jesus adopted the term for himself (Jn 10:11), and Peter referred to Jesus as the
"chief shepherd" and the "Shepherd and Guardian of your souls" (1 Pet 5:4 , 2:25).

It is not surprising, therefore, that the elders as leaders of God's people would
eventually be referred to by Paul (Eph 4:11) through the shepherding analogy of *pastors (poimen*—shepherd, pastor). As shepherds or pastors, elders know their flock well,
feed their flock, protect their flock, and lead the flock. The emphasis on shepherding
is on knowing the individuals; *"eldering"* or shepherding is a people-intensive ministry.
In a unique manner elders as shepherds are responsible for the souls of God's people.

They meet this responsibility not simply through administering a church program, but by knowing their people by name and being personally responsible for and involved with their flock. They nurture, feed, protect, and lead the flock.

The authority of the elder/bishop/shepherd lies in the responsibility God has placed on them to teach, lead, equip, care for, guard, and protect the flock. Their authority is functional, ministry related, and bound by their ministry.

Leaders. A primary function of elders as shepherds is to feed their flock. Much of this will be done through the teaching ministry of the church in which elders function as prominent teachers. Some of this teaching will be done in congregational classes, some of it in homes, some again in one-on-one private situations. Whatever the case, elders as pastors or shepherds will provide much of this teaching. In this capacity they are referred to as leaders in the biblical sense of *hegoumenois* (Heb 13:7) who "speak the Word of God" to their people. We are reminded that Ephesians 4:11 includes "pastors and teachers" or "teaching pastors" in the list of those teaching ministries responsible for *equipping* the church for the work of ministry. Elders function as leaders in a profound manner when they are teaching God's word.

Deacons. Deacons, as specially chosen servants with specific qualities, are appointed by the church for *special ministries*. These ministries are not specified, but we gather from Scripture, especially Acts 6:1-7,[163] that they are appointed to assist the elders and the congregation so that the elders may get on with their business of shepherding and teaching the congregation. It has been the custom in some situations for the work of deacons to be limited to the more "physical" responsibilities of the congregation such as the church building and grounds, and there is nothing essentially wrong with this practice. It should not be concluded from this practice, however, that deacons' work should be limited to the physical. Deacons may assist the elders and congregation in such "spiritual" matters as the Bible school program, benevolence, evangelism, missions, counseling, and a variety of ministries that enrich the congregation. It is a fallacy, however, to consider the church building and grounds as merely a "physical" entity in the life of the church without "spiritual" implications. In keeping the building and grounds in good shape, deacons are ministering to the people, not merely keeping the physical property in shape.

Some congregations select deacons for specific ministries and for a specific period. This practice is fine. Other congregations select deacons because they are already providing quality spiritual leadership, and then guide the deacons in the selection of ministries in which the deacons have a vital interest and giftedness. Often the deacons are given the opportunity to periodically rotate through different ministries.

It is a serious mistake to look on being a deacon as a stepping stone before "moving up" to become an elder. This practice results from a hierarchical structure of church polity. Deacons should be as spiritual, as mature, and as capable as elders. The chief difference lies not so much in the spiritual qualities of the two, but in the *ministries* to which they are appointed. If being an elder means sitting in an elders' business meeting making decisions for the congregation, then deacons are as well qualified and capable as elders to do this. The elders' ministry is not the "decision making" ministry of the congregation, but the "shepherding, teaching, guarding, caring for" ministry. The distinctive qualities required in elders relates specifically to their shepherding ministry. Making decisions is too easy a job for elders! It is my opinion that the elders/bishops/shepherds' role is more specifically focused on the teaching, nurturing, maturing ministry, whereas the deacons' role is more general. Elders are to be the guardians and leaders who give direction to the deacons who function in team with the elders.

The authority of the deacons lies in their spiritual qualities, example, and special ministries for which the congregation has selected and empowered them. Their authority lies in the function of their specific ministry.

Evangelists and Ministers. In 2 Timothy 4:1-5 Paul admonishes Timothy to "preach the word, be urgent in season and out of season...*do the work of an evangelist, fulfill your ministry.*" In Ephesians 4:11 he makes reference to evangelists as involved in the ministry of equipping the church through their teaching. In 1 Timothy 4:6-16 he encourages Timothy to "put these instructions before the brethren" and observes that by doing this he will be "*a good minister* in Christ Jesus." He becomes more serious when he charges Timothy to "command and teach these things...set the believers an example in speech and conduct, in love, in faith, in purity. Till I come, *attend to the public reading of Scripture, to preaching, to teaching.*"

It would be difficult to miss the emphasis given by Paul to the work of an evangelist or minister in preaching and teaching Scripture. It is unfortunate that many congregations and ministers have bought into the model of church ministry practiced by some denominations in which the minister has become either the counselor in residence or the local church administrator. Others in the congregation blessed with the gift of administration and counseling should be involved in these ministries. The evangelist should be freed to practice his God-given giftedness, namely, preaching and teaching the Word of God as an evangelist.

It is a decidedly unfortunate situation where Church of Christ ministry schools and universities prepare ministers to be "church chaplains" who take care of counseling, hospital visitation, and other such housekeeping jobs. It is little wonder that many Churches of Christ are not more evangelistic when their ministers are neither trained to be nor are practicing evangelism through preaching and teaching. In many instances, evangelists are doing shepherding work while the elders are sitting in meetings doing deacons' work and making decisions. Somewhere along the road to becoming part of the religious establishment in twentieth-century America, Churches of Christ lost sight of the biblical role of elders and ministers. Elders became "board room" executives and ministers became "church chaplains"!

The authority of the minister/evangelist lies in his God-given charge to preach the Word of God faithfully and to draw people, both church members and the unchurched, to Christ through his ministry of teaching and preaching.

CONCLUSION

In this chapter we have explored the concept of biblical authority. We have examined the term *exousia* in its various contexts and noticed that in Christianity normative authority pertains to God, Christ, the apostles, and Scripture. We observed that elders, deacons, and ministers also have authority, but in contrast to that of God, their authority is limited to their ministry function.

We observed also that authority in regard to elders, deacons, and ministers is the outgrowth of their ministry. The biblical terms translated elders, deacons, and ministers each are descriptive of the nature of leadership assigned to them by Scripture, and the authority to perform these ministries is inherent in the ministry itself. When authority is placed in the position or office, one is forced back into a Catholic or Episcopalian hierarchical model of church polity. Biblical authority stresses ministry and function rather than position or office. When biblical authority is seen in the context of ministry, one is freed from concerns of "usurping authority." *Biblical authority is freedom to function in ministry, not permission to take over, run, or domineer the church.*

In regard to all church ministries, whether that of the elder, deacon, minister, secretary, Bible school teacher, youth minister, or parent, how they exercise their authority to function is critical to both their effectiveness and the response of their followers. They, and in particular elders, are not to lord it over their people in a domineering manner. All should lead through their personal example, personal character and faith, and ministry function.

Chapter 16

CONGREGATIONAL ORGANIZATION

—⁓—

In this chapter we will propose a model of church organization which we believe is commensurate with a participative leadership model in which authority is perceived as real, yet ministry is functionally related. The proposed model contrasts with a traditional hierarchical model which emphasizes "office" and "authoritarian" leadership (see **Figure 12** at the end of this chapter). We will demonstrate how a congregation can organize itself into a practical, workable, participative model (see **Figures 13** and **14** at the end of this chapter).

BASIC ASSUMPTIONS

In this model we adopt a church of approximately 300–500 members with 8 elders, 20 deacons, ministers (or at least a minister), a secretary, and Bible class teachers. We will also assume that this church has a thorough participative mindset. It is worthy of observation at this point that what we are proposing is merely a good model that has worked in some congregations, yet may need modification in some cases.

As a fundamental operational model we will assume that the elders define their ministry primarily as a pastoral, shepherding one. They prefer to refer to themselves as shepherds rather than elders or bishops. The elders are all capable Bible students and teachers, although not all are as proficient in a large class setting. Some prefer to teach one-on-one or in small home groups, while others are "professional" teachers, some having served in the past as ministers. The congregation adopts a full participative ministry model under the participative leadership of the elders.

SELECTION OF ELDERS, DEACONS, AND MINISTERS

In keeping with their participative ministry and leadership philosophy, the congregation adopts a full congregational participative selection process when selecting its primary leaders, namely, the elders, deacons, and ministers. This process is initiated by the elders on a regular timetable (except in the case of the ministers) after considerable teaching on the biblical nature of the process and biblical qualities desired in the leaders of the church. This process will be discussed in full detail in a later chapter.

ELDERS MEETINGS

The elders meet once a week on Wednesday afternoon from 5:30 to 7:00 PM in regular meetings. These meetings are open meetings—the ministers are asked to attend all such meetings if possible, and members are invited to drop into the meeting whenever they feel the need. These meetings are structured around spiritual shepherding needs. Separate ad hoc meetings are called at a different time to discuss matters of a confidential nature.

Ministry group leaders (usually deacons) are requested to attend these regular elders meetings in rotation on a regular schedule in order to discuss their particular ministry with the elders. The elders refrain from making decisions for the deacons, but give advice when necessary. This form of accountability is essential to the participative model of church leadership. This practice also facilitates cross-ministry communication. This model may need modification in congregations where weekly meetings are not the most efficient use of time. Nevertheless, elders do need to meet in some form with ministry group leaders and deacons if they are to "oversee," or care for the congregation's well being. It should be noted again that, at times, more confidential elders meetings need to be held when deacons and others are not present.

MINISTRY GROUPS

The ministry groups are set up following a congregational meeting in which the elders lead the congregation through a process of determining what ministries the congregation wishes to conduct. The elders preface the meeting with several classes and sermons taught and preached by the elders and the pulpit minister in which the biblical nature of the church and the essentials of biblical ministry are emphasized. Eight ministry areas are identified and planned by the congregation.

The deacons are requested to indicate the ministries with which they prefer to be identified. They are requested to indicate three choices with a promise from the elders that they will try to have each deacon working in the ministry of their first choice. One proviso is mentioned. The elders request permission from the deacons to negotiate if need arises to shift a deacon to his second choice. With thirty deacons and eight ministry groups planned, at least three deacons can be on one ministry group. Based on their shepherding experience the elders choose the ministry group leaders, usually from the deacons. The deacons are assured that after two years they can be relieved of the leadership if they so request. They are also assured that after three years the ministries and the ministry groups will be evaluated by the elders and the congregation, and that some adjustment of ministries will be made when requested or necessary.

Deacons are encouraged to build their own ministry groups by recruiting and equipping team members from within the congregation. The elders and ministry group leaders visit new members to enquire what ministries they would like to be identified with. A congregational ministry group visits new members to inventory personality, family particulars, and ministry interest. Such information is entered into a computer system and the information is made available to ministry group leaders.

Elders do not serve on these ministry groups, neither do they attend the group meetings unless requested. An elder is, however, appointed to serve as liaison with each ministry group.

Elders form a separate ministry group. Since their ministry is a shepherding ministry, the elders take care of the preaching ministry, the counseling ministry, and the spiritual care of the congregation. They also coordinate or initiate the operation of the ministry groups, and coordinate the accountability to the congregation of the congregational ministries.

The deacons and ministry groups are requested to meet at least once a month prior to the regular, scheduled meeting with the elders, but the scheduling and number of meetings is left to the discretion of the groups.

Figures 13, 14 at the end of this chapter diagram the "flat" participative organizational structure of the ministry groups of the congregation. **Figure 15** diagrams the "accountability" relationship of these meetings to the congregation. Notice that all ministry groups in this model, including the elders, are accountable to the congregation. (We take it as a fundamental tenet that all ministry groups are ultimately accountable to the Lord.)

Periodic Ministry Group Meetings

At least three times a year, sometimes quarterly, the elders call a special ministry group meeting. This meeting is designed to facilitate communication between the ministry groups of the congregation. The group meets at some restaurant large enough to accommodate at least one hundred people in a private meeting facility. All ministry group members and their spouses are requested to attend the meeting. After a meal and enjoyable fellowship, the group undertakes some brief evaluation of the previous quarter or period of ministry and then plans for the coming quarter or half year. The group attempts to identify one or two special focus programs to unite and involve the total congregation in the ministry of the congregation.

Plans are also made at this meeting for the various ministry groups to report on a regular basis the activities of their respective ministries to the whole congregation at a Sunday evening service. **Figure 15** at the end of this chapter diagrams the "accountability" relationship of these meetings to the local congregations.

Budget Development and Finalization

Initiating the annual congregational budget is the responsibility of the Administration Ministry Group. This group is ably led by deacons who are professionally prepared as CPAs. Their ministry includes assisting the congregation in developing the annual budget, keeping the financial records, and monitoring the financial pulse of the congregation.

In October of each year this group sets a budget development calendar and calls an initial congregational meeting on a Saturday for preliminary work on the budget. Each ministry group is requested to submit their budget requests at this meeting. This information is entered into a computer and compared with the previous year's budget. These group members work until they have brought the new budget within reach of the previous year's budget before preparing a tentative budget for the congregation's consideration. At times, it is necessary to call a second congregational meeting for adjustments to the tentative budget before its presentation to the congregation.

Once the tentative budget is prepared, the Administration Ministry Group calls a congregational "spiritual business meeting" for open discussion of the budget. This meeting is usually planned for a Sunday evening. The normal evening worship is truncated in order to accommodate time for congregational discussion. The visitors at the service are invited to remain should they so desire. Members are encouraged to remain, although no undue pressure is brought to bear in order to get them to do so. The meeting is chaired by one of the elders with the leader of the Administration Ministry Group assisting. The congregation is asked for input. After open discussion and possible adjustment to the budget, the congregation is asked to approve the proposed budget by hand vote. By following this procedure the congregation buys ownership in the budget which is no longer perceived to be the budget of the Administration Ministry Group or the budget of the elders. It is now a truly congregational budget. In fact, the elders have little role to play in the process since the deacons are so well prepared for this leadership role. The elders function in their specific giftedness as one of the congregational ministry groups, but in this instance merely as members of the congregation. If and when problems arise in the development of the budget, the elders act in their shepherding role to lead the congregation through the problem areas.

The strength of this process is that no "we–they" mindset is developed since every member of the congregation is invited to participate fully in all of the meetings in the development of the budget, from the beginning through each stage of the final approval. The process is fully open and the opinion of everyone is requested and respected.

The drawback of this procedure is that it is not efficient in regard to time expenditure. The process takes at least three months to finalize. But then, efficiency is not the goal of this process. *Effectiveness and congregational ownership are the goals.*

An additional strength of this process is that it is an effective method of participative leadership. Since this is a congregational process, the budget becomes a congregational budget, monitored throughout the year by the congregation through the monthly business meeting where monthly budget reports are made to the congregation. Open information at every step in the process fosters confidence in the process; accountability to the whole congregation on the part of every ministry group, and increased giving by Christians who feel that they have some say in the distribution of the funds.

MONTHLY CONGREGATIONAL BUSINESS MEETINGS

The congregation conducts a regular monthly business meeting on a Wednesday night after Bible class. This is an open meeting, with every member of the congregation invited to attend, but all deacons, ministry group leaders, elders, and ministers are expected to be present. The meeting is chaired on a rotation basis by someone with proven ability to conduct an orderly meeting. Elders do not chair these meetings. Budget reports are made during this meeting, and regular business needing the attention of the whole congregation is conducted at this time. Elders, along with the other ministry groups, make reports of their ministries. The regular monthly congregational business meeting serves also as a means of accountability to the congregation and as a vehicle for communication.

CONGREGATIONAL "SPIRITUAL BUSINESS MEETINGS"

In addition to the "special congregational business meeting" for the approval of the annual budget, the elders initiate a quarterly congregational "spiritual business meeting." This, too, is held on a Sunday evening after a truncated evening service. An elder supervises and controls the meeting. Any matter of congregational interest, but especially the spiritual needs of the congregation, are covered. The meeting is an open meeting and all—young and old, male and female—are invited to participate. Visitors are invited to attend should they so choose. Opinion polls, congregational input, and congregational voting when necessary take place at this time.

Major congregational decisions are made on a congregational level during these "spiritual business meetings." When such occasions arise, the elders spend time discussing the primary doctrinal or congregational values with the congregation. When necessary, sensitive meetings are prefaced by several weeks of congregational preparation and biblical study. The elders, or some special guest speaker who may be recognized as a specialist in a specific field, and sometimes the regular preacher deliver sermons on specific relevant topics. The congregation is well informed and taught.

The elders and congregation do not practice a hierarchical model of church polity, but an open participative model. The elders provide insightful and decisive leadership, but are careful not to adopt a domineering or autocratic style of leadership. They are highly respected in the congregation for their personal example and ministry, and function with the full authority of their ministry as shepherds. The authority of the elders is real, but empowered by their faith, lifestyle, active leadership, shepherding role, teaching, and preaching, not by an "office" or position in a hierarchical structure.

Team Building in the Ministry Groups

The elders and ministry groups are actively involved in building team spirit in the ministry groups. Regular ministry group retreats and seminars are conducted for this purpose. The elders are careful not to stifle leadership potential, and to encourage creative leadership among the whole congregation. Because of their active shepherding ministry, participative commitment, and regular meetings with the ministry group leaders and congregation, the elders and ministers are well informed as to the life and needs of the congregation.

The congregation is not structured in a hierarchical pyramid model, but in a "flat" organization of networking ministries in which every person and ministry is esteemed for their ministry contribution. The biblical body model in which every member provides valuable service sets the environment for church life. The elders, minister, and deacons see themselves providing an equipping ministry for the congregation and an attempt is made to equip and involve every member in some form of active ministry.

Congregational organization can be graphically diagrammed or structured in a number of configurations. The following pages illustrate several ways in which congregations can function as teams. The first diagram (**Figure 12**) demonstrates a hierarchical model. Then follow two models (**Figures 13, 14**) of participative team function.

Figure 15 demonstrates the "accountability" relationship of ministry groups and meetings to the congregation. The final diagram (**Figure 16**) assumes a mature congregation, experienced in participative leadership.

The movement from the initial model to the final one may be perceived as a growth and maturation in leadership style and participative leadership in team ministry function.

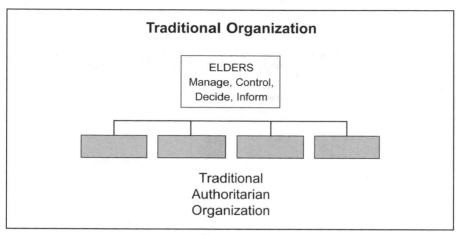

FIGURE 12

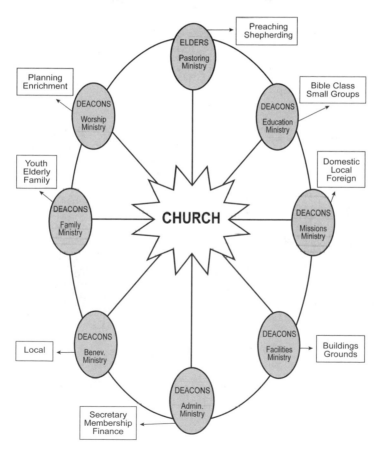

FIGURE 13: CONGREGATIONAL ORGANIZATION

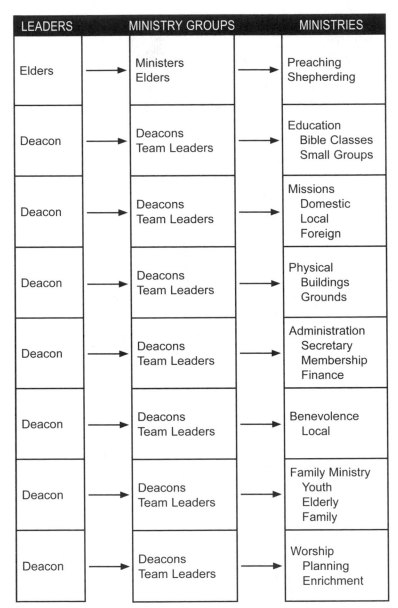

LEADERS	MINISTRY GROUPS	MINISTRIES
Elders	Ministers Elders	Preaching Shepherding
Deacon	Deacons Team Leaders	Education Bible Classes Small Groups
Deacon	Deacons Team Leaders	Missions Domestic Local Foreign
Deacon	Deacons Team Leaders	Physical Buildings Grounds
Deacon	Deacons Team Leaders	Administration Secretary Membership Finance
Deacon	Deacons Team Leaders	Benevolence Local
Deacon	Deacons Team Leaders	Family Ministry Youth Elderly Family
Deacon	Deacons Team Leaders	Worship Planning Enrichment

FIGURE 14: CONGREGATIONAL ORGANIZATION—MINISTRY

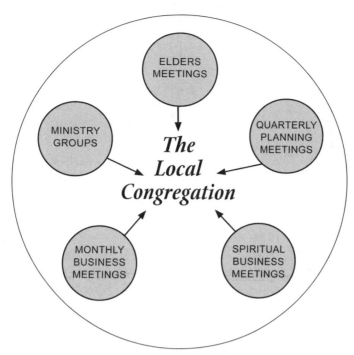

FIGURE 15: THE LOCAL CONGREGATION

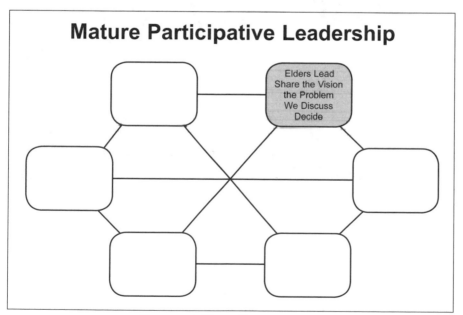

FIGURE 16: TEAM ORGANIZATION

CHAPTER 17

DECISION MAKING

—⁓—

It does not take a new member long to be mildly indoctrinated into the special colloquial language of Churches of Christ. Having been in Texas only one week as a Bible major at Abilene Christian College in the mid-'60s, I was visiting a rural congregation to preach one Sunday. The prayer immediately before the sermon was one I had never heard before, but one with which I have become familiar through the intervening years. "Lord, please grant the preacher a *ready recollection* of the things he has prepared to say today!" I needed that help, but wonder whether we are often merely repeating clichés. Prayers have a habit of becoming standardized in communities. In so doing, they paint a picture of the thinking and concerns or interests of the community.

A prayer often heard in Churches of Christ, at least in the South and Southwest, is "Lord, we thank you for our elders and pray for them that you would *grant them wisdom that they may make the right decisions.*" All elders are grateful for the sincere prayers of their people. We do need to pray for one another more that our ministries for the Lord may prosper. This prayer is interesting, however, in that it grants us a window into the mind of many Christians in regard to their understanding of the primary function of the elders, namely, *making decisions.*

Perhaps by our actions and style of leadership we have left the impression in the mind of our congregations that making decisions is the *primary role* of the elders. But is this the case? In our study of elders, bishops, and pastors in earlier chapters we observed that the primary role of elders is a shepherding, guarding, caring for, and teaching ministry.

We have already noticed, and will shortly develop this point more fully, that the biblical model established in both the Jerusalem and Antioch congregations was a participative model in which all the church played a part.

We should note at this point that all decision situations are not the same. Some decisions can and should be delegated and made at the ministry group level. Others can and should be made at the elder/shepherd level. Still others, however, need to be made with full congregational participation. In one sense mature congregations will shift decision making as far "down" the leadership continuum as possible. Mature congregations well equipped to delegate decision making in a participative manner will be selective in how and where decisions should be made. Notice this in the chart below.

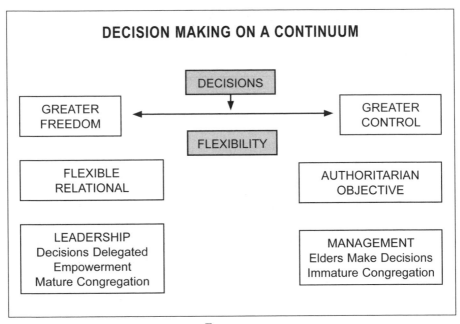

FIGURE 17

DIRECTIVE VERSUS PARTICIPATIVE DECISION MAKING

The *directive decision making process* takes place most often within the traditional hierarchical model of church polity, in which decisions are made at the highest level of the structure and passed down to the lower levels for administrative action. This is the classical directive model of managerial administration. In time past and under certain situations this model has been the preferred procedure in decision making. In any leadership or administrative model, there will be times when more managerial control is necessary in an organization, although this may not be the ideal. In a previous chapter we commented that effective leadership must move back and forth along the leadership-management continuum in any organization or church. We also observed that in immature organizations a top–down control style may be necessary on more occasions than may be desired. In a mature organization or church, the ideal would be for leadership to move toward the leadership-freedom-participative pole of the leadership-management continuum and away from the management-control pole. Decision making that takes place at the highest level in the organization is known as *directive decision making*.

In *participative decision making* the ideal model involves the whole organization or church in the process as in Acts 1, 6, and 15. If the ideal is not possible, then the process should take place as close as possible to the level of the workers who will administer the decision. A number of factors are necessary before an organization can adopt a participative model of decision making, chief among these will be the maturity of the organization or the members of the organization who will be involved in the process. Another significant factor will be the trust and confidence the leaders of the organization have in their workers. More will be said to this point in the following section. Primarily, however, a participative mindset is essential to the success of this process.

FACTORS NECESSARY FOR PARTICIPATIVE DECISION MAKING

Before any organization can successfully involve its members in a participative decision making process, a number of critical circumstances and attitudes must be in place. Participative decision making is a dynamic process which involves a number of factors.

A spirit of unity. The internal environment of the church is critical to all decision making. A frustrated, apathetic, or divided church will react negatively to any decision making process. It is imperative, therefore, that leaders in the church ensure that the congregation is healthy and in good spiritual shape. We are reminded of Ephesians 4:1-16 in which Paul discusses a growing and maturing congregation. He begins with a plea that the church strive to maintain the unity of the Spirit in the bond of peace, and concludes by stressing the need for every member of the body to work together. It is the responsibility of the elders and evangelists to equip the members through their teaching not only for ministry, but also for unity and peace.

Commonly shared values. Shared values serve to bind the organization or church together, giving it identity, meaning, purpose, and goals. Many of the values important to the life and identity of the church are doctrinal values. These must be communicated and encultured through the teaching ministry of the church. Other values are choices the congregation makes in their freedom within biblical parameters. These too must be shared, passed down to succeeding generations, explained, and likewise encultured.

Values also provide parameters within which the congregation or group must make their decisions. In Acts 1, 6, and 15, the Apostle Peter, the apostles in general, and James the brother of Jesus defined parameters within which their groups acted. Elders should lead the congregation and ministry groups in defining for the ministry group leaders and congregation the parameters of their ministry and decision making process. These parameters should be as broadly defined as the maturity of the group allows. Some parameters may be doctrinal, some cultural, others financial, but parameters of whatever kind are essential to the process. At all times accountability should be maintained through the regular meetings of the congregation as defined in the previous chapter.

As mentioned before, the participative model is not efficient in regard to time and energy, but it is effective as a teaching and maturing tool. We are reminded that church leaders are not in the task or goal business, but in the business of maturing people in Christ. This process of maturation, like the participative process, takes time and energy, but then, this is the ministry of the elders as teaching shepherds!

A sense of participative ownership. Nothing can be more devastating to the growth and maturity of a congregation than a "we–they" mindset in which the congregation looks at elders' decisions and asks, "Well, I wonder how they are going to achieve that goal!" In the process of maturing their congregation, elders and ministers must strive for a sense of participative ownership by the members. Directive decision making naturally works against this participative ownership mindset, whereas a participative process builds it. When someone is constantly "looking over the shoulder" of members and second guessing them, a sense of ownership is extremely difficult to achieve.

A spirit of openness. Nothing can destroy a feeling of confidence or trust in leadership among the members of the congregation quicker than a feeling that some are excluded from the "inner circle" or "in-group" of the congregation. In a participative process members must know that they are included in the process, that their opinion is valued, and that they are welcome. Whether they become involved or not is beside the point as long as they have been invited and know that they have a role if they so choose.

Furthermore, it is imperative that members do not perceive hidden agendas or that they are being manipulated. Full disclosure and openly shared information is essential to the process at every stage. If the members perceive that the decision is already made and that they are merely "rubber stamping" the decision, they will withdraw from the process.

Respect for the process. Leaders must project respect for the process. If leaders or elders demonstrate they do not fully support the process, the members will question whether the elders will abide by the decision. Again, the members must not perceive or feel that they are being manipulated by the elders who will in the end veto the decision.

A sense of mutual trust. Trust is an attitude based on trustworthiness and which must be earned. Stephen Covey includes trust and trustworthiness in his primary principles of "principle-centered leadership."[164] Open and full honesty, open and fully shared information, personal integrity on the part of the leadership, and mutual respect will have a profound impact on the viability of the process. Trust is like a bank account. It takes much time to establish a credible bank account and build it, but withdrawals are easy and quickly destroy or erode the account. Once depleted, the trust account is almost impossible to replenish.

Empowerment. Empowerment is a term that is often heard in discussion of participative leadership. Translated into the context of decision making, empowerment means that the members feel fully empowered to make the decision, and the elders and congregation will accept it. This should not mean that a decision may not be questioned or brought forward for review. It does mean, however, that due process has been respected and followed. Empowerment also means that the members have been freed up to make the decision and will be able to act on the decision once it is fully communicated.

One problem continues to surface in the mind of elders during leadership seminars. What if the decision is wrong? Or what if the members or deacons make a mistake? The answer is that mature leaders will then work gently and respectfully with the members or deacons as they work through the problem. The writer clearly remembers many years ago reading a journal article written in the context of a mission field. One of the natives said to the missionary, "What we need from you is for you to teach us to drive the car, then let us drive it. Yes, we will drive it into the ditch on occasions. What we need from you is not for you to take the keys away and to chastise us, but to help us get it out of the ditch, show us what we did wrong, and then let us drive the car into the next ditch!"

Furthermore, which eldership or elder never made a mistake?

THE PROCESS OF PARTICIPATIVE DECISION MAKING
In a previous chapter we explored a biblical model of church leadership by briefly examining Acts 1:15-26, Acts 6:1-7, and Acts 15:1-35. In these texts describing the church practicing its ministry, we noticed strong leadership initiating the participative process, setting parameters, drawing attention to Scripture, the Lord, and the Holy Spirit in the process, and much prayer.

Figure 18 below outlines the major components of the process in Acts 15:1-35.

Participative Decisions—*Acts 15*

• A Major Doctrinal Decision (15:1)	• Complete Representation (15:4,5)
• Strong Leadership (15:2, 7, 13) —Paul, Barnabas, Peter, and James	• Open Discussion (15:17-21)
• The Whole Church (15:4, 6, 12, 22)	• Establish the Process (15:22-23)
• Define the Problem (15:4)	• Define the Terms (15:22-29)
	• Own the Decision (15:22, 30, 31)

FIGURE 18

The process of participative decision making assumes that the congregation has already developed a participative philosophy, is comfortable with the process, and understands its workings. Several critical steps comprise a basic participative decision making process.

The leadership calls an open meeting. It is imperative that every member of the congregation or ministry group know they are expected to be involved in the process. Regardless of age or gender every member of the congregation or ministry group must feel free to participate. They should be assured that they will be heard and respected. Questions have been raised regarding teenagers participating in the process. It has been our experience that the teens do not have a significant impact on the outcome of a decision in that they comprise only a small percentage of the congregation. If certain members are eliminated from the process, the participative nature of the process will be prejudiced, and the congregation, or at least a group in the congregation, will justifiably feel that they have been manipulated. Furthermore, the meeting during which the decision is to be negotiated must be fully open, yet controlled.

The leadership provides adequate advance notice of the meeting. The purpose of the meeting must be clearly stated, and adequate time allotted for information regarding the decision to be collected, disseminated and studied. All the facts and information needed must be freely available to all. The leadership should warn the congregation not to politicize the process by campaigning for some particular cause. The congregation should be alerted to this possibility and encouraged to gently admonish those campaigning not to compromise the process.

The leadership reminds the congregation or group of its primary values. These values explain to the congregation or group those fundamental parameters by which the group lives. The congregation or group must be taught why the values are significant, and how they function in the life of the congregation. The decision process should be set in the context of the shared values of the group.

The leadership sets the primary parameters of the decision and process. A clearly worded agenda should be prepared setting out clearly the nature of the decision, the time limit of the process, and other pertinent information. This should be openly distributed to the whole congregation. The group should be informed as to the kind of decision desired and how the group should respond to the decision once it is made. Typical decisions may be majority, unanimous, or consensus decisions. We will shortly discuss the relative merits of these three kinds of decisions.

Some of the parameters may be doctrinal, in which case the congregation should be well prepared and informed in this regard. Other parameters may be cultural, in which case the congregation must understand the rationale determining the cultural web of the congregation.

The leadership opens the meeting. The leadership should define the rules under which the meeting will be conducted. The group should be informed whether a formal meeting under Robert's Rules of order will be the model or whether the meeting will be open and informal. The chair must take and maintain control of the meeting. All persons must be permitted to enter the discussion openly and freely. Fairness should be the goal in the control of the meeting by the chair. Adequate time must be made available for discussion.

The chair (leadership) summarizes the discussion and brings it to a vote. Once the discussion has been given adequate time for all interests to be developed, the chair should summarize the options and ask for approval of the summation. The chair should explain how the vote or decision is to be made, whether it will be by show of hands, by voice, or by writing on a ballot, and if so whether it will be signed or not. These process decisions should have been made in advance and the group notified of them.

The leadership shares the decision with the whole congregation. Communicating the decision, and as much information as necessary regarding the need for the decision and the process adopted in arriving at the decision, should be as immediate and complete as possible. The leadership should use the church bulletin and, if necessary, a letter to the whole congregation. Announcements should be made at appropriate church services and other similar meetings. The congregation should be encouraged to discuss any concerns or questions they may have with the leadership. If necessary, confidentiality should be guaranteed.

DECISION MAKING POSSIBILITIES

There are three basic possibilities in decision making. These decisions may be by unanimous approval, by majority approval, or by general consensus within the group.

Unanimous decisions. Although the announcement of a unanimous decision is pleasing to any group, the larger the group or the more complex the decision, the more difficult it is to arrive at a unanimous decision. In fact, given the pluralism of opinion in contemporary society, with the complexity of ethnic, generational, and gender interests in many larger groups, a unanimous decision is all but impossible, or to say the least, very improbable. Perhaps when congregations were more homogeneous unanimous decisions were possible. Today this is unlikely. Given the changing nature of generational interests, it is unlikely that a unanimous decision can be reached even among some elderships.

In the Center for Church Resources, when called to assist in a situation where an eldership is "frozen" in a divided decision, it has been our experience that the major reason for the "frozen decision" is the mistaken notion that all decisions should be unanimous. Many informed members today are extremely suspicious when an eldership claims a unanimous decision. They believe the congregation is either being manipulated or that the elders do not understand the nature of a unanimous decision and have mistakenly identified a consensus decision with a unanimous decision.

Majority decisions. The system of decision making most familiar to the American culture is that of the majority decision. This is the method by which we govern our communities, our states, and our nation. In this system a majority level is established in advance and, upon reaching that majority, a side or person is declared the winner. Either a simple majority, a two-thirds majority, or a percentage majority is set, but whatever the case, the majority receives the approval.

In congregational elder selection it has been almost the standard practice for a congregation to require at least three elders so that a simple majority decision may be arrived at. At other times, concern is voiced as to the number of elders required to be present at a meeting for there to be a quorum present. This is necessary in a system that requires a majority decision to be reached.

The problem is that in such a system, elderships are often also frozen when one or more elders provides a "swing" vote in decisions requiring a majority vote. It has been our experience that majority votes, when close in an eldership or congregation, can be extremely divisive or unsettling.

Perhaps the majority decision is the more efficient of the three options. It is, however, certainly not the most effective in all cases.

Consensus decisions. The advantage of consensus decisions is that they allow the participants to disagree and yet reach a decision. Consensus decisions will not work in every situation or organization. Unless the organization is highly motivated with a strong sense of identity, shared vision, and values, consensus decisions are not possible. Consensus decision making will also not be effective in organizations divided by strife or antagonistic attitudes. Organizations built on trust, integrity, values, and relational goals are in a much better position to reach consensus agreement.

The church, by reason of its value system and concern to "maintain the unity of the Spirit in the bond of peace," is in an ideal position and framework for consensus procedures. When the other person is esteemed highly, when the other person is placed before oneself, consensus decisions are not only possible, they are the best possible.

In consensus procedure the parties involved must be given adequate time for all opinions to be expressed. Sometimes a minority group may agree to go along with the majority. On other occasions the majority may concede to the minority.

It is held by some that consensus agreement is valid only in matters of opinion, but not for doctrinal issues. This is not necessarily the case! If this is the case, then the only possibility in doctrinal matters is a unanimous decision, since a majority decision often leads only to a division. In this case, many elderships are not being honest with their congregation, or with themselves, or among themselves, for even on some doctrinal issues there is disagreement among good, honest elders.

In doctrinal issues one or more elders may not agree with the others, but for the sake of the unity or harmony in the congregation decide not to make an issue over the matter while they and the other elders restudy the issue. They may never reach full agreement, yet they are able to function through consensus agreement.

When questioned by someone regarding such a consensus agreement, an elder may answer, "I do not agree with the decision, however, the problem may be mine so I plan to restudy the issue." Or the elder may respond, "The other elders are a good, honest, and capable group of men, and I recognize that I am not always right, therefore I plan to go along with the decision while we study the issue." A final statement could be, "I am going to submit to the wisdom of these good men and give the decision all the support I can." Any of these last statements will be a fine example to the congregation on how to handle difficult problems even when they involve doctrinal issues. One should always allow people the freedom of their conscience and permit them to stand down or excuse themselves from the decision should they feel that their conscience is so deeply involved and must, therefore, be honored.

CONCLUSION

In this chapter we have briefly examined three possible vehicles for making decisions. All three are valid procedures. The unanimous procedure sounds the most acceptable, but it faces serious concerns of honesty and manipulation—though it can and does work effectively in some situations.

The majority procedure has serious weaknesses. When there is a clear-cut margin, the procedure may work effectively, but there is still the feeling by some that they have been abused and not heard. When the margin is close, serious problems of division can surface.

Consensus agreement works well in mature organizations with a strong sense of trust and respect. When an organization is driven by integrity, shared values, and vision, the consensus procedure is most effective and provides a fine learning experience for all involved.

In a participative decision making process it is our opinion that, although the consensus procedure takes longer and is not always efficient, it is the better of the choices in the long run. It also provides the elders and the congregation a valuable learning process and opportunity for maturing.

CHAPTER 18

SELECTING AND APPOINTING ELDERS AND DEACONS

——◆◆◆◆——

A Participative Selection Process, Part 1

Although the New Testament speaks quite clearly to the need for elders and deacons, and although much has been written addressing those qualities desired in both ministry groups, little has been said or written regarding the *process* of selecting these special servants.

In Acts 14:23 we see Paul and Barnabas involved in "appointing elders in every church" they had established. Nothing, however, is said regarding the process they followed in appointing these elders. Years later, Paul wrote to Titus in Crete explaining his reason for leaving Titus in Crete. Titus was to "amend what was defective and appoint elders in every town." Again, nothing is said regarding any procedure to be adopted in the selection and appointment of these leaders.

Some indication, however, is given in Acts 1:15-26 and Acts 6:1-7 to the process of selecting certain church servants. From these passages we learn that a *participative* process was adopted in the early church community, with strong initiative being provided by the apostles. Some parameters were laid down and defined. Much prayer was offered to the Lord. Faith in the presence and operation of the Holy Spirit was evident. Finally, the cooperation and involvement of the whole group or congregation was elicited.

This chapter will recommend a participative selection process and suggest how this process can be adapted in churches today. Special attention will be given to the process recorded in Acts 1:15-16 and 6:1-7.

We learned in an earlier chapter that leadership style is fundamentally sociologically determined. We also observed that the sociological "culture" of the New Realities in which we now minister are conducive to a participative model of church leadership and leadership selection. It is impressive and somewhat amazing how much modern leadership theory is incorporating "biblical" models of leadership into contemporary leadership theory. Anyone reading the modern leadership "guru" Stephen Covey's works on principle-centered leadership will be impressed with this fact. Perhaps the reason for this can be found in contemporary emphases on people rather than on organizations and tasks. Christians naturally are delighted to find contemporary leadership theorists incorporating biblical principles into their theories of leadership.

A TRADITIONAL MODEL FOR ELDER SELECTION

Churches of Christ have traditionally adopted several models for selecting church leaders. Since leadership style is sociologically determined, this variety in methodology is understandable.

One model, however, has predominated in certain localities. This model calls for the existing elders to nominate a certain number of candidates for the "office" of elder, and to ask the congregation to inform the elders by a certain date whether any scriptural objections would disqualify any candidate from serving. If no objections are received by the appointed date, then the nominees would be installed as elders. This "top–down" model of selection fits well into a sociological culture comfortable with an autocratic or authoritarian, hierarchical model of church polity. In past generations more comfortable with an authoritarian environment this model served well. In contemporary society and culture, however, this model often leads to congregational discontent, discomfort, and apathy. For some reason, many Christians are unable to distinguish between respect for authority and an authoritarian mindset. They consequently interpret biblical and congregational authority along authoritarian lines. We have already observed in previous chapters that biblical authority is not vested in an autocratic concept of position and office, but in loving Christian service and ministry.

Apparently this "top–down" model has persisted in spite of firm criticism by past biblical scholars and church leaders. Robertson L. Whiteside, gospel preacher, minister to the College Church of Christ in Abilene, Bible scholar, and past president of Abilene Christian College, voiced strong opposition to this traditional model of leadership selection.

> The selection of bishops for the church is a serious and solemn matter, for the future usefulness of the church, and perhaps its destiny is involved....The duty and responsibility of selecting elders belong to the congregation as a whole. No man or set of men should undertake to do the selecting for the church....

> Another plan fraught with much danger to the church is for elders to select others to serve with them....Neither is it better for the elders to confer and decide that they want a certain man to serve with them, and then announce,

"We have selected Brother John Doe as an elder. If we have no objection, his selection stands approved." This is taking advantage of the church....

Either ignorance of Scripture, or a boss spirit that ignores the Scriptures, is at the bottom when a man, or set of men, does the choosing for the church....[165]

Howard Norton, Bible scholar, past missionary to Brazil, minister, professor at Harding University, and former editor of the *Christian Chronicle*, wrote these comments in a 1993 editorial:

People and churches must sometimes let go of the past....Just as individuals must be willing to say good-bye to attitudes or circumstances in their past in order to survive and prosper, congregations must free themselves from non-productive historical practices in order to be effective.

Some congregations are dying today, for example, because they will not turn loose of an obsolete leadership style that is autocratic and dictatorial. This type of leadership might have made sense in the Army or the Marines during a time of war, but it is as out of place in the Lord's church today as a ring in a swine's snout. Church leaders who insist on running the church business from behind closed doors in a climate of secrecy are killing the church, no matter how good their intentions.

Some congregations are dying today because they will not say good-bye to methodologies of the 1930s, 1940s, and 1950s that do not fit the cultural patterns of urban America in the 1990s. I am confident that a part of the generation gap in Churches of Christ today stems from this fact: Young Christians who grew up in urban America feel that many of the church's methods today are foreign to the world they live in. These young people love the church, but seriously question the way the church performs its task.

Not only individuals, but congregations must learn to say good-bye to some things in order to be productive in the present and be prepared for the future. Congregations must not say good-bye to biblical truth....However, they can be flexible in methodology.[166]

A Participative Model for Selection of Elders, Deacons, or Congregational Leaders

Here we outline a participative model of leader selection that is in keeping with the biblical tradition respected by Churches of Christ. A growing number of congregations, both small and large, over the past twenty-five years have adopted this model with satisfying results. The first use of this model to our knowledge was in Abilene, Texas, in

1966 when the South 11th and Willis Church of Christ selected their first elders. The model has been developed and adapted by congregations ranging in size from less than one hundred members to congregations of over one thousand members.

Several critical steps are essential in this participative process of selecting elders, deacons, and other church leaders such as pulpit ministers, youth ministers, and missionaries.

INVOLVE THE CONGREGATION IN THE PROCESS

In an article in the *Millennial Harbinger* of 1835, Alexander Campbell made the following astute observation:

> The voice of the church must be directly heard before any person be acceptably heard by it....To ordain is to appoint; and all appointments, from that of the successor of Judas as a witness of the resurrection, from an apostle to the messenger of a church, or an almoner, *was in the beginning by an election of the whole community* (italics added).

> The election or *choice of the community* (italics added), guided in that choice by the Living Oracles (Campbell's term for the New Testament), is essential consideration without which all forms would be unavailing.

Since the whole congregation is to be actively involved in the selection of their leaders, adequate time should be given for preparation, instruction, and maturation in order for the process to be effective. Significant time should be devoted to study of relevant Scripture and to prayer. This preparation can be done through leadership seminars, special sermons, well-prepared Bible class material, and specially called seasons of prayer. Every effort should be made to bring the whole congregation into the process. All members should be included, with special effort to include the women, the young people, and the elderly. The process of participative leadership selection, if conducted wisely, can be a wonderful learning and maturing experience for the whole congregation.

DETERMINE THE NEED FOR CONGREGATIONAL LEADERS

The first step in the process of leader selection is to *determine the need*. The need for church leaders may arise from two dimensions. One will be the "sociological" need within the congregation for strong, spiritual leadership. The other will be the need for congregations to follow a biblical model for church polity.

Church members should understand clearly why any process for selecting leaders has been initiated. Present leaders should clearly articulate their vision for church leaders. Unless the congregation "buys" into the need for leadership, the leadership will face the impossible task of leading people who see no need for leadership.

Primarily, it is a basic premise of conservative Christians that all leaders serve under the will and purpose of God, as prescribed in Scripture. Thus, congregations need to be well informed about the biblical model for church leaders, their biblical function or ministry, the necessary qualities for leaders, and the process of selecting leaders. Sufficient time and commitment must be given to preparing the congregation, scripturally and emotionally, for the process of selecting elders, deacons, ministers, and any other leaders.

Second, all leaders serve under the immediate will of the local congregation. Unless the congregation agrees to the selection of the leaders, owns the process, or initiates the process of leader selection, the "chosen" leaders will not be as fully accepted as they would if they were truly representative of the people. Church members, being good Christians, will submit to elders out of their Christian sense of responsibility, but this will be mainly as a matter of duty unless members feel they have had a significant role in selecting their leaders. Too often, a "we–they" mentality exists in congregations because the members feel disenfranchised from the process of selecting elders, or from the process of making such significant decisions.

Finally, congregational participation in selection is a well-documented biblical model for leader selection.

WHEN CONSIDERING THE NEED FOR LEADERS, SEVERAL SCENARIOS PRESENT THEMSELVES

The congregation may be serving without elders and deacons and the time has come for the selection of biblical leaders. In some ways congregations which have never had elders and deacons are in an advantaged position. They can move into the process without having a traditional model to live down. In other situations, congregations may have had elders and deacons previously, but for a variety of reasons, and often because of disharmony in the eldership or congregation, the eldership has been disbanded. Such situations can be difficult if previous elders remain in the congregation. Congregations selecting elders and deacons for the first time have in the process of participative leader selection an opportunity for congregational edification and unity building. When the process is handled in a spiritual manner through prayer and careful Bible study emphasizing spiritual qualities and the need for love, the mind of Christ, and the need for unity, much good can result. Considerable attention to study and prayer should take place before any process of elder selection is considered.

A congregation may be in an unfortunate situation where, because of problems within the eldership or congregation, desperate measures are being considered to rectify the problem. In some situations an eldership may be "frozen" and consequently unable to lead because of a faulty model of decision making or other similar situation.

Whatever the case, appointing new elders before biblical and spiritual conflict mediation and spiritual healing has taken place will be futile. The process of participative leadership selection, although a fine occasion for congregational growth, is not a panacea for all ills. Effective leadership can take place only in a congregation in which the "unity of the Spirit in the bond of peace" is a reality (Eph 4:1-16, especially vss. 1-3).

One would wish that a spirit of unity was the normal experience in congregational life, but this is not always the case. However, when a congregation sees the need for additional leaders as an opportunity for spiritual growth through improved shepherding and ministry, good things can happen.

The congregation should understand clearly why it is considering the process of leader selection, the positives and negatives of the process, and what steps they need to take in order for the process to be conducted in a godly and effective manner. Before we discuss in detail a participative leader selection process in which the whole congregation is involved, we stress, even to the point of overstating the case, the *unconditional need for considerable biblical teaching, meditation, soul searching, and prayer* throughout the process. Much needs to be said of the power of prayer in the lives of godly people who are determined to do God's will according to his spirit and purpose.

PRESENT BIBLICAL TEACHING ON LEADERSHIP AND LEADERSHIP QUALITIES

Everyone who is to be involved in the process—the congregation and those nominated for the specific ministry being considered—must understand clearly the biblical principles of the process and the requisite qualities involved in the leadership ministry being considered.

We underscore as before that there are many biblical principles involved in the qualities of leaders beyond those mentioned in 1 Timothy 3 and Titus 1, as important as these may be. When these two passages are reduced to a list of necessary *qualifications*, injustice is done to the biblical principles involved in these two great passages, as well as to the full range of spiritual qualities desired in elders, deacons, and ministers.

The following Scriptures and biblical principles, to mention just a few, help us understand the *kind of persons* church leaders should be:

> ***The Church is the Body of Christ.*** We are all baptized into one body by the same Holy Spirit. This contributes to a *Spirit of unity* created by the Holy Spirit and the new birth. This unity of the spirit must be maintained in a spirit of peace. In this one body no one member is more important than any other, and all contribute to the well being of the others. It is only in a body in which all members work together in harmony and in mutual support that growth can be possible. The unity of the Spirit in the bond of peace in the

body of Christ is absolutely essential to effective leadership (1 Cor 12:1-31; Rom 12:3-8; Eph 4:1-17).

Ministries are Gifts of God's Grace. Leadership in the body of Christ is not a matter of position or authority, but of ministry. Whatever ministry we are called to is the result of God's grace working in our lives, and not one's own ability or position (1 Pet 4:7-11; Rom 12:3-8; Eph 4:7,11; 1 Cor 4:1-2; 2 Cor 5:18-19; 1 Cor 12:27-31).

Qualities of Elders and Deacons. Several passages stress the quality of life desired in leaders. In each of these the role model is Jesus Christ. As his disciples and servants we seek to be like him. We are being transformed by the renewal of our minds, and renewed in our inner man after the image of our creator (Rom 12:1, 2; Col 3:10; 2 Cor 3:18).

Each of the following Scriptures, although representing only a few possibilities, speaks to the kind of person "the man of God" (1 Tim 6:11; 2 Tim 3:17) should be if he is to be God's leader.

John 13:3-15; James 3:1-12, 13-18; Matthew 5:1-12; Matthew 18:1-20; Galatians 5:26–6:10; Hebrews 13:7; Romans 12:9-21; 2 Peter 3:9; 2 Corinthians 2:14-17; 2 Corinthians 5:17-20; 1 Timothy 3:1-13; Titus 1:5-9; 1 Peter 5:1-4; Hebrews 13:7, Ephesians 4:11; 1 Timothy 5:17; Acts 20:28-35; John 19:1-18.

BIBLICAL EXAMPLES OF PARTICIPATIVE LEADERSHIP SELECTION IN ACTS

The process we have identified as a participative model of leader selection has its roots in the book of Acts. The Greek term from which our title Acts derives is *praxis*, meaning "activity, function, way of acting, business, or conducting affairs." It is to the book of Acts that one goes to see the apostolic church functioning or carrying on its "business." Several passages in Acts demonstrate the church, under the leadership of the apostles, following a participative model of church leadership. The occasions range from the selection of Matthias to take the place in the apostolic ministry vacated by Judas (Acts 1:15-26), through the selection of "special servants" (possibly deacons) in Acts 6 to minister to the widows of the church in Jerusalem, to the meeting of the whole Jerusalem church to discuss the problem created by certain Judaizers from Jerusalem who attempted to bind the law of Moses on Gentile Christians (Acts 15).

In the significant selection of an apostle to replace Judas in Acts 1:15-26, Peter provided the *initiative* in leadership by calling on the *120 believers* to become involved in the process. Peter set out the *parameters* of the decision (a witness to the ministry of Jesus and his resurrection), and led the group through the process which involved much *prayer* (Acts 1:24). The names of Barsabbas and Matthias were put forward by the *whole group*, who after much prayer and dependence on the working of the Holy Spirit in their lives, *cast lots* (voted) under the guidance of the Lord, and selected Matthias. In this participative process we see *creative initiative* (Peter), *involvement* of the *whole group* (the 120, Acts 1:15, 26), some *advanced preparation in parameter setting* (Acts 1:21), *faith* in the working of the Lord (Acts 1:24), *prayer* (Acts 1:24), and the *corporate participation* of the *whole group* by *voting* (casting lots, Acts 1:26).

A sensitive and delicate problem had arisen in the nascent life of the church in Jerusalem over care of the widows. The problem held both sociological and doctrinal implications. The Hellenists (Greek-speaking Jewish Christians who had adopted some Greek cultural characteristics) felt they were being overlooked in the daily food distribution. They felt the Hebrews (Aramaic-speaking Jewish Christians who resisted Greek and pagan cultural influences) were being favored in this distribution. The apostles, providing the *initiative*, set out the *parameters* for the solution by *instructing* the *whole congregation* to select from among themselves seven men with *specific spiritual qualities*, namely, being of good repute and full of the Holy Spirit, to assume the responsibility of caring for the equitable distribution of food. The congregation set seven such men before the apostles who first *prayed* for, then installed the seven men in this new ministry. This process pleased the *whole multitude* (the church, Acts 6:5), and led to remarkable growth (Acts 6:7).

We learn several significant lessons from this process. The apostles understood the nature of their personal ministry (prayer and preaching the word, Acts 6:4.) They did not presume on their apostolic authority, knowing that it would be much more effective to involve the whole congregation in this sensitive matter. We also learn that not all members of the church have the same ministry, yet all are important to the life and growth of the church.

Finally, Acts 15:1-35 provides perhaps the most striking example of participative leadership within the context of the whole Jerusalem church making a major decision with serious doctrinal implications for the whole apostolic mission. The occasion for this scenario was that certain men had come to Antioch from Judea demanding that Gentile converts adopt the "customs of Moses." After much debate, the church in Antioch "appointed" Paul, Barnabas, and others to go to Jerusalem to discuss the matter with the elders and apostles in that city. In Jerusalem Paul and Barnabas met with the elders and the apostles, together with the *whole church* (Acts 15:6, 12, 22), to discuss the matter. It is significant that the discussion did not take place in a private meeting of the elders and apostles. *The whole church was present in the assembly!* *Initiative* was provided by Peter (Acts 15:7), followed by James, who presented the *framework of a solution* (Acts 15:13-21). After *open discussion*, a letter was written to the church in Antioch proposing a solution to the problem.

In Antioch the *whole church* gathered together to hear the proposed solution (Acts 15:30). What is interesting about this scenario is that it involved a major theological and doctrinal problem which would have a significant consequence for the future of the gospel. Yet such a discussion with such profound implications for the whole church was not decided behind closed doors by a few authoritarian leaders and then communicated "down" through the ranks to the church. Certainly, the apostles had the authority to act in such a manner, but in their wisdom they knew that such a decision would not be widely accepted unless it had been openly discussed. The process obviously was not the most *efficient* resolution to the problem, but it certainly was the most *effective*. *Sometimes efficiency must concede to effectiveness!*

In the above three illustrations we see the church in Acts *practicing* its faith. We have watched as the church *conducted its business* under the guidance of apostolic men and the Holy Spirit. The model adopted, at least on these three significant occasions, was a *participative model. Participative leadership and leadership selection is a biblical model!*

The above principles of participative leadership selection have been with us for some time. On several occasions throughout the history of the Restoration Movement these sentiments have surfaced. Alexander Campbell articulated them in the *Millennial Harbinger* of 1835 by stating clearly that it is the duty of the whole church to select its leaders, not that of one or two men. J. W. McGarvey argued much the same in his work, *A Commentary: Acts of the Apostles* (1863) while commenting on Acts 6:2-4: "It seemed good to the Holy Spirit and the apostles that the whole 'multitude of the disciples' should take part in the selection of these officers." Likewise, in 1918, and in agreement with "Brother Campbell," T. W. Brents cited Acts 6:2-5 in support of his view that the whole church should be involved in the selection process *(Gospel Sermons*, pp. 353ff).

CONCLUSION

The point of this chapter has been to demonstrate that a participative model of leader selection is contemporary in sociological terms and biblical in theological concerns. We have emphasized that the congregation must be well prepared through biblical teaching and prayer for such a process, and that an environment in which the unity of the Spirit prevails is essential to the success and operation of the process. In the next chapter we will outline a participative process in more detail.

CHAPTER 19

SELECTING AND APPOINTING ELDERS AND DEACONS

—⁓—

A Participative Selection Process, Part 2

DEFINE THE PROCESS
The process of participative leader selection must be carefully defined before the process begins so that all may know the parameters of the selection process. This chapter will be devoted to defining this process. The details of the process should be clearly outlined, documented, and made public. Sound wisdom declares that a process that is allowed to "shift" once initiated will lead to dissatisfaction among the nominees for leadership and the congregation itself. Either the existing elders or preferably a committee appointed by the congregation should draft a model to be followed by the congregation in the selection process. Even when elders exist in a congregation, an impartial committee appointed by the congregation itself could act as an initial steering committee for the process. In participative selection it is always advisable to follow a "from below" (grass roots) process. The process, once initiated by the elders or steering committee (however defined), should be open to every member. Finally, the congregation should be given the opportunity to confirm its willingness to follow the process regardless of its outcome. If the elders or steering committee have judiciously led the congregation through an extended period of congregational study and preparation, few fears should exist as to the effectiveness and biblical nature of the process.

REAFFIRMATION OF EXISTING ELDERS
Discussion should be engaged as to whether the existing elders are to be reaffirmed in the process or whether only new elders are to be selected. It has been our experience

that on occasions when a participative process is being initiated for the first time it is wiser not to include the existing elders in a reaffirmation process. The process can be repeated after approximately two years once the congregation has become familiar with the process and the present elders then included in a reaffirmation process.

CONFIRM THE PROCESS

Once the process of selecting leaders has been defined and presented to the congregation, the process should be confirmed by the whole congregation in an open congregational meeting. One method for handling such a meeting and confirmation process is for the elders, or congregational steering committee, to appoint a chair who is capable of leading such a meeting to a conclusive decision in regard to the process. Neither the chair nor the steering committee should have any responsibility at this point other than to move the congregation to a decision. The chair of the meeting should provide adequate time in the meeting for open discussion. Finally, at an appropriate time, a vote should be taken among all the members either adopting the process as defined or adjusted, or rejecting the process. Once the process has been approved by the congregation it should be followed exactly as approved. Failure to follow the process as defined and approved will prejudice both the process and the credibility of those leaders selected by the process.

SELECT AN ADMINISTRATIVE COMMITTEE

The process of participative leader selection begins with the selection of an *administrative* committee. In some instances, elders have chosen to serve as this administrative committee. It has been our experience that it is not in the best interests of this congregational participative process for elders to serve on this committee, especially when the reason for the selection process arises out of problems within the eldership, or between the elders and deacons, or the congregation itself. When elders serve on this committee they are perceived by some members, even those members who have no hidden agenda, to prejudice the participative process. Even under circumstances where no problems exist, it is healthier for the nature of the process for elders not to serve on this administrative committee. *We should stress, however, that this committee will not serve in any capacity of making decisions for the congregation.* The role of this administrative committee will be to steer the congregation through the process of selecting the leaders. The sole role of the administrative committee is to direct the flow of the process in behalf of the congregation, and to move the process toward its ultimate conclusion, namely, the selection of leaders.

An administrative committee of approximately seven members is ideal for the execution of the process. This committee should be selected by nomination in an open meeting of the congregation called for this specific purpose. The congregation should be advised not to permit the process to become politicized, and to select a committee who have some administrative experience. Care should be taken to warn the congregation to be individually alert to some who would politicize the process and turn the process into a popularity contest. No prospective leaders should serve on this committee. The committee should select its own chair. This committee's tenure is limited to the duration of the selection process. Once the process of selecting leaders has been completed, the administrative committee is dissolved.

Prepare a Schedule or Timetable for the Process

The first task of the administrative committee, after selecting its own chair, is to prepare a schedule for the process. This process should be presented to the congregation in a brief meeting, possibly after a worship service, for congregational approval. The approved schedule should be printed and made available to the congregation.

Refine the Process

At this stage of the process, the committee should provide some occasion for the process and schedule to be refined. Furthermore, some additional decisions that present themselves for consideration at this stage of the process could include the congregation setting the desired number of leaders to be selected, deciding whether existing leaders should be reaffirmed in the process (it is our opinion that this should not be the choice in situations where congregations are adopting the process for the first time), setting percentages or numbers of nominations that nominees should receive before being included in the process, how the process of eventual voting will be conducted, and the level of percentages necessary for final affirmation. Each of these factors will be discussed in greater detail below, but the decisions relating to these could be determined at this stage.

Approve the Process

Before the process is finally set in motion the refined process should be brought back to the congregation for final approval. The ultimate success and dynamic of the participative process is *absolute openness* to the congregation, and the full cooperation of the whole congregation. Every effort should be made to ensure that every member of the congregation is encouraged and enabled to participate. We should note that the process will involve some areas of confidentiality which must be respected, but in regard to the process itself, every effort must be made to maintain openness to congregational involvement. Some provision should be made for members to have "absentee" participation should they be unavoidably absent on any appointed occasion of congregational involvement. It is of utmost importance that all members are well informed as to the process and that all have occasion to participate.

The final congregational approval could be obtained by a simple majority decision on a show of hands. If the process has become so politicized that a simple majority show of hands is unsuitable, then the congregation manifests problems of a nature far greater than can be solved by the selection of leaders by any process. If this is the case, the congregation is displaying profound spiritual problems which demand considerable biblical teaching and biblical conflict management.

We have stressed above that the process of participative leader selection is one that takes considerable time and effort. It is not the most *efficient* process, but one should prize *effectiveness* over *efficiency* in matters that relate to congregational relationships and leadership.

NOMINATE POTENTIAL LEADERS

The administrative committee, having called a congregational meeting for this specific purpose, leads the congregation through the process of nominating potential leaders. Ample lead time should be given between calling the meeting and the date for the meeting. The congregation should be reminded of the spiritual qualities required in such leaders. The called meeting should be fully open to all baptized members of the congregation.

An excellent time for such a meeting may be immediately following the morning worship service. Visitors may be invited to remain through the process should they be interested. All members should be encouraged to remain and participate. In cases where a congregation holds multiple worship services, special arrangements should be made to accommodate such, but we have found some arrangement around the Sunday morning assembly to be the most effective for such meetings. With adequate notification, the Sunday evening service may be used, but Sunday evening attendance being lower than Sunday morning tends to limit the effectiveness of the process.

Nomination forms should be prepared for the occasion. These forms should include some comment as to the spiritual qualities necessary for the specific ministry, and should *make provision for the person responding to sign the nomination. The signature on the nominating form tends to add an element of seriousness to the process, and facilitates feedback to those making the nomination.* On every occasion we have found that someone nominated chooses not to be considered in the process. Feedback to the person making the nomination ensures that no one feels that the process has been manipulated so as to eliminate any nominee. In fact, feedback at every stage of the process to both the nominee and those participating in the process is absolutely essential to the effective dynamic of the process.

Members should be reminded not to permit the process to become politicized, and to make no attempt to prejudice the process.

The administrative committee will have already determined the number of nominations necessary for a nominee to be carried forward in the process. This decision will have been determined through congregational participation at a previous stage in the process and will be influenced by the size of the congregation. All nominees should be informed of the status of their nomination, and those having reached the required level for nomination should be interviewed as to their desire to be carried forward through the process. The results of this stage of the process should be communicated to the congregation before the next stage of the process is begun.

If the existing elders or deacons are to be re affirmed in the process, they become automatic nominees at this point unless they choose to step down from their specific ministry.

INTROSPECTIVE QUESTIONNAIRE

Every nominee should be required to complete an introspective questionnaire, the design of which is twofold. *First,* the questionnaire will enable nominees to engage in an introspective examination of themselves as suitable persons for such a ministry. *Second,* the completed questionnaires serve to inform the congregation of those personal and spiritual qualities the nominees have identified as their strengths and weaknesses. The process of acquainting the congregation with nominees that they may not know very well enables the congregation to engage in the process better informed than otherwise.

Nominees should know in advance of the nomination stage that they will be required to complete an extensive personal introspective reflection which will be made public to all members of the congregation who desire to be so informed. Members of the congregation may read as many, or all, of the questionnaires as they desire. Copies of the completed questionnaires may be photocopied and made available to the congregation through the church library, or some other means. The questionnaire should be developed by the administrative committee in such a manner as to be meaningful to the ministry involved and the nature and needs of the congregation. The questionnaire should explore biblical, spiritual, emotional, and personal family matters.

BIBLICAL EVALUATION OF THE NOMINEES BY THE CONGREGATION

Following the completion of the introspective questionnaires, and after adequate time for reflection on these, members of the congregation must be given an opportunity to express their opinion regarding the *biblical* suitability of each nominee for the ministry to which they have been nominated. We stress here that this examination of the nominees is solely along legitimate *biblical* lines and not personal likes or dislikes.

The congregation should be informed that this phase of the process pursues only *biblical* objections. *Personal* concerns or objections should be held until the final congregational selection process when a final decision will be made by congregational vote expressing confidence in or disapproval of the nominees. This biblical examination phase is not the "I don't think he will be a good leader" kind of consideration or the "I don't like him" phase. That expression of lack of personal confidence should be reserved for the final selection process taken by congregational vote for that very purpose.

This biblical examination should be expressed via a printed form provided for this purpose. *The response should be in written form and signed by the person making the objection or examination.* Having the examination in writing and signed ensures that no one takes indiscriminate "pot shots" at the nominees without due process.

The congregation should be admonished as to the serious and sensitive nature of this step in the process. Once more, the congregation should be warned against politicizing the process. Persons making the objections should be instructed to keep their objections confidential and not to discuss them with any other persons. The congregation must be assured that their objections will be kept in the strictest confidence, and that the nominees will not be informed of the names of the persons making the objections without the objector's prior permission. The persons making the objections must be informed that the administrative committee may discuss the objection with the nominee and with the person making the objection (both in private), and that the existing elders may be brought into the process should the occasion or objection be serious enough to warrant this.

It is imperative that the members of the administrative committee be sworn to honor confidentiality in the short- and long-term future. They should be admonished not to discuss any spiritual and confidential objections with anyone other than the committee, the nominee, the objector, and the elders should the case demand such. They should not discuss such matters under any circumstances with their spouses or family.

The congregation must be assured of the complete confidentiality of the objections as defined above.

If *legitimate biblical* objections are raised as to the suitability of the nominee, these should be discussed immediately and confidentially with the nominee, maintaining the confidentiality of the objector. If the objection, however, comes from only one objector, the objection should be judged on that basis. This fact should be communicated with the objector. However, if the objection is strong enough or serious enough, it should be explored in greater detail. If the objection comes from more than one objector, then the matter should be evaluated and followed up in the appropriate manner. Should doubt arise as to the seriousness of the objection, the existing elders may be brought into the process at this point. The administrative committee should be mature enough to make wise decisions in such cases. We must stress here that if the objection is not considered to be based on a biblical principle or if it is considered to be poorly founded, this should be communicated to the objector. We stress once more that as much feedback as possible is essential to the success of the process.

Every objection and situation should be dealt with on its own merits. There are no easy solutions to objections. The administrative committee should be prepared to deal with such objections in a mature, balanced manner, assigning appropriate reaction and response to each objection.

It has been our experience that most persons against whom substantial objections are raised will voluntarily remove their name from the list of nominees. Whenever a name is removed from the list of nominees for whatever reason, the person having made the original nomination should be informed of this in the appropriate confidential manner.

In some cases, the nominee may refuse to accept the objection as being valid. When this occurs, the administrative committee should return to the objector for more information. In such occasions it has been our experience that the objector withdraws the objection. When, or if, this does not take place, the objection must be brought once more to the nominee's attention with the observation that the objector feels strongly enough about the situation to emphasize once more the seriousness of the objection. This dialogue may prolong the process, but must take place until resolution to the objection is finalized. The objection may be brought to the elders for examination. On occasion it may be necessary to inform the nominee that the objection is serious enough that additional information is necessary and that the objection must be made public in order to be fully explored. When such drastic steps are taken, either the objector or the nominee or both will withdraw from the process.

The nominees should also be encouraged to maintain the confidentiality of the process in order to prevent personality conflicts in the congregation from getting out of hand and thus negating the positive nature of the process.

It has been our experience that such a biblical objection process, properly handled in a biblical and spiritual manner, can be a growing and maturing experience for both the objector and the nominee.

Once the objection phase is completed, the administrative committee should present to the congregation, in writing, a list of those nominees considered by the congregation to be biblically qualified to serve as leaders.

GUIDED COST COUNTING

It is advisable at this stage of the process to lead the nominees through an analysis of the emotional and spiritual pressures and stresses they will experience as the process nears the final stages of selection. All of the nominees will at this stage have been approved as nominees biblically qualified for the leadership role under consideration. This does not mean, however, that they will be recognized by the congregation as persons suitably qualified by experience, personality, or nature to be leaders. This final process of congregational selection still lies ahead and can be the most traumatic stage of the process for the nominees.

Nominees must face the distinct possibility of rejection. At the time of nomination they may be convinced they can handle this traumatic experience, and this may well be the case. However, the families and friends of the nominees may not be as well prepared as the nominees themselves to handle rejection. It has been our experience, however, that nominees overestimate their ability to work through the trauma of being rebuffed by those whom they thought respected and loved them. An added ingredient is present with heightened emphasis if existing elders are being included in the process for reaffirmation.

A special time of self-evaluation and cost counting is essential at this stage of the selection process to enable the nominees to work through these emotions in advance of the final selection, and if possible, close family should be included in this advance therapy. Where possible, an experienced Christian counselor should be invited to conduct these group therapy sessions. Much loving care should be devoted at this point in order to "redeem" hurt feelings and egos in advance of the rejection.

In addition to the proactive concern for those who may not be selected, those who are selected should be instructed in regard to the reality of the time and energy investment demanded by the particular ministry being sought. Devotional time, prayer, personal reflection, meditation, and group sharing should become a vital and integral aspect of this stage of the process of elder and deacon selection.

Some effort in Bible class lessons and sermons should be devoted to the spiritual and emotional price paid by everyone in the congregation throughout the process of participative leader selection. This stage of the process in particular is most deserving of such effort.

CONGREGATIONAL APPROVAL

The process of participative leadership selection involves all members of the congregation participating at every stage of the process. The final vote representing the willingness of the congregation to accept certain persons as leaders is perhaps the most crucial and sensitive stage of the process. By this time the congregation will have determined that the remaining nominees are biblically qualified or, to be more precise, manifest those biblical qualities essential for congregational leadership. The final stage is for the congregation to express willingness to appoint such persons as leaders in the congregation. Prior to the final vote the congregation must set the percentage standard for approval in the voting. This should be clearly stated and known by everyone in the congregation, especially the nominees. Experience over the years has determined that a percentage approval for elders runs between 70 and 75 percent.

VOTING

We have already observed from several passages in Acts (1, 6, and 15) that it was the *practice* of the early church to involve the whole congregation in the process of congregational decision making, especially in the case of leader selection (Acts 1 and 6) and a major doctrinal decision (Acts 15). This process involved the whole group or congregation and eventually some form of voting in which the members expressed their opinion.

There will always be those who are sensitive to the process of voting in matters of church governance. Reformers during the formative years of the Restoration Movement among Churches of Christ struggled as they searched for a biblical pattern of church polity in opposition to Episcopalian and Catholic models in which bishops ruled over large dioceses. As early as 1835 Alexander Campbell discussed this concern at length in his journal, *Millennial Harbinger*. About fifty years later, in 1891, the topic was still of such concern to some that T. W. Brents devoted a full chapter to it in his work *Gospel Sermons*. This chapter was the outgrowth of several revisions of earlier articles by Brents addressing church organization. Brents drew heavily from Campbell's earlier work. The flow of thought in these writings is of particular interest to leaders of Churches of Christ today as they lead in the context of the *New Realities* of the century that lies ahead, in particular the era of the *Boomers'* and *Busters'* reaction to hierarchy and institutions. Since many do not have access to this interesting work of Brents and Campbell, and at the expense of some space, we include excerpts of these two works at this point, with some relevant comment.

Brents begins his chapter by including a lengthy article by Campbell[167]:

—◄◄◇►►—

ORGANIZATION OF A CHURCH—BY A. CAMPBELL

When a society of disciples agree thus to walk as Christians under the New Testament...They need bishops and deacons...

It is disorderly, in the fullest sense of the word, for any person to assume any thing in an organized community. *The voice of the church must be directly heard before any person can be acceptably heard by it...*

ORDINATION OF BISHOPS

(1) *What is ordination* as respects the Christian Church?

It is the solemn election and appointment of persons to the oversight and service of a Christian community. To ordain is to appoint; and all appointments, from that of the successor to Judas as a witness of the resurrection, from an apostle to the messenger of a church, or an almoner, was in the beginning *by an election of the whole community.*

...The election or choice of the community, guided in that choice by the Living Oracles (Campbell's translation of the New Testament), is the essential consideration without which all forms would be unavailing. *Vox populi, vox Dei,* or in English, "the voice of the people" is in this case "the voice of God," calling the persons elect to the work of the Lord.

CONGREGATION HERSELF ELECTS AND ORDAINS ALL HER OFFICERS

No person can take any part in these forms of consecration or separation to the work of the Lord, but only as far as they are regarded as members of the congregation...

...*Who may, or who ought to lay hands on bishops, or deacons, or messengers elect?* I answer, without dubiety, and in a few words, the whole community, or such elders of the community as may be approved on behalf of the congregation...

The jurisdiction of such bishops is always circumscribed by the congregation which ordained them. A single church is the largest diocese known in the New Testament. Neither does his election and ordination give him an indelible character, nor a perpetual office. Should he leave the church, which, under the direction of the Holy Spirit, created him, and become a member of another church, he enters it as a private member, and so continues until that church elect and ordain him, should they call for his services. The bishops and deacons of the church in Philippi were the bishops and deacons of the church in Philippi, and no other church; and so of Ephesus, Antioch, Rome, and Jerusalem.

At this point Brents resumes his own comments under the heading:

IN THE PRESENTATION OF OUR VIEWS

...I then ask, who shall judge of, and decide upon the qualifications of the party who shall undertake the work? Not every one for himself, surely;

for, as Brother Campbell has well remarked, the one least qualified will likely be the first to volunteer his services. Do you say the *church* shall make the selection? So do I. Then *what shall we call these parties thus selected* to take the oversight of the flock...*bishops* and *deacons...elders.*

How Shall Bishops and Deacons Be Selected?

Or, rather, how shall material be selected of which to make bishops and deacons? Or, to be more plain, *who* shall make the selection? And *how shall they do it?*

As they are to serve the *congregation*...they must be selected by the congregation in the interest of which they are to labor;...

When the seven deacons were to be selected in Jerusalem, 'the twelve called the multitude of the disciples unto them, and said,...look ye out among you seven men of honest report....Here we learn that the apostles addressed the *multitude of the disciples,* and told *them* to look out persons, and the saying pleased *the whole multitude* and *they elected the parties* to be appointed...the whole multitude made the selection; or, if you please, *elected* the parties, for elect simply means to choose or select.

...We see it did obtain in the section of Matthias to succeed Judas in the apostleship; then if it obtained in these cases of which we have record, why shall we not concede that it obtained in all cases where the procedure is not recorded?

But we may be asked if Titus did not select the elders ordained in Crete? We suppose not. He was commanded to ordain them, but it is not recorded that he selected them, or that he was commanded to do so.

How Was the Will of the Congregation Expressed?

Paul speaks of a brother whose praise was in all the churches, "who was also chosen of the churches to travel with us" (2 Cor. viii: 19). Here was a *choice* or *election* of a person by the churches; and while there is nothing in the English words *choose* and *chosen* to indicate the *manner* of choosing, yet in the Greek word here rendered *chosen* there may be light on this point. Chosen is here a translation of *cheirotonetheis,* which is a form of *cheirotoneo,* which Young defines, "to extend the hand (in voting)." [We note that Bauer, Arndt, Gingrich in the 1957 edition of *A Greek-English Lexicon of the New Testament* render the same word *"choose, elect by raising hands",* IAF]. While it is possible that this does not exhaust the meaning of this word, we can see no other reason for its employment here than to express the manner of electing the person chosen. Taking this as true, it is entirely scriptural for the members of the congregation to express their choice *in matters of character* by voting with the hand.

We are fully aware of the prejudices existing in the mind of good brethren against voting in the congregation, yet we know no better way of getting at the will of the congregation in many cases which may come before it, than to allow the members to express their choice by vote....We know of no congregation which does not practice voting in some form. Suppose we say, in the congregation, that "if there is no objection by any one, *thus* and *so* will be done." We pause for objection—none is made, and the thing is done; did not the congregation, by its silence, vote for the thing done, just as clearly as if the question had been put before it in any other form, and voted upon it in any other way? Most assuredly it did; and yet this is the general practice of those who object to voting!

Brother Campbell has given us some excellent thoughts in his Extra to the *Harbinger* for 1835, from which, by the reader's indulgence, we will reproduce an extract...

A. Campbell on Voting in the Church

Some Christians are opposed to voting in the church. They only vote against voting! They will give their *voice*, but say they will not *vote*. Now upon a little reflection, it may, perhaps, appear to them that to vote and to give their voice, is identically one and the same thing. To express their mind or their wish on any question, is certainly to vote—whatever form may be chosen, whether standing up, stretching forth the hand, or simply saying yes or no, aye or nay.

Wherever there is an election, or choice of persons, or measures, there must be voting, or casting of a lot...

We need not labor to show that Christians under the very eye, and with the approbation of the apostles, voted; for the apostles commanded them to vote...

But in all matters not of faith, piety, or morality; in all matters of expediency, and sometimes in questions of fact pertaining to cases of discipline, there is no other way of deciding but by vote of the brotherhood.

Procedure for "Yes," "No," and "I Don't Know" Votes

The participative model for finally selecting the leaders to be "ordained" or appointed by the congregation involves establishing a system for determining the congregation's will in the matter to be decided. It has been our experience that a written and signed ballot is the most effective method of reaching such decisions.

There are three categories of congregational opinion that relate specifically to the process: A "YES" vote, signifying approval; a "NO" vote, signifying disapproval; and an "I DON'T KNOW" vote, signifying that the person voting does not know the person well enough to have formed an opinion. There will always be the tendency of some to want to vote "I DON'T KNOW" rather than "NO." To some, this provides a way out of voting against a nominee. The congregation should be carefully instructed in regard to the use of the "I DON'T KNOW" vote.

The "I DON'T KNOW" vote should be reserved for those who, being new to the congregation, legitimately do not know the person well enough to form an opinion. Members of reasonable standing will have had time to form an opinion through personal contact and the availability of the introspective questionnaires provided during the process for this very purpose. Furthermore, members should have been encouraged during the process to get to know the nominees through personal contact with them.

At a certain point, the "I DON'T KNOW" votes can, and should become a "NO" vote. If enough members in the congregation legitimately feel that the nominee is not well known, this becomes tantamount to the nominee not being able to effectively serve that congregation as a shepherd or deacon. The congregation, therefore, under the guidance of the administrative committee, should set a limit to the number of "I DON'T KNOW" votes that would disqualify the nominee. This decision should be made *before* the final vote is taken.

Two possibilities are open for determining this limit. The nominees themselves could set the limit or the congregation could do so. Either procedures has been found to be effective following meaningful instruction in regard to the nature and impact of the limit. The limit to "I DON'T KNOW" should be set as a percentage of the votes returned by the congregation. If, say, the limit is set at 25 percent of the final vote, and a nominee receives 26 percent "I DON'T KNOW" votes, this would consequently disqualify that nominee from being an elder or deacon. Both the nominees and the congregation *must be carefully instructed* on the nature and use of the "I DON'T KNOW" vote standard.

Setting such a limit, once the nature of the limit has been carefully described to the nominees and the congregation, discourages some from taking the easy path out of voting "NO" to a nominee. It is imperative, however, that the congregation be well informed as to the impact of the "I DON'T KNOW" vote. An "I DON'T KNOW" vote, in essence, can become a "NO" vote. We have found that a 25 percent limit to the "I

DON'T KNOW" votes is a reasonable and effective limit for a congregation of approximately 300–500 members. For congregations larger than 500 membership, a percentage higher than 25 percent may be more appropriate. Each congregation, however, should determine for itself the limit with which it feels comfortable.

One final standard must be set before the critical vote affirming or denying a nominee as an elder or deacon. The congregation must determine what percentage of the final vote is necessary for the nominee to be affirmed as an elder or deacon. We caution congregations adopting a participative model of leader selection for the first time not to set the standard too high. It has been our experience that a 75 percent for elders and a 65 percent for deacons are reasonable initial standards. Once the congregation has become familiar with the participative model, these standards may be raised in proportion to the comfort level of the congregation, or its "maturity" in working with this model.

It is a good practice to have the nominees verbally express willingness to abide by the standards set by the congregation, and to admit to one another and to the administrative committee that should they not be affirmed by the percentage chosen they would automatically, and without contesting the standard, remove their names from the list. Some congregations have taken this step so seriously as to ask the nominees to make this statement before the whole congregation. The means of such expression has a positive effect on the whole congregation and stresses once more the serious nature of the process.

We stress again that the participative procedure of leadership selection is not by any measure a *time-efficient* one, but when handled well, accompanied by careful instruction, biblical study, and prayer, it can become an *effective* maturing experience for the congregation.

Care should be given, however, not to permit the process to take longer than necessary, otherwise it becomes tiring to the congregation. Congregations can suffer from "burn out" as a result of the process. After the initial instruction and decision to adopt a participative model of leader selection, it has been our experience that a congregation should not take longer than two months before bringing the process to the final selection by vote.

FINAL CONGREGATIONAL SELECTION

Once the percentage standards for the approval/denial selection process have been determined and agreed upon, preparation for the selection through congregational vote remains as the final step to affirmation or denial. Considerable time for prayer, both private and congregational, should be devoted to this final stage of the process. Furthermore, we cannot overstress the importance of admonishing the congregation not to politicize the process, thereby prejudicing the integrity of a truly participative model. Extreme care should be taken not to permit this stage to degenerate into a popularity contest. No congregational campaigning whatsoever should be tolerated. The congregation should be encouraged to be on the alert for any members who may campaign for a nominee and to gently warn the persons involved against such practice.

It is necessary to have the ballot forms signed so the administrative committee can check the ballots against the church roll and ensure that only one ballot is returned per member. The persons voting should be assured that their vote will be held in strict confidence in order to ensure that the process is not prejudiced by the voters' sensitivity in the process. All ballot forms should be destroyed immediately after the final count is affirmed.

INDUCTION OF THE SELECTED LEADERS

We have found it extremely important to formalize the process of inducting elders and deacons into their ministry. Some form of ordination or appointment helps solemnize the occasion and the ministry to which the leaders are being appointed. This can be more or less formal as meets the needs of the congregation. A special time of prayer, Scripture reading, and "laying on of hands" as a sign of ministry identification, will add a serious note to the occasion. Meaningful comments regarding stewardship, the grace of the Lord working in the lives of the leaders, and ministry as a gift of God's grace are appropriate. Such a formal identification of leaders with ministry is biblical (1 Tim 4:14, 5:22).

LEADER RETREAT

Meaningful retreats for elders and deacons, both individually and combined, should be planned. During these retreats, leaders can discuss the style of leadership they will adopt, how they plan to work together and make whatever decisions fall within their ministry, and similar matters. Considerable time for prayer and Scripture reading confirms the leaders in their relationship to the Lord and their responsibility to the congregation.

Some form of group dynamic exercise should be employed as a beginning step toward team building. We have found it effective to employ someone skilled in group dynamics and team building to work with the leaders on such retreats. It is useful to have elders affirm that, although they are shepherds, they are also sheep who need pastoring by the remainder of the elders. It is also a healthy procedure to have elders repeat that, should they ever be asked by the remaining elders or the congregation to step down from their ministry, they will do so without argument.

AFFIRMING THOSE NOT SELECTED

It is possible in this process that some will not be chosen by the congregation. Although possessing those spiritual qualities desired in leaders or deacons, some may not be perceived by the congregation as leaders. Such rejection can be hurtful to those not selected, and especially hurtful to their families. Much care should be given, prior to the final voting and subsequent to the voting, to preparing nominees for and helping them through such rejection. The nominees rejected should be affirmed by the new leaders and the congregation, and be surrounded and nurtured by loving support.

WRAP UP

The final responsibility of the administrative committee is first to destroy any confidential materials they may have in their possession. The administrative committee should be reminded of their initial charge to deal throughout the process with extreme confidentiality.

It is a good practice to request the administrative committee to prepare a detailed report of the process for the congregation's future examination, refinement, and adaptation. Once this is done, the administrative committee disbands.

PART FOUR

DEVELOPING LEADERS
IN THE CHURCH

CHAPTER 20

DEVELOPING LEADERS IN THE CONGREGATION

———

Thus far in the first three parts of this book we have focused attention on leadership style in general, in the New Testament, and in the contemporary local congregation. In this section we will pay attention to developing leaders in the local congregation, a dynamic that is too often overlooked, taken for granted, or assumed to take place by osmosis.

We will propose three models of leadership training that have proven effective in the process of developing leaders at the congregational level:

Formal Training. Formal training takes place in formal institutions of learning such as colleges, universities, and similar institutions. Normally this form of training in the congregation is left to the minister or some specialist in ministry as they pursue advanced education in ministry. The ongoing benefit provided by those receiving formal training in the university context is that they combine their academic experience with practical ministry experience and produce learning material such as textbooks and leadership manuals. Examples of this combination of academic and ministry experience might be this textbook, and the one by Lynn Anderson, *They Smell Like Sheep*.

Informal Training. Informal training is that which is experienced at the congregational or ministry group level in seminars on leadership training, leadership development classes in the congregation, or ministry group training sessions. In most instances informal training in congregational seminars should draw on the experience of those who have received formal training and have considerable experience in leadership instruction. In some instances informal training may be through the use of textbooks and leadership manuals written by those involved in formal training in a university or college or experienced in leadership development.

Non-Formal Training. Non-formal training is hands-on, participative, simulated and mentored training. Non-formal training is normally "in-house" training in settings where someone (or a group) is being mentored by an existing practitioner in the specific ministry.

Each training model has a rightful place in leadership development. The goal is to maximize leadership development by drawing on the strengths of each of these models. Notice there is a natural progression in the threefold model of instruction, from formal training, through informal training to non-formal training. Although non-formal training in and of itself is an excellent vehicle for leadership development, such hands-on training can be exponentially increased if built on sound leadership principles. Non-formal training is enhanced by congregational seminars where all are made aware of where the ministry leadership is going and what parameters are relevant for that congregation or group. The remainder of this chapter will be devoted to discussing the salient values of each of the training models presented above.

FORMAL TRAINING

As mentioned, formal training is that which normally takes place in universities, colleges, and similar institutions which teach specialist leadership development courses. Because of the very nature of this model, set in "off-campus" institutional settings, many are not able to benefit personally or directly from such instruction. The benefit of the formal instruction provided in institutional settings is enhanced by research materials and the resources provided by cultural and religious pollsters such as Harris Interactive, Inc., and The George Barna Group. The cutting edge information provided by many of these institutions and settings is normally handed down to popular use via the production of specialized video instruction, Internet instruction, and various journal and textbook publications. In addition, it is often in such institutions and seminaries that ministers and church leaders receive specialized instruction. Standing alone, formal instruction is not the most effective form of learning, especially in regard to congregational leadership development. The real value of this form of instruction lies in the cutting edge materials and research data provided for dissemination by practitioners in localized settings.

INFORMAL TRAINING

Informal training is the next step in the progression of leadership development. Informal training introduces a group to the resources provided by formal training through the vehicle of written resources and specialists in leadership instruction. In the church setting informal training can be experienced in local congregational seminars, regional seminars, and church-related university and college lectureships and workshops.

Informal seminars may be related to church eldership development where the seminar is focused purely on the work of elders, bishops, and shepherds, or they may be dedicated to the development of specially dedicated and appointed ministry group leaders such as deacons. In some cases congregational leadership seminars may be broader and more global in their view of congregational leadership development.

In view of the tendency of some traditional leadership biases to negate leadership growth, it is often advisable to bring in outsider specialists who are not inhibited by congregational history and traditions, and who are able to present challenging new concepts of leadership that can be dialogued and adapted by the local congregation within the parameters of the local congregation's values. Such issues as congregational values and parameters will be discussed later in this chapter.

INFORMAL LEADERSHIP SEMINAR CURRICULUM

Congregational leadership seminars leading up to leadership development should provide some of the more prominent leadership principles and values. This is necessary in view of the fact that new leaders may not be familiar with fundamental leadership principles. Topics to address and include are Leadership versus Management, What Leadership is Not, What Leadership Is, Leadership and Authority, The Descriptive Nature of Leadership Terms such as Elder, Bishop, Shepherd, Deacon, and Decision Making should be reviewed. (Each of these topics is discussed in some detail in Part Two of this book.) Potential leaders must understand clearly the values and parameters of the congregation regarding leadership. Failure to understand these principles will inevitably lead to frustration and interpersonal friction within the congregation and ministry group.

NON-FORMAL TRAINING

Non-formal training involves hands-on experience in ministry. A common term encountered in non-formal training is mentoring. Mentoring is the process of a teacher or leader working "on the job" with learners. The strength of mentoring is the individual expertise and involvement by leader example. One advantage of non-formal mentoring is that it provides immediate feedback in a non-threatening manner. Non-formal training is proactive leadership preparation in the sense that new leaders are gently and gradually introduced to the responsibility of ministry leadership.

Non-formal training should build on informal training sessions but has the advantage of contextualizing the informal seminar learning experience. In non-formal settings the leader or teacher may ask the learner how he or she would apply what has been learned to a specific ministry or problem, giving advice as necessary.

In non-formal training the learner must understand clearly the parameters and values to be adopted in a particular ministry.

Non-formal training can take place in real live settings of ministry, or in simulation situations and case studies.

Case studies are specially prepared problem-oriented narratives in which the learner is introduced to the specific issue under guided study settings. A problem is set and the group is asked how they would address the problem. Parameters and concerns are set and explained. Case studies may be based on real instances of ministry or may be designed to address certain vital issues to ministry. A movie such as *Dead Poet's Society* could provide the case study for the group to critique leadership style.

Simulation refers to live situations or acts (games) in which the group or developing leader is required to act out certain responsibilities of leadership. In this kind of learning experience the learner is required to simulate the leadership process under the guidance of the teacher or leader. Alternate suggestions can be made by the leader as to how a situation could be addressed. In simulation the group is also involved in reflecting on the leadership style played out by their colleagues.

SMALL GROUPS AS AN IDEAL SETTING FOR NON-FORMAL LEADERSHIP DEVELOPMENT

Many congregations have restructured their Sunday evening worship services into small group "house church" experiences. Since there is extensive research and written materials available discussing the dynamic of small groups, it will not be my purpose to engage in a detailed discussion on small groups other than to mention them as an ideal laboratory for leadership development. Small group leaders are encouraged to persuade members of their group to participate actively in the group discussion and dynamic of the group. In this dynamic, latent leaders can be surfaced and given opportunity to lead the group. The parameters of the group dynamic are already established and easy to emulate. The self-confidence of the individuals in the small group has already been developed. In the nonthreatening environment of friends, individuals are encouraged to "try their wings and fly."

A variety of other small groups are available in most congregations. Bible classes, youth groups, ladies' classes, men's classes, ladies' breakfasts and men's breakfasts, and various ministry groups are small group experiences that can be used for leadership development. Every opportunity should be taken to maximize the small groups already in existence in congregations.

Using the Bible Class to Develop Bible Class Teachers. The Story of Dennis is a wonderful example of using the Bible class to develop leaders and Bible class teachers. This is a real story, only the name has been changed. Dennis was a relatively new member of our congregation and adult Sunday morning Bible class. He had limited experience in Bible class teaching but was sincere about his faith and becoming an effective servant leader. I am the regular Sunday morning auditorium Bible class teacher, but on several occasions I have to be away due to my work with the Center for Church Resources. I asked Dennis if he would teach my class for me. He was willing but reticent because he had no classroom teaching experience and doubted his ability. I had spent some time with him on non-formal occasions and had confidence in his Bible knowledge and felt he could handle the class. In addition, since Dennis is a regular member of the class he had some idea of how I teach and what I am looking for in the class.

I suggested that I could write a lesson outline which he could follow with the class. I suggested that I could include some discussion questions and possible answers for him to use. He was willing to try. The class went reasonably well. As soon as I returned I tactfully asked several members how the class had gone. They were complimentary of Dennis's effort. I then met with Dennis, mentioned that several in the class had been complimentary regarding his teaching, which set him at ease. I asked him how the class went. He felt he had done a reasonable job.

We repeated this procedure on several occasions. Each time Dennis felt more at ease with the class. Eventually I suggested to Dennis that I should give him only a broad outline for the class material and he could fill in what he felt needed to be stressed. This would give him the opportunity to shape the class in a style with which he would be comfortable. We repeated this on several occasions. Eventually I asked Dennis to teach the class, giving him only the topic for the class. Now when I am away I merely ask Dennis to teach the class and leave the topic to his discretion within the general topic of the class. On occasion I ask Dennis to teach the class and select any topic he feels is suitable. I ask him to let me know in advance what he is planning to teach.

Notice in this teacher-mentoring model of leadership or Bible class teaching we have a non-formal learning style in which case studies (lesson outline) and mentoring are combined. Positive feedback and accountability are immediate in the process.

STRATEGIC PRIORITY AND PLANNING IN LEADERSHIP DEVELOPMENT

As we learned in Part Two of this book, leading involves providing vision and goals for people, leading them beyond horizons which before were distant but now have become reality, setting values and parameters, and managing accountability. Clear vision, however, involves strategic thinking and planning. Visionary leadership development requires new leaders to think strategically and develop new ideas within predetermined parameters. Visionary leaders must be able to think ahead, "outside the box," and formulate new policy and strategy. This process is defined as *strategic thinking* or establishing *strategic priority*.

In establishing strategic priority several salient considerations come to mind. First, we should remember that leadership involves constructive and effective change. Leadership means that we are not simply satisfied with the status quo. However, change and resistance to change should be carefully and sensitively managed. Second, we should recognize that we learn from prior experiences. We can learn what worked and what did not work, and why that was the case. But we should not be haunted by failure or be overconfident from previous success since situations change steadily and what worked before may not work again. Third, we should be intentional in our strategic thinking. We need to work on strategic thinking well in advance of the need. Fourth, we need to be able to work through traditional reluctance to change and attempt new initiatives. Traditional excuses such as, "We have tried that before and it did not work!" or "This is too new for us!" or "We have no potential leaders!" or "Leaders are born, not made!" are common and need to be dealt with sensitively yet firmly.

LEADERSHIP DEVELOPMENT AS A SPECIFIC GOAL OR STRATEGY

When applying strategic thinking to leadership development we should have specific goals in mind. Too often congregations and leaders fall into the pitfall of leaving leadership development to crisis times rather than conducting a constant process of leadership development or "equipping the saints for the work of ministry," which is a primary ministry of ministers and elders (Eph 4:12).

Leadership development should involve everyone in the congregation, "from the cradle to the grave." Spiritual development within the congregation should be a primary and ongoing function of the ministers, elders, and ministry group leaders. Spiritual development should include challenging the members to be actively involved in the life and ministry of the congregation, and this should include leadership development and formation. The leadership of the congregation should set as a high priority involving every family and every member in some form of congregational ministry.

Several factors should feature prominently in developing leaders within the congregation. Active involvement of young people in the communion service, in song leading, in leading prayers, in Bible reading, all prepare them for leadership roles in later life. In developing future leaders, elders should be proactive in inculcating in prospective leaders those goals and ingredients for becoming deacons, special ministry leaders, and elders.

SOME PRACTICAL OBSERVATIONS

The following are observations from a real-life congregation that took leadership development seriously.

First, they applied the principle of teach–practice–apply seriously. They adopted the principles of formal instruction, informal instruction, and non-formal instruction, providing good reading material to leaders, inviting experienced instructors to conduct learning seminars (both biblical and methodological seminars), and setting up mentoring situations within specific ministries such as missions and youth ministry.

Second, they made some strategic demographic observations. They attempted to ascertain where the greatest need in their congregation lay. They asked simple questions such as, "Where is the best place to begin?" On this occasion they determined that the greatest need was in their youth ministry and missions programs. They then strategically decided to get the families of their youth more involved in the youth program. They then worked on a strategic "job description" defining the goals and nature of their youth ministry program. When this had been achieved they involved the parents and youth in the process of hiring a youth minister. Working with the elders they set up an organizational outline of who would be involved in specific tasks, who would be the primary leaders in the ministry (in this case, it was not to be the youth minister), who would receive reports from the various aspects of the youth ministry program, and who would make such reports to the elders and the congregation. Working with the elders and ministers, they invited experienced youth ministry leaders to conduct seminars within the youth ministry groups to gain knowledge of what was working in other congregations.

In regard to their missions program, they began a two-year study and survey of the several mission fields and missionaries they supported. They had several of their missions committee members visit the mission fields in order to gain firsthand knowledge of their mission work. Working through a strategic analysis of their mission outreach, they then decided to focus their outreach in specific geographic areas. In order to broaden their leadership team they encouraged families to visit various mission initiatives and gain mission experience. They invited their missionary families to furlough and spend time with families in their congregation, especially with the mission committee families. This enabled the mission committee to build deeper relationships with the missionaries and gain firsthand knowledge of mission issues. By involving the mission committee families, the leaders of the mission committee were actively mentoring their members in the role of strategic planning and hands-on involvement in mission leadership.

SOME ORGANIZATIONAL STRATEGIC MENTORING OBSERVATIONS

First, begin by identifying mentor/leader relationships. If the leader who is to mentor a new leader is a "loner" who does not easily enter into close relationships with others, it might mean that that person should not be mentoring another. This should not be interpreted that that person is not a good Christian. It merely means he may not be effective in mentoring relationships.

Second, some prospective mentors may themselves need to be mentored. A good policy is to get outside help from a skilled mentor to guide a group of prospective mentors through the process of mentoring. "Boot strap" mentoring is not often effective.

Third, think in terms of ministry leader apprenticeships in which a potential leader works alongside an experienced leader as a co-leader in the process.

RECOGNIZING AND DEVELOPING LEADERSHIP GIFTEDNESS

Although I do not consider leadership to be a natural, innate gift, all of us possess some form of giftedness which we may have learned in our growth process from parents, school, and church experiences. Developing one's personal giftedness, however, is a fundamental Christian principle. Through our study of Scripture, prayer, the example of Christ, and support and help of God's Holy Spirit, we do believe that Christian growth can take place and mature. Developing one's giftedness is part of the process of leadership development.

Several texts are germane to the concept of Christian giftedness and the responsibility that we should use our gifts in ministry in the body:

> Romans 12:3-8. For by the grace given to me I bid every one among you not to think of himself more highly than he ought to think, but to think with sober judgment, each according to the measure of faith which God has assigned him. [4] *For as in one body we have many members, and all the members do not have the same function,* [5] *so we, though many, are one body in Christ, and individually members one of another.* [6] *Having gifts that differ according to the grace given to us, let us use them*: if prophecy, in proportion to our faith; [7] if service, in our serving; he who teaches, in his teaching; [8] he who exhorts, in his exhortation; he who contributes, in liberality; he who gives aid, with zeal; he who does acts of mercy, with cheerfulness. (italics added).

> 1 Corinthians 12:14-26. For the body does not consist of one member but of many. [15] If the foot should say, "Because I am not a hand, I do not belong to the body," that would not make it any less a part of the body. [16] And if the ear should say, "Because I am not an eye, I do not belong to the body," that would not make it any less a part of the body. [17] If the whole body were an eye, where would be the hearing? If the whole body were an ear, where would be the sense of smell? [18] But as it is, God arranged the organs in the body, each one of them, as he chose. [19] If all were a single organ, where would the body be? [20] As it is, there are many parts, yet one body. [21] The eye cannot say

to the hand, "I have no need of you," nor again the head to the feet, "I have no need of you." [22] On the contrary, the parts of the body which seem to be weaker are indispensable, [23] and those parts of the body which we think less honorable we invest with the greater honor, and our unpresentable parts are treated with greater modesty, [24] which our more presentable parts do not require. But God has so composed the body, giving the greater honor to the inferior part, [25] that there may be no discord in the body, but that the members may have the same care for one another. [26] If one member suffers, all suffer together; if one member is honored, all rejoice together.

An important text that suggests we should work with the Holy Spirit and Christ in developing our giftedness for Christ is Ephesians 3:14-21, "For this reason I bow my knees before the Father, [15] from whom every family in heaven and on earth is named, [16] that according to the riches of his glory he may grant you to be strengthened with might through his Spirit in the inner man, [17] and that Christ may dwell in your hearts through faith; that you, being rooted and grounded in love, [18] may have power to comprehend with all the saints what is the breadth and length and height and depth, [19] and to know the love of Christ which surpasses knowledge, that you may be filled with all the fullness of God. [20] Now to him who by the power at work within us is able to do far more abundantly than all that we ask or think, [21] to him be glory in the church and in Christ Jesus to all generations, for ever and ever. Amen."

The point I am making is that in leadership development those mentoring new or potential leaders should work closely with their elder/shepherds and evangelists in this task. It is primarily the responsibility of the elders and evangelists to develop leadership and ministry giftedness among their members. However, elders need all of the support and help they can get from existing leaders. Together they work toward equipping the saints for the work of ministry by encouraging their learner leaders to develop their giftedness for use in the body. The following are some ideas for working on this:

First, work with potential leaders in the congregation in identifying their giftedness. This may involve recognizing skills learned through the years, mindsets relating to ministry, personal, spiritual, and ministry interests, age, maturity, spiritual growth, and growth habits like prayer and Scripture reading, Bible class attendance, and regular worship habits.

Second, expose potential leaders to the various aspects of ministry in the congregation, to the need for leaders, and to ministry seminars such as "job fairs" within the congregation.

Third, ask potential leaders where they might like to be involved. When they have identified certain ministry areas, take them to lectureships related to those ministries such as youth ministry lectureships, education ministries, mission seminars and workshops, and other such opportunities to see the church at work. One might also arrange with other congregations involved in specific ministries to have prospective learners visit with their ministry leaders as they address certain ministry issues.

Fourth, spend time with potential leaders in study, prayer, and hands-on mentoring opportunities. We should challenge them incrementally to become involved in some aspect of ministry leadership. Positive affirmation at all steps of the learning process does more to encourage growth than one might suspect. Be a Barnabas, a "son of encouragement."

PRINCIPLES AND PITFALLS IN LEADERSHIP TRAINING

The Danger of Silo Thinking in Leadership Training[169]

Figures 19, 20, and 21 on Silo thinking depict the dangers of compartmentalized thinking in congregational ministry organizations. When one stresses the importance of any one ministry, the ministry group tends to isolate and emphasize their ministry at the expense of other ministries. For instance, custodial and building and grounds ministries tend to be taken for granted and in many cases seen as physical jobs and not as spiritual ministries. Congregations should learn that these ministries cater to people and not physical facilities. Since the education ministry is an every Sunday and Wednesday experience, this ministry also tends to be taken for granted. Highly visible ministries that tend to receive an aura of glory such as missions, benevolence, and evangelism sometimes overshadow so-called lesser visible ministries.

Congregational leaders and those being mentored in ministry leadership need to constantly be aware of the fact that all ministries in the body of Christ are equally important. Ministry leaders should see their role as that of *jointly* bringing glory to Christ rather than that of *personal* ministry. In Ephesians 4:11-16 Paul stresses the point that evangelists (ministers) and teaching pastors (elders as shepherds) should *equally* be involved in equipping the saints for the work of ministry. *Together* they are involved and building up the body (the congregation) into maturity in Christ. The teaching responsibility of ministers and elders/shepherds must be focused on working toward the goal of every member being joined and knitted together to where they are working properly together in love. It is only when they are united in this manner that they are able to bring glory to Christ and are built up together in love. Silo thinking tends to mitigate against such harmony.

As is illustrated in **Figure 21**, vertical and horizontal thinking must be integrated into a dynamic where each individual ministry is seen as essential to the life and growth of a congregation. However, each ministry must also see itself cooperating and working together with other ministries in the mature ministry of the congregation. The question is, how is this achieved? The following proposals can work toward this goal.

DEVELOPING CONGREGATIONAL MINISTRY TEAM HARMONY

It is important that the congregation be informed on a regular basis of the "success" and importance of each ministry. This can be achieved through bulletin articles; periodic sermons relating to congregational ministries supported by visual aids, photographs and charts; leadership comments and commendations during congregational announcements; and visual reports on overhead screens (this is one of the better uses of overhead and video announcements using the modern technology now available and used by many churches).

Church leadership should plan strategic congregation ministry fellowship gatherings on a quarterly basis in which each ministry is highlighted and commended for their work and contribution to the whole congregation's welfare.

During regular congregational business meetings (I recommend these as a valuable vehicle for developing congregational responsibility by all members), each ministry should report on its work and concerns, as well as be held accountable for its budget expenditure and function. Such shared concerns, when handled in an environment of mutual respect and love, build congregational unity in regard to the various ministries.

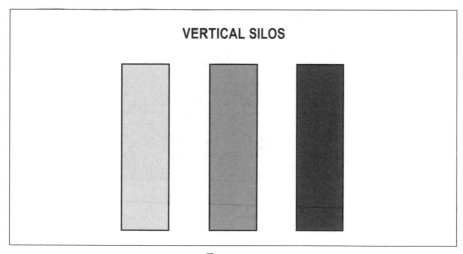

FIGURE 19

The congregational leadership should ensure that such meetings are held in a spirit of mutual respect and love. Prayers should be led for each of the congregation's ministries.

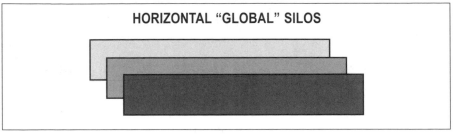

FIGURE 20

Ministry groups tend to think in terms of their own ministry.
First, the danger in Silo thinking is that specific ministries see themselves as "lone rangers," capable of functioning independent of other ministries.

Second, an additional danger is that one ministry sees itself as the most important ministry in the congregation. *Third,* Silo thinking can lead to problems in budget and manpower allocation within the congregation.

Congregations tend to treat all ministries as part of the general congregation's responsibility.
This silo represents a view in which no ministry is given specific attention in the understanding that ministry "just happens."

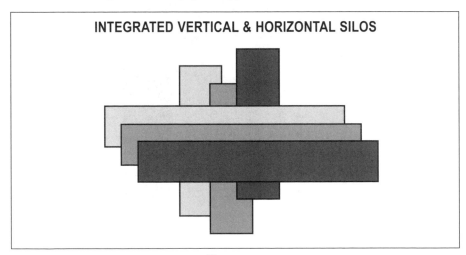

FIGURE 21

There is no specific responsibility manifested for any specific ministry—the whole congregation is expected or thought to be responsible for the ministry.

The danger of the horizontal global ministry concept is that individual ministries become lost in the overall ministry of the church.

The church knows it should be engaged in some ministry but no one accepts specific responsibility or charge of the ministry.

The congregation makes a serious effort to give each ministry individual leadership responsibility but integrate all ministries into a dynamic whole.

The individual ministries need to be made aware of other ministries in the congregation.

They need to know that they work together with other ministries in achieving the total congregational responsibility.

They need to realize that they are all equally important in the overall ministry of the church.

This can be achieved in a number of different ways:

- Church bulletin ministry news articles
- Congregational ministry announcements (audio and video)
- Congregational ministry fairs
- Congregational ministry organizational fellowship meetings
- Congregational business meetings
- Special prayers during worship for the many church ministries

VALUES-DRIVEN LEADERSHIP

The values that shape a congregation's psyche are both simple and significant. Every group or congregation is shaped by several value sets such as doctrinal values, congregational cultural values, and community cultural values. Doctrinal values may relate to the style of worship or membership that drives and "controls" a congregation. The role of women in congregational life, however this may be interpreted, must be clearly articulated. In addition, the congregation may have set certain mission/purpose values such as where and how they desire to support global evangelism and church planting. Leadership and shepherding values should be clearly defined. The congregation must be well informed as to how elders work with deacons, ministry group leaders, and the congregation in general. Congregational cultural values may include dress standards, worship times, the architecture and decorative nature of the building, the rural/urban culture of the congregation, etc. Community values speak to dress values, family values, ranching/business values, etc. Potential or new leaders must understand these values in order to be able to lead within the sociocultural mores of the congregation and community. New leaders should be wary of introducing initiatives that run opposed to the value parameters of the congregation.

ETHICAL LEADERSHIP

How one respects congregational values impacts the effectiveness of leadership and the stability of the congregation or ministry group in significant ways. Every community has certain standards of ethics that must be respected. These ethical values are directly related to the congregational values that shape the congregation. For leaders not to respect such values has ethical significance. Leaders should always lead within the values of the congregation. The values of the congregation may be "challenged" in an appropriate manner through the correct avenues such as discussion with the elders, teaching under the oversight of the elders, and biblically based sermons that contribute to congregational growth. A sectarian or divisive spirit should at all times be avoided and guarded against. Congregational values should be addressed at the congregational level and not at the ministry group level. Effective and meaningful leadership can take place only within the values of the congregation and a respect for ethical leadership.

ACCOUNTABILITY LEADERSHIP

When working with a participative, values-driven, and ethical model of leadership in which ministry is shared or delegated, it is imperative that responsibility be stressed and that some model of accountability be established.

First, elders need to know that they too are responsible and accountable. They are responsible to the congregation for the trust the congregation has placed in them to be their shepherds. They need to be accountable to God and to the congregation for the manner in which they conduct themselves and carry out their ministry. In Ephesians 4:11ff. ,Paul encourages evangelists and shepherds (the elders) to use their God-given gifts effectively in "equipping" the saints for the work of ministry, which includes developing future leaders for the congregation.

Second, deacons and ministry group leaders likewise have a fiduciary responsibility to the congregation and the ministries they are leading. They need to realize that they are accountable not so much to the elders, but to the congregation that has chosen them and "ordained" them to their ministry. In the ministries of missions, education, youth, and women's service, the leaders must accept responsibility for their role in leadership and in developing new leaders.

Third, the congregation must understand that they, too, are accountable in regard to ministry leaders in the sense that there can be no leadership without followers who are willing to "join the team" and get involved in the diverse ministries of the congregation.

How to Manage Accountability. In a previous section of this book we have stressed that elders especially are not to be domineering over the congregation, acting as the lords of the congregation, but are to be examples (cf. 1 Pet. 5:1-4). This principle cannot be overstressed when considering managing accountability. Nothing will discourage ministers, deacons, ministry leaders, and members of the congregation more than an overbearing eldership or leadership group.

Building Good Relationships. Ministry leaders (elders, deacons, and others) with the responsibility of leading teams of ministry workers need to spend considerable time building good relationships with their team members or ministry group. Building good relationships demands dedicated and special time spent with the group. This needs to be both formal time in meetings and informal time in social relationships.

Ongoing Training. No matter how capable ministry group members are, they will need specialized training before becoming ministry leaders, and then continuing mentoring and guidance. Repeated mention of the values, goals, purpose, and parameters of the ministry group helps focus the group's attention on their ministry. This can be achieved through special sessions for this purpose, but most likely the most effective will be in social settings where the group meets just to fellowship and discuss their ministry.

Guided Self-Evaluation. Adopting a "client-centered" model, the leader can ask the learners in the ministry group how they feel about their achievement. By reminding the group or learners of their ministry values and goals, the leader can set the scene for self-evaluation. By beginning with his or her own self-evaluation, the leader can set the tone for the evaluation. The teacher or leader may make some suggestions for the learner to work on for the next round of self-evaluation.

Regular Evaluation Schedule. By setting a schedule for evaluation the leader can have the group prepared for the exercise. An agenda mentioning goals and purposes can be announced for the group to work on. It is imperative for effective leadership that leaders and ministry groups know in advance that they will be evaluating themselves in regard to their ministry. I would suggest quarterly mild evaluation occasions and annual serious evaluation, study, and prayer occasions.

ENDNOTES

[1] J. J. Turner, *Christian Leadership Handbook* (West Monroe, LA: Howard Publishing, 1991), p. xi.

[2] For instance, members of the Nsawam Road Church and students from the Heritage Christians College planted over 620 new churches in West Africa in five years. It is estimated that there are more congregations and members of Churches of Christ in Africa now than in the United States. The message is still powerful, especially when the leadership is bold.

[3] Peter Drucker, *The New Realities* (New York: Harper & Row, 1989).

[4] George Barna, *The Frog in the Kettle* (Ventura, CA: Regal Books, 1990), pp. 66ff.

[5] This term and other similar terms defining generational groups will be discussed in detail in a chapter on Generations.

[6] Suneel Ratan, "Why Busters Hate Boomers," *Fortune 500*, October 4, 1993, pp.56ff.

[7] The English word *church* actually derives from the Germanic word *kirche* which in turn derives from the Greek *kuriakos*, meaning "belonging to the Lord." It would be better to translate *ekklesia* as *congregation* or *community*, but we are stuck by long usage with *church*.

[8] Warren Bennis and Burt Nanus, *Leaders: The Strategies for Taking Charge*. (New York: Harper & Row, 1985), pp.2, 3.

[9] Bennis and Nanus, *Leadership*, pp. 1, 2.

[10] Ibid., p.1.

[11] James M. Kouzes and Barry Z. Posner, *The Leadership Challenge* (San Francisco: Jossey-Bass Publications, 1987), p. xxi.

[12] Dan Quayle, Opinion USA, *USA TODAY*, July 8, 1993.

[13] John Naisbitt, *Megatrends: Ten New Directions Transforming Our Lives* (New York: Warner Books, 1982).

[14] Thomas A. Stewart, "Welcome to the Revolution," *Fortune 500*, December 13, 1993, pp.66ff.

[15] The term "Baby Boomer" or "Boomer" refers to those born between 1946 and 1964. This group has become a dominant force in shaping the American psyche or mind set in recent years. More will be said later regarding the impact of generational segmentation on American society.

[16] Generation X is a term considered by that generation to be pejorative, indicating the independent mindset of those born in the 1960s and 1970s and maturing and entering the marketplace in the 1980s and 1990s. Generation Y, or The Millennials, refer to the generation born in the 1980s and 1990s and maturing and entering the market place in the twenty-first century. More will be said of these generations at a later point in this study.

[17] Both the terms modernity and postmodernity are extremely elusive and difficult to define. Fundamentally, they are sociological and epistemological constructs that refer to a change in the way man perceives reality and progress.

[18] Drucker, *New Realities*, pp. 3-9.

[19] Doug Murren, *The Baby Boomerang* (Ventura, CA: Regal Books, 1990), p. 8.

[20] Refer to the discussion of this under the heading, *Generation Segmentation*, in chapter 4.

[21] Leith Anderson, *Dying For Change* (Minneapolis, MN: Bethany House Publishers, 1990), p.26.

[22] Ibid., pp. 26, 27.

[23] Ibid., p. 43.

[24] George Barna, *The Frog in the Kettle* (Ventura, CA: Regal Books, 1990), pp. 186-192. All population statistics for the population survey are drawn from this survey of demographics by Barna.

[25] Jeff Magee, *Jeff Magee International*, http://www.jeffreymagee.com/articles_show.aspx?categoryID=32&id=268.

[26] William Strauss and Neil Howe, *Generations* (New York: William Morrow, 1991).

[27] Among them one would include Abraham Zaleznik, Peter Drucker, Warren Bennis, Burt Nanus, James M. Kouzes, Barry Z. Posner, Joseph L. Badaracco, and Richard R. Ellsworth. For a full list of significant writings in the field of business management and leadership that relate to the topic under consideration, refer to the bibliography at the close of the book.

[28] Kenneth Blanchard, Patricia Zigarmi, and Drea Zigarmi, *Leadership and the One Minute Manager* (New York: William Morrow and Company, 1985).

[29] Ibid., p.68.

[30] Ibid., p. 27.

[31] Named for Max Weber, well-known sociologist of the 1940-50 era, father of much American organizational and management theory.

[32] Warren Bennis, *Leaders on Leadership* (Boston, MA: Harvard Business School Publishing, 1992), p. x.

[33] Abraham Zaleznik, *The Managerial Mystique: Restoring Leadership in Business* (New York: Harper & Row, 1989); James M. Kouzes and Barry Z. Posner, *The Leadership Challenge* (San Francisco: Jossey-Bass, 1990).

[34] Peter Drucker, *Managing for the Future* (New York: Truman Talley Books/Dutton, 1992), p. 157.

[35] Ibid, pp. 337ff.

[36] Ibid., p. 340.

[37] Ibid., p. 3.

[38] Ibid., p. 340.

[39] Ibid., p. 342.

[40] *Conservative* as it is used in this instance does not necessarily mean *theologically* conservative. The term is used in its basic sense for one uncomfortable with or opposed to change.

[41] Michael E. Gerber, *The E Myth* (Harper Business, 1986), p. xiii.

[42] Ibid., p. 20.

[43] Ibid., p. 19.

[44] We are aware that Bolman and Deal argue that the relational aspect of leadership is but one of several "frames" through which leadership must be approached. We are not overlooking the other three components that Bolman and Deal surface, and will consider them at the appropriate time. It is the conviction of this writer, however, that the relational frame is of profound significance to leadership in the sociological milieu in which we find ourselves at the close of the twentieth century. See Bolman and Deal, *Reframing Organizations*, 1991.

[45] Kouzes and Posner, *The Leadership Challenge*, p.16.

[46] Ibid., p. 302.

[47] Badaracco and Ellsworth, *Leadership and the Quest for Integrity*, p. 209.

[48] Cited in Kouzes and Posner, *The Leadership Challenge*, p.1.

[49] Edwin A. Locke, *The Essence of Leadership* (New York: Macmillan, 1991), pp. 2, 3.

[50] Philip B. Cosby, *Leading: The Art of Becoming an Executive* (New York: McGraw-Hill, 1990), p. 23.

[51] Max DePree, *Leadership Is an Art* (New York: Bantam Doubleday Dell, 1989), p. 3.

[52] James MacGregor Burns, Foreword to *Leadership: Multidisciplinary Perspectives*, Barbara Kellerman, ed. (Englewood Cliffs, NJ: Prentice-Hall, 1984), p. vii.

[53] Cited in Kouzes and Posner, *The Leadership Challenge*, p. xv.

[54] Zaleznik, *The Managerial Mystique*, pp.16ff.

[55] Stephen R. Covey, *Principle-Centered Leadership*, (New York: Summit Books, 1991), p.31.

[56] Kouzes and Posner, *The Leadership Challenge*, p.267, cite research in support of this claim.

[57] Ibid., p. 81.

[58] Ibid., pp. 83, 84.

[59] Gardner, *On Leadership*, p. 130.

[60] Locke, *The Essence of Leadership*, pp. 49-61, passim.

[61] Max DePree, in *Managing the Non-Profit Organization* by Peter Drucker (New York: Harper Collins, 1990), p. 40.

[62] In Warren Bennis, *On Becoming A Leader*, p. 83.

[63] Kouzes and Posner, *The Leadership Challenge*, p. 94.

[64] Badaracco and Ellsworth, *Leadership and the Quest for Integrity*, p. 65.

[65] Drucker, *Managing for the Future*, p. 116.

[66] Ibid., pp. 116, 117.

[67] Kouzes and Posner, *The Leadership Challenge*, p. 187.

[68] Stephen R. Covey, *Principle-Centered Leadership*, (New York: Summit Books, 1991).

[69] Badaracco and Ellsworth, *Leadership by Integrity*.

[70] Kouzes and Posner, *The Leadership Challenge*, pp. 267, 268.

[71] Ibid., p. 267.

[72] Gardner, *On Leadership*, pp. 42, 52, 117.

[73] Drucker, *Managing for the Future*, p. 122.

[74] Bennis and Nanus, *Leaders*, p. 8.

[75] Kouzes and Posner, *The Leadership Challenge*, p. 141.

[76] Nanus, *The Leader's Edge*, p. 101.

[77] Covey, *Principle-Centered Leadership*, p. 31.

[78] Drucker, *Managing the Non-Profit Organization*, p. 116.

[79] Ibid., p. 125.

[80] Gardner, *Leadership*, p. 33.

[81] Bennis and Nanus, *Leaders*, p. 184.

[82] Covey, *Principle-Centered Leadership*, p. 31.

[83] Kouzes and Posner, *The Leadership Challenge*, p. 150.

[84] Elmer L. Towns, *10 of Today's Most Innovative Churches* (Ventura, CA: Regal Books, 1990).

[85] Drucker, *Managing the Non-Profit Organization*, pp. 152, 153.

[86] Lynne Joy McFarland, Larry E. Senn, and John R. Childress, *21st Century Leadership* (New York: Leadership Press, 1993), pp. 247, 248.

[87] Drucker, *Managing for the Future*, pp. 175, 176.

[88] Bolman and Deal, *Reframing Organizations*, pp. 100-116.

[89] Gardner, *Leadership*, p. 118.

[90] Gardner, *On Leadership*, pp. 26, 27.

[91] Benjamin B. Tregoe, John W. Zimmerman, Ronald A. Smith, Peter M. Tobia, *Vision in Action* (New York: Simon and Schuster, 1989), p. 19.

[92] Tom Peters, *Thriving on Chaos* (New York: Harper Perennial, 1987).

[93] Ibid., p. xiii.

[94] Lynne Joy McFarland,Senn, and Childress, *21st Century Leadership*, p. 246.

[95] Max Weber, *The Theory of Social and Economic Organization* (New York: Oxford University Press, 1947).

[96] Gardner, *On Leadership*, p. 23.

[97] Ibid., p. 166, 167.

[98] Bolman and Deal, *Reframing Organizations*, p. 261.

[99] William F. Glueck and Lawrence R. Jauch, *Business Policy and Strategic Management* (New York: McGraw-Hill, 1984), p. 155.

[100] Ibid., p. 163.

[101] Cited by Bob Buford in a plenary address at a Leadership Network seminar on "The Church in the 21st Century," June 1992, Los Colinas, Dallas, Texas.

[102] Pluralism as used here describes the contemporary view that suggests the existence of a number of equally valid authority sources, or centers of authority, to which one may turn in contrast to the more traditional or conservative view that suggests one central institutional center of authority.

[103] Drucker, *Managing for the Future*, p. 340.

[104] Joseph L. Badaracco, Jr., *Leadership and the Quest for Integrity* (Boston: Harvard Business School Press, 1989).

[105] Edgar H. Schein, *Organizational Psychology*, 3rd ed. (Englewood Cliffs, NJ: Prentice-Hall, 1980).

[106] Ibid., p. 107.

[107] Ibid., p. 108.

[108] Blanchard, Zigarmi, and Zigarmi, *Leadership and the One Minute Manager*.

[109] Ibid.

[110] Adapted from Badaracco and Ellsworth, *Leadership and the Quest for Integrity*, p. 40.

[111] Ibid., p. 42.

[112] Ibid., p. 39.

[113] We do not intend to imply that the only qualification of elders, bishops, or shepherds is one of age or gender. We simply mean that many members of the church are of equal spiritual maturity and experience, but by reason of age are not suitably prepared for the ministry of shepherding.

[114] Badaracco and Ellsworth, *Leadership and the Quest for Integrity*, p. 32.

[115] Ibid., p. 22.

[116] Lorne C. Plunkett and Robert Fournier, *Participative Management* (New York: John Wiley and Sons, 1991), pp. 4, 5. It is unfortunate that Plunkett and Fournier incorporate the word "management" in the term "participative management." In view of the unfortunate connotation of management, which speaks more to tasks and goals rather than to people and relationships, it may be more appropriate to speak of "participative leadership."

[117] Ibid., p. 40.

[118] Ibid.

[119] Ibid., pp. 20, 21.

[120] Badaracco and Ellsworth, *Leadership and the Quest for Integrity*, pp. 65ff.

[121] Stephen C. Covey. *Principle-Centered Leadership* (New York: Summit Books, 1991).

[122] Ibid., p. 19.

[123] Ibid., p. 9.

[124] Badaracco and Ellsworth, *Leadership and the Quest for Integrity*, p. 67.

[125] Ibid., pp. 66, 67.

[126] Ibid., p. 72.

[127] John H. Zenger, Ed Musselwhite, Kathleen Hurson, and Craig Perrin, *Leading Teams: Mastering the New Role* (New York: Irwin Professional Publishing, 1994).

[128] Plunkett and Fournier, *Participative Management,* devote considerable space to the discussion of team building in participative management, pp. 107-169.

[129] The possibility of women serving as special servants or "deaconesses" cannot be overlooked. The difficulty arises over the fact that no clear statement is made of such in the New Testament other than possibly Romans 16:1 in the RSV. 1 Timothy 3:11 has been used as the basis for such a ministry. See the discussion of this in J. W. Roberts, *Letters to Timothy,* The Living Word (Austin, TX: Sweet Publishing Company, 1961), pp. 37ff. Roberts argues in this context for the possibility of some "ministry" for a certain group of women who met specific spiritual qualifications. Church of Christ discomfort with this concept arises over the fear of women "usurping authority" over men. The term "usurping authority" in itself is an unfortunate translation. The term simply means to teach in a "domineering manner." The major difficulty encountered by many with this concept of the possibility of women serving as "deaconesses" lies in misunderstanding these ministries as "positions of authority" rather than unique services. We will address this problem in greater detail in a study of "authority" in a later chapter of this book.

[130] The translation of the Greek word *prohistemi* as "rulers" in 1 Timothy 5:17, RSV) is unfortunate and unnecessary. The same word is translated in Romans 12:8 (RSV) as "give aid." In the NIV translation of 1 Timothy 5:17 the word is rendered as "direct the affairs" of the church. In 1 Thessalonians, 1Tiomthy 5:12 (RSV and NIV) the word is translated as "are over you." Literally meaning "stand in front of," the term is better translated as "lead" or "provide leadership," as is the case in Romans 12:8 in the NIV. In both 1 Thessalonians 5:12 and 1 Timothy 5:17, therefore, the meaning of *prohistemi* is more accurately understood as "provide leadership."

[131] Acts 20:17-35 is unique in the New Testament in that Luke uses the terms *elder, bishop, pastoring* to describe the same ministry, clearly explaining that in the New Testament the terms are used descriptively and interchangeably for the same ministry.

[132] See the discussion on this in J. W. McGarvey, *The Acts of the Apostles* (Nashville, TN: B. C. Goodpasture, 1958), p. 76. see also Joseph A. Fitzmyer, *The Acts of the Apostles,* The Anchor Bible (New York: Doubleday, 1998), pp. 344ff; F. F. Bruce, *The Book of Acts* (Grand Rapids, MI: Eerdmans, 1954), pp. 127ff.; I. Howard Marshall, *Acts* (Grand Rapids, MI: Eerdmans, 1980), pp. 126f.

[133] The term *diakonos,* often translated "servant" or "deacon," can also be translated "minister," Colossians 1:7, 23. The term can have either a generic application to all members, or a specific application to certain special ministries.

[134]Cf. my comments above. Cf. also the discussion of 1 Timothy 3:11 in J. W. Roberts, *The Letters to Timothy* (Abilene, TX: Abilene Christian University), p.37. Cf. the discussion of this in Joseph A. Fitzmyer, *Romans,* The Anchor Bible (New York: Doubleday, 1992), pp. 728ff; Thomas R. Schreiner, *Romans* (Grand Rapids, MI: Baker Books, 1998), pp. 786ff; James D. G, Dunn, *Romans 9-16* (Waco, TX: Word, 1988), pp. 886ff; C. E. B. Cranfield, *The Epistle to the Romans,* vol. 2 (Edinburgh: T. & T. Clark, 1979), pp. 780ff. W. Sanday and H. C. Headlam, *The Epistle to the Romans* (Edinburgh: T. & T. Clark, 1979), pp. 416f; Jack Cottrell, *Romans,* Vol. 2 (Joplin, MO: College Press, 1998), pp. 460ff; Leon Morris, *The Epistle to the Romans* (Grand Rapids, MI: Eerdmans, 1988), pp. 528ff; Ernst Kasemann, *Romans* (Grand Rapids, MI: Eerdmans, 1980), pp. 409f.

[135] The author served for 15 years as a missionary in South Africa, working among both black and white urban churches and rural black churches.

[136] Some members of Churches of Christ are uncomfortable with the concept of a Restoration Movement. The argument is that we are a church or a religious group, not a movement. One needs to understand that there are several ways of looking at religious groups. Churches of Christ are a religious group and should be defined in such terms. However, Churches of Christ are also part of a sociological or historical development, and as such should be studied and defined in a sociological or historical framework. Within the framework of sociological studies, Churches of Christ are a religious *movement*.

[137] We should note, however, that Bible classes as part of congregational practice are seriously questioned by some members of the American Restoration heritage.

[138] Although not always clearly understood in some quarters, or perhaps not clearly articulated in their doctrine, Churches of Christ believe the Word of God to be comprised of the whole Bible, both Old and New Testaments. When properly interpreted, both Old and New Testaments are equally fundamental to faith and practice.

[139] Again we stress that this study is not intended to be a definitive definition of Roman Catholic polity, but merely serves as a survey to demonstrate where this system has made an impact on Protestant and Church of Christ thinking.

[140] To be more precise, we should point out that the King James Version was itself significantly influenced and shaped by a succession of translations, each made from within a distinctly Roman Catholic or Church of England environment. Most modern mainstream translations of the Bible have been made with the stated purpose of revising that tradition established by William Tyndale, Miles Coverdale, the Geneva Bible, and the Bishops' Bible.

[141] *Traditionally conservative* is understood here to mean that one is inclined to canonize one's religious tradition, culture or sociological heritage, rather than be willing to reexamine and change past practice if necessary for future growth.

[142] That Acts is a theological sequel to the Gospel of Luke is a commonly accepted view among New Testament scholarship.

[143] The Greek title to Acts is almost certainly not original, but is an *inscription* added to the work at an early date. Although commonly known as *The Acts of the Apostles*, it is in reality more correctly *The Acts of the Apostle Paul*. It is perhaps more accurate to understand the book as a record or theological account of *The Acts of the Early Church* in which Paul was very active.

[144] Church of Christ theology would be more comfortable with the term "Jerusalem Meeting" than with the more formal term "Jerusalem Conference."

[145] It is approximately at this stage in Paul's ministry that he writes the heated letter to the Galatians in which he forcefully argues for his gospel of grace by faith unencumbered by the law. Cf. Galatians 1:6-10.

[146] At this moment we merely stress that elders and other ministry leaders do have authority. The point in question is the nature or kind of authority.

[147] Abraham Zaleznik, "Managers and Leaders: Are They Different? *Harvard Business Review* (May-June 1977): 67-78, and *The Managerial Mystique* (New York: Harper and Row, 1989).

[148] Craig M. Watson, "Leadership, Management, and the Seven Keys," *Business Horizons*, 26, 2 (March-April 1983), pp. 8-13.

[149] Zaleznik, "Managers and Leaders: Are They Different?"

[150] Joseph L. Badaracco and Richard R. Ellsworth, *Leadership and the Quest for Integrity* (Cambridge, MA: Harvard Business School Press, 1989).

[151] Zaleznik, "Managers and Leaders: Are They Different?"

[152] Ibid.

[153] Ibid.

[154] Reuel Lemmons, "Editorial: Elders," *Firm Foundation* (June 1972).

[155] Selected statements from 1 Timothy.

[156] See also the discussion of this text in J. W. Roberts, *Letters to Timothy*, pp.26-33.

[157] We do raise the question, however, in regard to the proper interpretation of this term, and question whether the literal interpretation is what Paul had in mind, regardless of what our present sociological and religious preferences may be. A guiding principle of interpretation should always be to determine how the term was understood in its original sociological and theological context. In attempting to determine the original understanding and use, other literary sources from the period can be of assistance.

[158] The RSV renders this as "that is your charge." The NIV understands this as "that is under your care." The Greek *en humin* literally means "in, or among you," but the context supports the RSV and NIV translations. The NIV translation seems to us to be more in keeping with the context of shepherding.

[159] It is my view of that the translation and interpretation of the Greek "*didaskein...oude authentein*" in 1 Timothy 2:12 as "having authority" or "usurping authority" is a most unfortunate translation and, in fact, an incorrect translation. A more precise interpretation should be "teaching in a domineering manner."

[160] The history of the translation of the English Bible is interesting and informative for our study of "office". If we take as our beginning point the translations of William Tyndale (1525-1530) we notice that it was a fundamental principle that Tyndale retain as much of the ecclesiastical language of the Latin Vulgate as possible. The same principle applied for the successive translations which were all significantly influenced by Tyndale. Several fine English Bibles continued this tradition: Miles Coverdale (1535), John Matthew (1537), the Great Bible (1539), the Geneva Bible (1560), the Bishop's Bible (1568), and the King James Version (Authorized Version, 1611). The 54 translators of the KJV, reflecting a preference for the Bishop's Bible, were commissioned to alter this translation as little as possible, and to retain as much of the ecclesiastical language as possible.

[161] See the discussion of elders' authority and *exousia* in Jack Lewis, *Leadership Questions Confronting the Church* (Nashville, TN: Christian Communications, 1985), pp. 7-12.

[162] Acts 11:30 is the earliest reference to church elders in the book of Acts. Acts 14:23 mentions that Paul and Barnabas "appointed elders for them in every church."

[163] Although this passage as translated into English does not specifically mention deacons, the men appointed are special servants who assist the congregation and relieve the apostles from a ministry not specifically that of the apostles so that the apostles may continue with their specific ministry. The infinitival form of *diakonos* (servant, deacon, minister), namely, *diakonein* from the verb *diakoneo*, translated "to serve tables," does appear in verse 2. Whatever views one may take of this passage, special servants are chosen by the congregation to serve the congregation in a special ministry. This is precisely what deacons do; they serve the congregation in special ministries.

[164] Stephen Covey, *Principle-Centered Leadership*, 1991.

[165] Robertson L. Whiteside, *"Concerning Elders": Doctrinal Discourses* (Denton, TX: Inys Whiteside, 1955), pp. 82-89.

[166] Howard Norton, "Currents," *Christian Chronicle*, December 1993.

[167] T. W. Brents, *Gospel Sermons* (Nashville, TN: McQuiddy, 1918), pp. 353-410.

[168] Much of this material is from a class on developing leaders presented at the 2005 ACU Lectureship by Ian A. Fair, Mitch Mitchell, and Deon B. Fair.

[169] The three charts on Silo thinking used in this chapter are used by kind permission of Deon B. Fair.

I. JOURNALS AND ARTICLES

Time. "On Leadership" (July 15, 1974).

Time. "On Leadership" (November 8, 1973) p. 38.

Executive Excellence. August 1988.

Executive Excellence. October 1988.

Conger, Jay A. "Inspiring Others: The Language of Leadership." *Academy of Management Executive* 5, No. 1 (1991), 31-45.

Goodwin, Doris Kearns. "True Leadership: An Interview with James MacGregor Burns." *Psychology Today*, October, 1978, pp. 46ff.

Huey, John. "Managing in the Midst of Chaos." *Fortune 500*, April 5, 1993, pp.38ff.

———. "The New Post-heroic Leadership." *Fortune 500*, February 21, 1994.

Ingram, Larry C. "Leadership, Democracy, and Religion: Role Ambiguity among Pastors in Southern Baptist Churches." *Journal for the Scientific Study of Religion* 20, No. 2 (1981), 119-129.

Jaques, Elliott. "In Praise of Hierarchy." *Harvard Business Review* (January-February 1990), 127-133.

Keys, Bernard, and Thomas Case. "How to Become an Influential Manager." *Academy of Management Executive*s 4, No. 4 (1990), 38-51.

Kim, W. Cahn, and Renee A. Mauborgne. "Parables of Leadership." *Harvard Business Review* (July-August 1992), 123-128.

Kirkpatrick, Shelley, and Edwin A. Locke. "Leadership: Do Traits Matter?" *Academy of Management Executive*s 5, No. 2 (1991), 48-60.

Kotter, John. "What Leaders Really Do." *Harvard Business Review* (May-June 1990), 103-111.

Lard, Moses E. "Ordination of Church Officers." *Lard's Quarterly* (July 1865), 350-360.

Lemmons, Reuel. "Editorial: `Who Calls the Shots?'" *Firm Foundation*, August 2, 1977. See also several articles in subsequent issues of the *Firm Foundation* in response to this editorial.

———. "Elders." *Firm Foundation*, Jan 31, 1978. This issue was devoted to the topic of elders.

Lipscomb, David, "Elders and Officialism in the Church of God." *Gospel Advocate* 9 (July 18, 1867), 567-568.

———. "Church Work." *Gospel Advocate* 13 (August 31, 1871), 793-795.

———. "Church Authority." *Gospel Advocate*, 19 (April 12, 1877), 232.

Nolan, Richard L. "Too Many Executives Today Just Don't Get It!" *Cause/Effect* 13, No. 4 (Winter, 1990), 5-11.

Oldenburg, Don. "More Americans Growing Cynical About Fellow Man." *Dallas Times Herald*, Wednesday, June 28, 1989.

Ratan, Suneel. "Why Busters Hate Boomers." *Fortune 500,* October 4, 1993, pp. 56ff.

Rosner, Judy B. "Ways Women Lead." *Harvard Business Review* (November-December 1990), 119-125.

Sewel, E. G. "Elders." *Gospel Advocate* 15 (September 5, 1972), 829-834.

Sherman, Stratford. "A Brave New Darwinian Workplace." *Fortune 500*, January 25, 1993, pp. 50-56.

Squires, Sally. "Depend on It: Learning to Trust Takes Time." *Dallas Times Herald.* Thursday, July 21, 1988.

Stewart, Thomas A. "Welcome to the Revolution." *Fortune 500*, December 13, 1993, pp. 66ff.

Watson, Craig M. "Leadership, Management, and the Seven Keys." *Business Horizons* 26, No. 2 (March-April, 1983), 8-13.

Wright, Jim. "What Has Become of Trust?" *Dallas Morning News*, Tuesday, September 26, 1994.

Zaleznik, Abraham. "Managers and Leaders: Are They Different?" *Harvard Business Review* 73 (May-June 1977), 67-78.

_____. "The Leadership Gap." *Academy of Management Executive*s 4, No. 1 (1990), 7-22.

"Leadership." *Theology, News and Notes.* Fuller Theological Seminary June 1989, pp. 4-31.

II. BOOKS

Adams, Arthur Merrihew. *Effective Leadership for Today's Church.* Philadelphia: Westminster Press, 1978.

Adizes, Ichak. *Corporate Life Cycles.* Englewood, CO: Prentice Hall, 1988.

Allen, C. Leonard. *Distant Voices.* Abilene, TX: ACU Press, 1993. pp. 100-107.

Anderson, Leith. *Dying For Change.* Minneaplis, MN: Bethany House, 1990.

_____. *A Church for the 21st Century.* Minneapolis, MN: Bethany House, 1992.

Badaracco, Joseph L., and Richard R. Ellsworth. *Leadership and the Quest for Integrity.* Cambridge, MA: Harvard Business School Press, 1989.

Baird, Lloyd S., James E. Post, and John F. Mahon. *Management.* New York: Harper & Row, 1990.

Bass, Bernard M., and Richard M. Stogdill. *Bass and Stogdill's Handbook on Leadership.* New York: Free Press, 1990.

Bass, Bernard M. *Leadership and Performance Beyond Expectations.* New York: Free Press, 1985.

Below, Patrick J., George L. Morrisey, and Betty L. Alcomb. *The Executive Guide to Strategic Planning.* San Francisco: Jossey-Bass Publishers, 1988.

Bennis, Warren. *Why Leaders Can't Lead.* San Francisco: Jossey-Bass, 1989.

_____. *On Becoming a Leader.* Reading, MA: Addison-Wesley, 1989.

Bennis, Warren, and Burt Nanus. *Leaders: The Strategies for Taking Charge.* New York: Harper & Row, 1985.

Bolman, Lee G., and Terrence E. Deal. *Reframing Organizations.* San Francisco: Jossey-Bass, 1991.

Brents, T. W. "Church Organization." *Gospel Sermons.* Nashville, TN: Gospel Advocate, 1891. pp. 353-410.

Bryan, Barry W. *Strategic Planning Workbook for Non-Profit Organizations.* Management Support Systems, Amherst Wilder Foundation, 1985. (Fuller Theological Seminary)

Bryman, Alan. *Charisma and Leadership in Organizations.* Newbury Park, CA: Sage Publications, 1992.

Burns, James MacGregor. *Leadership*. New York: Harper & Row, 1978.

Callahan, Kennon L. *Twelve Keys to an Effective Church*. San Francisco: Harper & Row, 1983.

_____. *Effective Church Leadership*. New York: Harper & Row, 1990.

Certo, Samuel C., and J. Paul Peter. *Strategic Management*. New York: McGraw-Hill, 1990.

Clemmens, John K,. and Douglas F. Mayer. *The Classic Touch*. Homewood, IL: Business One Irwin, 1987.

Cousins, Don, Leith Anderson, and Arthur DeKruyter. *Mastering Church Management*. Sisters, OR: Multnomah, 1990.

Covey, Stephen R. *The 7 Habits of Highly Effective People*. New York: Simon & Schuster, 1989.

_____. *Principle-Centered Leadership*. New York: Summit Books, 1991.

Covey, Stephen R., A. Roger Merrill, and Rebecca R. Merrill. *First Things First*. New York: Simon & Schuster, 1994.

DePree, Max. *Leadership is an Art*. New York: Dell Publishing, 1989.

Drucker, Peter F. *The New Realities*. New York: Harper & Row, 1989.

Fiedler, F. E. *Leadership*. New York: General Learning Press, 1971.

Gardner, John W. *On Leadership*. New York: Free Press, 1990.

Geneen, Harold S. *Managing*. London: Grafton Books, 1984.

Glueck, William F., and Lawrence R. Jauch. *Business Policy and Strategic Management*. New York: McGraw-Hill, 1984.

Gordon, Judith R., R. Wayne Mondy, Arthur Sharplin, and Shane R. Premeaux. *Management and Organizational Behavior*. Boston: Allyn and Bacon, 1990.

Greenleaf, Robert K. *Servant Leadership*. New York: Paulist Press, 1977.

Howe, Neil, and Bill Strauss. *13th Gen*. New York: Random House, 1993.

Hunt, James G. *Leadership*. Newbury Park, CA: Sage Publications, 1991.

Jaques, Elliott. *Requisite Organization: The CEO's Guide to Creative Structure and Leadership*. Cason Hall/Gower, 1989.

Kellerman, Barbara. *Leadership: Multidisciplinary Perspectives*. Upper Saddle River, NJ: Prentice Hall, 1984.

Kouzes, James M., and Barry Z. Posner. *The Leadership Challenge*. San Francisco: Jossey-Bass, 1987.

Kurfees, M. C., ed. *Questions Answered by Lipscomb and Sewell*. Nashville: McQuiddy Printing Company, 1957.

Leas, Speed B. *Leadership in Conflict*. Nashville, TN: Abingdon Press, 1982.

Lowry, L. Randolph, and Richard W. Meyers. *Conflict Management and Counseling*. Waco, TX: Word, 1991.

MacGregor, James. *Leadership*. New York: Harper & Row, 1978.

Manz, Charles and Henry Sims. *Super-Leadership: Leading Others to Lead Themselves*. New York: Simon & Schuster, 1989.

McGavran, Donald Anderson. *How Churches Grow*. New York: Friendship Press, 1967.

_____. *Understanding Church Growth*. Grand Rapids, MI: Eerdmans, 1970.

McFarland, Lynne Joy, Larry E. Senn, and John R. Childress. *21st Century Leadership*. New York: Leadership Press, 1993.

Nanus, Burt. *The Leader's Edge*. Chicago: Contemporary Books, 1989.

Nouwen, Henri J. M. *In the Name of Jesus*. New York: Crossroads, 1989.

Ogden, Greg. *The New Reformation: Returning the Ministry to the People of God*. Grand Rapids, MI: Zondervan, 1990.

Peters, Tom. *Thriving on Chaos*. New York: Harper Perennial, 1987.

Plunkett, Lorne C., and Robert Fournier. *Participative Management*. New York: John Wiley and Sons, 1991.

Richards, Lawrence O., and Clyde Heldtke. *A Theology of Church Leadership*. Grand Rapids, MI: Zondervan, 1980.

Schein, Edgar H. "Why is it Difficult to Analyze Leadership?" (ch. 7), "Theories of Leadership and Participation" (ch. 8). *Organizational Psychology*, 3rd ed. Englewood, CA: Prentice Hall, 1980. Pp. 104-139.

Sims, Henry P. Jr., and Peter Lorenzi. *The New Leadership Paradigm*. Newbury Park, CA: Sage Publications, 1992.

Smith, Peter B., and Mark F. Peterson. *Leadership, Organizations, and Culture*. Newbury Park, CA: Sage Publications, 1988.

Steiner, George A. *Strategic Planning: What Every Manager Must Know*. New York: Free Press, 1979.

Strauss, William, and Neil Howe. *Generations*. New York: William Morrow and Company, 1991.

Towns, Elmer L. *10 of Today's Most Innovative Churches*. Ventura, CA: Regal Books, 1990.

Tregoe, Benjamin B., and John W. Zimmerman. *Top Management Strategy: What It Is and How to Make It Work*. New York: Simon and Schuster, 1980.

Wagner, C. Peter. *Strategies for Church Growth*. Ventura, CA: Regal Books, 1987.

Whetten, David A., and Kim S. Cameron. *Developing Management Skills*. 2nd ed. New York: Harper Collins, 1991.

Whiteside, Robert L. "Concerning Elders." *Doctrinal Discourses*. Denton, TX: Inys Whiteside, 1955. pp.82-89.

Zaleznik, Abraham. *The Managerial Mystique: Restoring Leadership in Business*. New York: Harper & Row, 1989.